THE WORLD VIEWS OF
THE US PRESIDENTIAL ELECTION

THE WORLD VIEWS OF THE US PRESIDENTIAL ELECTION

2008

Edited by

Matthias Maass

First published in 2009 by
PALGRAVE MACMILLAN®
in the United States—a division of St. Martin's Press LLC,
175 Fifth Avenue, New York, NY 10010.

Where this book is distributed in the UK, Europe and the rest of the world,
this is by Palgrave Macmillan, a division of Macmillan Publishers Limited,
registered in England, company number 785998, of Houndmills,
Basingstoke, Hampshire RG21 6XS.

Palgrave Macmillan is the global academic imprint of the above companies
and has companies and representatives throughout the world.

Palgrave® and Macmillan® are registered trademarks in the United States,
the United Kingdom, Europe and other countries.

ISBN: 978–0–230–61868–8

Library of Congress Cataloging-in-Publication Data

The world views of the U.S. presidential election: 2008 / edited by
Matthias Maass.
    p. cm.
Includes bibliographical references.
ISBN 978–0–230–61868–8 (alk. paper)
    1. Presidents—United States—Election—2008. 2. United States—
Foreign public opinion. 3. United States—Foreign relations—2001–
I. Maass, Matthias.

JK5262008.W67 2009
324.973'0931—dc22   2009014842

A catalogue record of the book is available from the British Library.

Design by Newgen Imaging Systems (P) Ltd., Chennai, India.

First edition: December 2009

10 9 8 7 6 5 4 3 2 1

Printed in the United States of America.

Für Max

CONTENTS

Acknowledgments

In 2004, I was invited by Tomasz Pludowski to contribute a chapter on the upcoming U.S. presidential election from the South Korean perspective. Even if the edited book's focus ended up being much broader than just the contest between Bush and Kerry, I found the exercise to be immensely fruitful.[1] In particular, with a potentially historic 2008 US election on the horizon, a study centered on the foreign perspectives of the US presidential election appeared useful.

Robyn Curtis, Asa Johnson, Farideh Koohi-Kamali, and Rachel Tekula at Palgrave were immensely helpful in moving this project from idea to reality. Here at Yonsei University I received tremendous help from student assistants, namely, Dongyoon Chung, Tim Gitzen, and Holly Stephens.

This project has been a collaborative and intercontinental effort, and much gratitude is due to all those who provided the IT-infrastructure at universities. Yonsei University and its Graduate School of International Studies provided all the logistical support I could have hoped for. Both contributions may sound banal, but were crucial for this project.

There were many friends, whom I do not need to name here, and also family, who were a constant source of advice and encouragement.

NOTE

1. The 2004 American Presidential Election and the Korean Peninsula: US Foreign Policy toward the Korean Peninsula after 2004. The South Korean Perspective," in Tomasz Pludowski (ed.), *American Politics, Media, and Elections, Contemporary International Perspectives on US Presidency, Foreign Policy, and Political Communication* (Warsaw and Torun: Collegium Civitas Press and Adam Marszalek, 2005).

Introduction

THE US PRESIDENTIAL ELECTION IN 2008: AN INTRODUCTION TO A "GLOBAL EVENT"

Matthias Maass

On November 4, 2008, Barack Obama was elected 44th President of the United States. The world approved. When President-elect Obama proclaimed in his victory speech "a new dawn of American leadership,"[1] he did so to a broad popular acclaim across the globe.

The 2008 US presidential election was more than a domestic political event in the United States. It was, first, the election of the US President of choice of most, although certainly not all, countries across the globe,[2] the selection of a "global leader" in which most of the world felt it had a stake. Globally, it was perceived as a political event that could not be disregarded and its implications beyond the borders of the United States not be discounted. Second, it was perceived widely as a rebirth of sorts of the idea of America. The return, as it was seen, of the United States as an inspiration and aspiration was greeted globally with much relief.

This book investigates selected foreign perspectives of the US presidential election in an effort to compile a picture of how the event was perceived abroad and how the viewpoints were similar or differed across the globe. How were this election, its candidates and issues seen, its importance judged, and its impact evaluated outside of the United States? Thus, this edited volume analyzes the 2008 American presidential election by taking various foreign perspectives—by looking at this event from the vantage points of other countries. Adopting such international perspectives, and putting the election in a global context, allows the volume to investigate if and how the 2008 US presidential contest can be seen as a "global election."

The key assumption underlying this collaborative effort is that the US election was seen to matter far beyond the borders of the United States. This election was, in many ways, a "global event." But how and why was that the case? In other words, the following chapters investigate the causalities that made an election in the United States be seen as relevant in other countries. Each country study further analyzes what exactly the perceptions were with regard to the candidates, the issues, and the process of the election, as well as the anticipated implications of the choice of Obama for the respective bilateral relationship.

RELEVANCE OF THE 2008 US PRESIDENTIAL ELECTION

US presidential elections have relevance far beyond America's borders. To be sure, neither is the fact new nor the insight novel. However, the degree to which this is true or is perceived to be true outside of the United States is arguably much higher today than in the past. In most, if not all, countries around the world, the US presidential election is not only perceived as *important* news, but as *relevant* news—relevant for those countries themselves. In fact, in a hegemonic system, the domestic politics of the hegemon almost by definition cease to be purely domestic. Since US influence can and frequently does reach into even the remotest corners of the world, key developments in America are then ipso facto of international relevance.

Moreover, given the multifaceted way in which the United States is tied into global affairs and constantly interacts with other countries, how the United States is perceived abroad, it is argued here, also matters for the United States itself. Neither the political leadership in Washington, DC, nor the country as a whole can be ignorant of how its domestic affairs are viewed outside its borders if it wants to conduct its foreign affairs effectively. In this sense, the following essays deal with a key ingredient of US foreign policy. In its bilateral relationships with other countries, the US administration will have to deal with their concerns, perceptions, and expectations as much as with any of the realities that shape bilateral relations. Therefore, the chapters assembled in this volume draw a picture of US perceptions abroad and thus describe and analyze parts of the landscape that forms the backdrop for US foreign policy today.

To be sure, practically all major elections or other key changes in government across the globe get international coverage, some to a greater degree and some less. Many countries are so important that any change in their leadership will be taken note of by others. There is a system-wide significance regarding who holds executive control in major powers. In other cases, the way power transition takes places warrants a broader, international coverage. Alternatively, possible changes in government of even smaller and less powerful states are being paid close attention worldwide if these countries hold key positions in other regards, for example, economically or geopolitically.

However, the depth of international interest in US presidential elections stands out, and for two reasons: first, because of the hegemonic position of the United States at the beginning of the twenty-first century, and second, because of what "America" represents ideationally. Regarding the former, since the end of the Cold War, the United States has been the only remaining superpower and has achieved a hegemonic position in international affairs, reigning supreme in various dimensions of power. Beyond that, the country's global connections and its international interdependence across all corners of the globe are such that the United States matters almost universally. Simply put, the United States is too big, too powerful, and too interconnected for its major domestic affairs—such as key elections—to be ignored by other countries.

However, there seems to have been an additional issue at play with regard to the 2008 US presidential election, which relates to the latter, conceptual point. At least implicitly and as appropriate in each individual case, the studies compiled here also tackle the question of what, in the eyes of foreign observers, the US election was about, beyond the concrete choice of either the Democratic or Republican candidate. Were there broader and ideational issues perceived to be at stake? In a number of countries, both candidates were not only linked to their respective party lines, but also, it seems, to certain broader ideational concepts. In fact, Obama's call for "change" was a direct appeal to such a more general rethinking of US politics and policies.

In many countries, the United States represents ideas, attitudes, and viewpoints, both good and bad, that often go far beyond the level to which other countries too are frequently associated with certain characteristics. Critically, the United States is regularly associated with the "American Dream." Although it has different connotations to different people, the "American Dream" remains a powerful mode of association with the United States, and the 2008 presidential election was an event in which foreign observers, too, saw this aspiration and inspiration, implicitly at least, on the agenda. In this sense, one may argue, the clash between Obama and John McCain was not just about individuals but also about a particular idea that is intrinsically associated with their country.

Moreover, the relevance of the 2008 US presidential election grew out of it being a uniquely "global event." Not only was the election seen internationally as important with regard to bilateral relations or as relevant in terms of ideational aspects of "America," the election was also one that generated a global "constituency" that felt it had a stake and thus a justified say in the election. Therefore, it was the world as a whole that "participated" in the national elections of the United States. There were many societies across the globe that felt they were partaking in the US presidential election, even if they had, of course, no vote. In most cases, such participation went far beyond an explicit expression of prefer-ence in another country's election, which is not an uncommon phenom-enon, rather, the global involvement was to such a level that it frequently bordered on making it a domestic event. It is in this sense that the 2008 vote for the White House was an event with international attendance and participation, in effect, a "global event."

Following this approach, this work develops, applies, and advances the notion of the US presidential election as indeed a "global election." The purpose is to better capture, conceptualize, and understand the rel-evance of the US presidential election worldwide. By doing so, the book also points toward a triangular relationship—the US electorate, the American Presidency, and an international "pole" of stakeholders.

Finally, this study is concerned with how the Obama administration is perceived with respect to bilateral relations and global affairs from the perspective of foreign countries. The truism that "elections have consequences" has been regularly brought up by Democrats in order to defend policy choices against the critique of Republicans soon after the November 2008 elections. While this is generally meant to refer to domestic politics, it is also true of foreign relations. The choice of Obama over McCain, together with majorities for the Democrats in both houses of Congress, meant that the George W. Bush presidency ended with a political exclamation point. Thus, the new political leader-ship in Washington may also implement major changes in US foreign policy. This was certainly anticipated by other countries. Hence, each of the following chapters concludes with an analysis of what the outcome of the US presidential election now may mean in the eyes of the coun-tries being discussed. What policies do these countries think will the Obama administration now pursue bilaterally, and what course will it chart in multilateral affairs?

Assumptions Made and Questions Asked

This book targets the perception of the US election abroad. Thus, the focus of the following chapters is not primarily to discuss how impor-tant or irrelevant the 2008 US presidential election was, but rather to investigate how it was *seen* overseas. It is, in other words, a study of the "image" of the United States, or a part of the image, to be precise, as perceived by other countries. In this sense, the chapters in this volume build up an implied constructivist argument to put forth the claim that how other countries view the United States matters analytically and prac-tically. Further, the chapters also discuss how and by what means vari-ous countries form different images of the United States and also point toward the possible inaccuracies that can crop up in their perception. In such cases, the gap between the perceived views and actual relevance of the United States to the country in question are then investigated further. What emerges then on the basis of this analysis is a picture of how other countries responded and reacted to the US election and what this reaction may tell us about the country in question and its bilateral relationship with the United States.

Given the choice of the subject—the election of the US President—the book clearly puts forth the argument that individuals do matter in an event of such significance. That is to say, throughout this study, it is argued that it mattered to all countries who was being selected to be the presidential candidate, though it mattered more for some and less for others. The US Constitution endows the head of the executive branch with considerable power. In addition, the US President becomes, for good or for worse, the face of the United States during his time in office. And finally, in the early twenty-first century, the US President steers a hegemon in world affairs. Thus, it is argued here, who occupies the White House matters immensely, domestically in the United States and also internationally.

To be sure, even if the interpretation of the 2008 US election as a "global event" made above is accepted, one cannot reasonably assume all countries to show a uniform response. First, there are major differences between countries, and this book accounts for some of those differences. In fact, the rationale for undertaking a study of this sort involving the views of different individual countries, instead of one larger, thematic treatment of how "the" world viewed the US election, is exactly that, the fact that the differences between countries are too significant and their individual views too relevant not to be studied individually. Second, even within countries, the election in the United States was seen differently by different groups of people, and each of the following chapters takes this into consideration as well. Each author considers carefully where to focus the analysis, taking into account the particular domestic environment. In other words, French "Obamania" was a popular phenomenon, for example, whereas Japanese thinking about the election was much more driven by the country's political intelligentsia.

As in most other countries, major election campaigns in the United States are also characterized to a large extent by very differing messages from a single candidate. The messages are targeted at particular domestic audiences, allowing different segments of the electorate, to some degree, to pick and choose messages or to disregard some positions and rely on other promises of one and the same candidate, thus enabling them to make their choice as a voter. What works domestically also works internationally, and the election-promises of each camp, the different candidates' speeches, and the respective foreign policy standpoints of each party's nominee were viewed and analyzed differently and selectively overseas, too. This study takes this issue into careful consideration and attempts to disentangle the candidates' messages and their perception(s) in an effort to clarify what other countries understood when they studied the candidates' foreign policy standpoints.

The same logic applied for the issues that the foreign audience focused on. In some ways, this might be stating the obvious. For example, Palestinians looked at the presidential candidates almost exclusively in light of the still unresolved and frequently violent conflict in the Middle East; nothing else mattered much, and for obvious reasons. In Japan, on the other hand, the primary criterion for evaluating the candidates was their respective approaches to address the global economic crisis. And for many countries, a mix of issues was at play and shaped their view of what the choice before the American voter was about. In short, different countries saw different issues, or combinations thereof, on center stage at this election. Each chapter looks at these issues and investigates why they were seen as critical and what is now expected or hoped for from the Obama administration to tackle them.

Finally, if and where appropriate, the country-wise studies in the following chapters analyze links between the US presidential election and the domestic politics in the country under investigation. In some European countries, the mere possibility of a minority candidate winning the highest office was a cause for considerable soul searching. The question asked was whether such a happening would in fact be possible in these European countries, too. Yet other countries felt reminded of the inadequacy of their own political structure, as their systems seemed not permeable enough to allow for the fast rising of a young and unproven but dynamic and inspiring candidate. Such "Obama envy" was not at all uncommon across the globe.[3] Needless to say, the link between the election in the United States and domestic politics of countries across the globe differed from country to country. Nevertheless, where there is proof of such a link, an attempt is made to investigate it in detail.

Layout and Organization

As expected, considering the importance of the US presidential election indicated above, it received wide, continuous, and insightful coverage across the globe. However, much of it was done in the form of reporting of particular events, opinion pieces, and occasional opinion polls. What has been lacking was a sustained qualitative investigation of a cross-section of foreign perspectives. This book attempts to bridge that gap. The express purpose is to allow the reader to delve deeper into particular foreign perspectives than news reporting generally permits, and to explore the causality for perceptions from abroad more thoroughly than opinion polls may allow. However, this is not to disqualify either the newspaper coverage or the opinion polls that were conducted. In fact, both were vital sources for the individual studies that follow. Rather, the following chapters attempt to contribute a better understanding of the 2008 US election from the overseas perspectives by adding depth-of-analysis and breadth of coverage to the existing discussion.

In essence, it has been the editor's and authors' collective ambition to bring together in one place a substantial selection of country-wise studies, all dealing with the US presidential election from unique national perspectives, in an effort to advance our understanding of this election as a "global event" of international importance.

The chapters are ordered roughly, for reasons of simplicity only, according to the geographical location of the countries studied. With the exception of the chapter on the United Arab Emirates and Gulf States, each chapter focuses on a single country and looks at two broader streams of questions: First, the chapters discuss how the presidential election was interpreted as an American event—what were perceived to be the major issues, the positions of the candidates, and the importance of the outcome on the United States itself. In other words, what was the "take" of other countries on the US presidential election? Second, each chapter deals with the perceived impact of the US presidential election's outcome on that country or on broader issues. Particular attention has been paid to drawing out causalities and interconnections that link the US election with the domestic setup of each country in order to further our awareness of how and to what extent the US presidential elections matter domestically across the globe. Within this rough framework, each chapter takes note of peculiarities and focuses on the major issues that characterized each particular country's unique perspective on the US presidential election in 2008.

Notes

1. America.gov, "Obama's Victory Speech," November 5, 2008. http://www.america.gov/st/elections08-english/2008/November/200811051 01958abretnuh0.580044.html (accessed February 12, 2009).
2. BBC News, "World has 'high hopes' for Obama," January 20, 2009. http://news.bbc.co.uk/2/hi/americas/obama_inauguration/7838475.stm (accessed February 10, 2009).
3. Anand Giridharada, "A New World is Turning, and It's Obamaesque," *International Herald Tribune*, 2, February 13, 2009.

1

MEXICO: BETWEEN SKEPTICISM, HOPE, AND DISILLUSION

Thomas Cieslik

INTRODUCTION

Worldwide, the election of Barack Obama as the 44th president of the United States of America was the top news story when it broke. Due to the fact that an estimated 25 million individuals with Mexican roots are living in the United States the Hispanic dimension was a crucial topic in the election campaign of both principal candidates, Obama of the Democratic Party and the Republican John McCain. Like other Latin Americans and Hispanics in the United States, people of Mexican heritage first preferred Hillary Clinton. However, after Obama's nomination as the Democratic candidate, the sympathy turned toward him, and a huge wave of support developed because of his fresh election campaign. Critically, Obama promised not only a change within the United States but also a change in US relations to Mexico and Latin America. Of the US Latinos, 67 percent voted for Obama, only 31 percent for McCain.

This 2:1 ratio reflects also the sympathy of the Mexicans toward Obama and the Democrats. The Mexican political establishment and people are expecting from the new president a quick decision on immigration, the future development of the NAFTA (North Atlantic Free Trade Agreement), and support in the Mexican war on drug trafficking. Overall, Mexico hopes for closer relations with the United States after eight years of negligence by the George W. Bush Administration.

The crash of an airplane with the Mexican Interior Secretary Juan Camilo Mouriño on Election Day, however, overshadowed, in Mexico, the victory of the Democratic Senator from Illinois. The death of Mouriño was the top headline on television, radio, and in the newspapers. He was the most trusted confidante of Mexican President Felipe Calderón from the conservative party PAN (National Action Party). He was responsible for a hardliner concept against the drug crime that has been spreading throughout Mexico. The government jet crashed into a main city-road near the president's office, killing nine passengers and staff aboard the plane and six people in the avenue. Among the victims was also the former antidrug prosecutor Jose Luis Santiago Vasconcelos, who had been the target of different assassination attempts in the past. More than forty people were injured. Until today, rumors and speculation claim that the accident was engineered by one of the leading drug cartels in Mexico. Since Calderón took the presidency in December 2006 and ordered the deployment of the National Army to fight drug trafficking, especially at Mexico's Northern Border, almost 8,000 people have been killed. In 2008, around 5,600 were murdered. The drug cartels, among them the Sinaloa, Juarez, Tijuana, and the Gulf Cartel that is now run by the Los Zetas, have killed especially security officials and police forces. Therefore, security is still the number one priority on the bilateral agenda of United States and Mexico.

The Relevance of the US Election for Mexican Politics

An old Mexican saying goes: "Mexico is too far from heaven, and so close to the US." It reflects the asymmetric and ambivalent relations of the two states that share a common border of almost 2000 miles. Mexico has always been the less developed state, in contrast to the United States. Ever since the loss of California, New Mexico, and Texas in the context of the North American-Mexican War in 1846–1848, Mexicans felt inadequate in relation to US citizens. US ascent in world politics, its democracy, the rule of law, the booming and dynamic economy over the decades, and the creation of a large middle class have presented an example of a successful state for many Mexicans. The Mexicans have become disappointed by their revolution in 1910–1918, the subsequent autocratic regime of the ruling PRI (Institutional Revolutionary Party) with its oppression and corruption, as well as the lack of opportunities for millions of poor people migrating from the provinces into the cities.

This paradoxical love-hate relationship is typical for the Mexican identity toward the United States. In contrast to US citizens, Mexicans mostly feel envious about the ascent of other people, generally speaking. They do not appreciate others for their efforts and performance or the opportunities that others were able to take advantage of. But they are keen to realize the dream of their co-citizens in the United States, although their own government has not provided them with the same opportunities.

Since 1994, with the pattern of the European Union in mind, Mexico has aimed at a similar integration with North America. With the foundation of NAFTA, Mexico has orientated its activities strictly to the North. The technocratic elite that studied at North American universities wants to transform the country into a modern society through neoliberal reforms and a tentative democratization process, which mainly was realized by the last president of the PRI, Ernesto Zedillo (1994–2000), who is now the Director of the Center for the Study of Globalization at Yale University.

Within the NAFTA integration process, trade and capital investment have become easier. However, in contrast to the European Union, the treaty does not pay attention to labor mobility. Moreover, the market has not been affected so far by multilateral policies intended to design the harmonization of social policies and equalize economic infrastructure by regional cohesion funds. But NAFTA caused two phenomena: first, the creation of *maquiladoras* along the Mexican border, located in cities like Tijuana or Ciudad Juarez. These factories import materials and equipment from the United States on a duty-free basis for assembly and manufacture in Mexico, and then they reexport the products. The factories profit from low wages, tariffs, and taxes.

Maquiladoras lured many workers from the Central American and Mexican provinces, who came to find a job at the border first, with further prospects of transmigrating finally into the United States. This is the second phenomenon: according to data from the *Department of Homeland Security Yearbook of Immigration Statistics*, in the fiscal year 2006[1] only 9,247 Mexicans were admitted into the United States for temporary employment under the TN (Trade NAFTA) status, 2,904 persons under the treaty national's dependent status, like spouses or children. This special nonimmigrant status allows Mexican citizens to work in certain professional occupations in the United States for up to three years at a time. However, the procedure is complex and applicants are subject to an annual quota that does not really consider the needs of the labor force. The complex dimension of migration, with different interests of lobbying groups, has actually overwhelmed politicians and specialists and prevented a comprehensive migration reform in the United States. With such lack of willingness, US-Mexican relations have been permanently damaged. The facts, however, are clear:[2] There are twelve million Hispanics who are undocumented but living and working in the United States. All reforms to accept reality and find a path to legalize illegal immigrants and thus tackle the current situation have failed.[3] Meanwhile the Secure Fence Act was passed, while the Senate's Comprehensive Immigration Reform Act of 2007 failed eventually.[4]

In the US election campaign both McCain and Obama had huge congruence with respect to plans to address the migration problem: both favored improved border security, a legalization process and path to citizenship, a temporary guest-worker program, the introduction of an electronic employment verification system, family visas, and support of the *Development, Relief and Education for Alien Minors Act* (DREAM Act) of 2005. , which includes sponsorships for children of illegal migrants with respect to university fees. Only in the question of language (Obama spoke out against English as the official language) and driver's licenses (McCain objected to making them available to illegal immigrants) did the Democratic and Republican candidates differ. In the end, due to their high level of agreement, the topic of migration became actually a "nonissue" in the presidential campaign.

A significant aspect of US-Mexico relations is the dependence of the Mexican economy on remittances from migrants. According to data from the *Banco de México*, remittances to Mexico from migrants grew from US $4.6 billion to US $25 billion from 1996 to 2006. Meanwhile the number of undocumented migrants increased annually by some estimated 500,000 individuals. Remittances have approached 2 percent of the GDP (Gross Domestic Product), which came second only to oil exports, but ranked above tourism as the main source of foreign currency. The United States is also the largest country with foreign direct investment (FDI) in Mexico. In the first twelve years of NAFTA, the total FDI was US $109 billion.[5]

The dependence on remittances, like the dependence on the development of the US economy, is fundamental for the Mexican relationship with its northern neighbor. In the past few years, an average of 86 percent of Mexican exports went to the United States in a volume of up to US $190 billion, mainly manufactured goods and oil. The average GDP per capita has steadily increased to around US $9,000 in the past twenty years. According to data from the World Bank, 40 percent of Mexico's population is poor, and 18 percent lives in extreme poverty, although this situation has improved through economic growth and the federal housing programs.[6]

After the terror attacks of September 11, 2001, the United States envisioned the development of NAFTA into a zone of mutual cooperation against terrorism. In Waco (Texas), President Bush, President Fox of Mexico, and the Canadian Prime Minister Paul Martin signed the Security and Prosperity Partnership of North America on March 23, 2005. It is a regional level dialogue forum with the purpose of providing deeper security and economic cooperation toward the building of a North American community in the long run.[7]

The *Plan Mexico* or *Initiative Merida* is a product of the Security and Prosperity Partnership of North America. In March 2007, President Bush and President Calderón met in the Yucatan city of Merida in order to sign a cooperation agreement in security issues to fight "narco-terrorism." In Mexico the word "narco" refers to a person who is involved in drug trafficking. The term "narco-terrorism" was invented by former president Fernando Belaunde Terry of Peru in 1983 when he described terrorist-type attacks against his nation's antinarcotics police. Later it was used during the Guerilla War of the FRAC in Colombia and the drug cartel of Pablo Escobar, and now for attacks and killings by the Mexican drug cartels. In light of this treaty, the US Congress, led by a Democratic majority, authorized US $1.6 billion for a three-year initiative. In 2008, the Congress released US $400 million (US $100 million less than originally agreed) for modern communication technology, helicopters, surveillance airplanes, nonintrusive inspection equipment such as iron scanners and gamma ray scanners for the Mexican army, and also for the training of Mexican soldiers and special police forces. US $73.5 million of this bill will be used for judicial reform and institution-building; a further US $50 million is devoted to the Central American states to deepen security cooperation between Mexican and Central American authorities against drug cartels and the notorious Maras. The latter are criminal gangs whose roots hark back to the civil wars in Central America and today live in brutal rivalry.

The current *Merida Initiative* between the United States and Mexico hints at the *Plan Colombia* that was developed in 1999 between the United States and the Colombian governments in order to halt drug trafficking and violence in the Andean country. The United States invested US $4.4 billion to support the formation and training of the Colombian military and police. Though it failed in its objective to reduce the cultivation and distribution of cocaine, it improved noticeably the security situation in many cities. The German think tank *Stiftung Wissenschaft und Politik* has interpreted the agreement as a new form of regionalization of the US security structure. Though the United States could exercise control over the distribution routes of drug trafficking, the authors fear that the conflict might spread out to Central America and the Caribbean and will worsen the current instability in the region.[8] Drug trafficking has always been a problem between the United States and Mexico due to high drug consumption in the former:

U.S. law enforcement officials estimate that $12 to 15 billion a year flows from the United States to the Mexican traffickers. And that is just the bulk currency amount, actual dollar bills, and doesn't include all the money sent by wire transfers. "In that sense, the U.S. is already financing this war. It is just financing it on the wrong side," Attorney General Medina Mora said grimly. "Another problem is that most of the weapons used by the traffickers come from the United States. Typically, the drug smugglers have much more firepower than local police departments, and sometimes can even outgun the federal police and the Army with high-caliber machine-guns and grenade launchers. "Most of the weapons, I would say around 95 percent of the weapons that we have seized, come from the U.S.," said Mora. "If the U.S. would stop the flow of weapons to Mexico the equation would change very rapidly here. We need the U.S. to stay committed in this war in reducing demand, in stopping the flow of weapons and stopping the flow of cash.[9]

In order to gain full political legitimacy after the Mexican presidential election in 2006, when Calderón won with a margin of 35.71 to 35.15 percent against the candidate Andres Manuel Lopez Obrador from the socialist PRD (Revolutionary Democratic Party), the newly elected president sent 6,500 federal troops to the state of Michoacan in order to stop drug violence. However, they could not even stop the violence from escalating. As of today, over 25,000 troops are involved in his antidrug campaign, and the government has spent approximately US $7 billion. Without having an exit-strategy the war will remain endless. Indeed, Calderón has won respect and confirmation within the Mexican population because he instrumentalized the army—along with the Catholic Church, the two most respected institutions in the country—for his goal. Unfortunately, he could not achieve a resounding success due to the corruption in police and judiciary.[10] Consequently, the transformation process in Mexico is stagnating. Democratic institutions and the rule of law are still in transition. The war on drug trafficking has subordinated democratic reforms. Tightened security has restricted civil rights and transparency. *Freedom House* has evaluated that human rights and civil liberties are under pressure, although the country is still classified as "free."[11] According to *Transparency International*, Mexico is, however, a corrupt country as of 2008, ranked seventy-two worldwide.[12] Politicians, policemen, attorneys are all on the payroll of the drug cartels. Press Freedom is also in danger. According to statistics from the organization *Reporters Without Borders*,[13] in the Americas Mexico is the state in which the lives of journalists are most threatened. In 2008, four journalists were killed and six kidnapped. Recurring violent attacks on the largest Latin-American media center *Televisa* in Monterrey reflect the degree of aggression against journalists who report about drug crime. Self-censorship is often the consequence, thus the quality of press suffers, and as a consequence the role of the "fourth estate" to control the political system has become tenuous at best, obsolete at worst.

In conclusion, any decision that is taken in the United States may have a direct impact, positively or negatively, on Mexico's security, economy, and migration policy. Therefore, every US presidential election has become more and more decisive for the future and fortune of Mexico.

The Viewpoints of Mexican Society on the US Election

Mexican society has observed carefully and curiously the election campaigns of all candidates from the Democratic and Republican sides.

Through family linkages—40 percent of Mexicans have at least one relative living in the United States—and solidarity feelings, they have a traditional sympathy toward the Hispanic community in the United States. Mexicans have paid particular attention to topics such as the economy and migration because any decision on these issues would have impacts on their personal life.

The presidential candidates, too, took the political debates to the Hispanic community in the United States. They published and broadcasted political statements and advertisements in Spanish newspapers, magazines, radio, and television shows. Currently at 46 percent, Hispanics have become the largest ethnic minority group in the United States, and have overtaken African-Americans. Approximately 14 percent of the US population belongs to the Latino group, but it only represents 9 percent of the electorate. Many Hispanics are ineligible to vote as they do not satisfy the age conditions or have uncertain legal status.

Though Hispanics are inclined toward more conservative values based on their catholic religion and tradition, 57 percent identified themselves in December 2007 as Democrats, only 23 percent as Republicans according to data of a Pew Hispanic Center poll,[14] because Democrats showed more concern on immigration issues than Republicans. Hispanics have become a sizeable factor in four of the so-called swing states, where Republicans and Democrats fight for any vote in a neck and neck race to win over the electorate. President George W. Bush won by only a small margin his reelection in New Mexico (with 37 percent Hispanic voters), Florida (14 percent), Nevada (12 percent), and Colorado (12 percent) in 2004. In the same year, the Democratic presidential candidate John Kerry lost New Mexico only by 6,000 votes, where 40,000 Hispanics did not vote. In the above-mentioned poll, presidential candidate, former First Lady, and Senator from New York, Hillary Clinton, stayed ahead by 59 to 15 percent against Obama. Clinton enjoyed high popularity in Mexico due to the legacy of her husband Bill Clinton who strongly supported NAFTA and oversaw its ratification in the United States. He was also instrumental in the creation of the North American Development Bank, designed to assist development along the Mexican border. Last but not least, President Clinton demonstrated a general concern for the problems of the growing Latino community in the United States. Finally, in the Democratic presidential primaries, Hispanics voted for Hillary Clinton by a margin of two to one, especially in states like California and Texas where the proportion of Latinos rose dramatically between 2004 and 2008. Hispanics comprised 30 percent of the turnout in California and 32 percent in Texas. The Pew Hispanic Center came to the conclusion that Hillary Clinton's electoral result would have been even worse if she had not received the support from the Latinos.[15]

The survey showed further an interesting note: "Hispanics (28 percent) were more likely than whites (13 percent) to say that the race of a candidate is important in deciding their vote. However, Hispanic voters who said that race was important were equally likely as Hispanic voters who said that race was *not* important to have voted for Clinton—64 percent versus 63 percent."[16] In general, the most important motivation for the Latinos to vote for Clinton was her experience as a politician and her position on economic issues and health care.

Furthermore, New Mexico Governor Bill Richardson, whose mother is Mexican and father Nicaraguan, hardly registered any gains in the primaries' polls. After his withdrawal he supported Obama's campaign and stated in Mexican newspapers that a migration reform would be a priority in the first one-hundred days of a Democrat assuming power. He emphasized that the Latin vote should go in favor of Obama after his nomination because he would identify them as "real" American citizens and had promised that, as president, he would pay more attention to Latin America. However, he actually did not make the latter promise in his electoral campaign. Richardson further announced that any migration reform should include three main elements: first, an increase in the number of legal immigrants; second, strengthening border security; and third, a plan that helps to legalize undocumented workers.[17] After the election, Obama appointed Richardson to become his secretary for commerce in the cabinet. But he withdrew his nomination because of a federal grand jury investigation. Mexican media and politicians regretted his decision because they had put much hope in Richardson's understanding of Latino issues and the growing commerce between the northern Mexican states and the United States.

Mexican politicians and press observed the attitude of Obama as president toward the Hispanic community in the United States. In July, Obama visited the 40th Annual Convention of the National Council of La Raza (NCLR) in San Diego in an attempt at approaching Latin-American issues. The NCLR was founded in 1968 and is the largest national Latino civil rights and advocacy organization in the United States. There, Obama promised to push for an immigration reform in Congress in the first one-hundred days of his Presidency. This reform would also include improvements of access to health services and education.

In January 2008, before the primaries started, only 23.1 percent of Mexicans were interested in the US elections, but 88 percent remained without preferences. In March, the number rose to 32.7 percent and then reduced marginally to 30.7 percent in June; finally, 43.6 percent of Mexicans with family links observed the elections with interest. According to data from the leading poll institute in Mexico, *Consulta Mitofsky*,[18] Mexicans gradually became more interested in the preelection campaign of the Democrats when it came to the neck and neck race between Clinton and Obama before the official nomination at the

Democratic National Convention took place on August 27, 2008. On June 3, Obama gained the majority of the delegates when he won 29 of 50 states' primaries and caucuses; even though in Texas he won the caucuses, he lost the primary.

A high number of Mexicans did not pay attention to the selection process (52.8 percent in January, 42.0 percent in March, and 45.5 percent in June). Further results of the poll showed that the higher the educational level, the more number of people are interested in elections: 36.2 percent among those with a university degree and 34.5 percent of the younger generation aged between eighteen and twenty-nine years showed interest in it. The majority of them identified themselves as supporters of the PAN. Only a minority of PRI supporters demonstrated high interest in the election. This reflects the Mexican post-PRI society: young professionals, mostly members of the middle class, but also of the lower middle classes, identify themselves stronger with the US model than the corporatist-centric and very national old PRI clientele. Geographically, the election was at the center of the public debate in the region of Bajio, which lies in the center of the country and is the area from where there are a high number of emigrants. The Mexicans then preferred Hillary Clinton over Obama as president, with 38 percent favoring Clinton and 21 percent favoring Obama. But the poll institute evaluated that through the impact of mass media the name of Obama became more popular. In January 2008, only 3.6 percent of Mexicans knew the candidate.

In general, Democratic candidates led their Republican counterparts in voter appeal by a proportion of 2 to 1. *Consulta Mitofsky* identified the same trends in Mexico as the polls about Hispanics in the United States had indicated. Among those Mexicans with relatives in the United States, 39 percent favored Obama over McCain, who was favored by 6.8 percent. The numbers for those individuals without family links were 25.4 percent and 6 percent, respectively.[19]

THE MEXICAN PERCEPTION OF THE US PRESIDENTIAL ELECTION AND DOMESTIC POLITICS IN MEXICO

Since Mexican President Vicente Fox from the PAN assumed power and in 2000 brought the seventy-one-year rule of the PRI to an end, the perception of the US presidential election has grown in meaning for Mexican domestic politics. An impressive example is the relation between Fox and US President Bush. Since 1992, every president-elect in the United States has a meeting with the Mexican president a few days before the official inauguration. Mexican President Carlos Salinas de Gortari invited for the first time Bill Clinton, when he was elected, for a discussion of the bilateral agenda. Usually, incoming American presidents have visited

Canada on their first foreign trip due to the deep economic and political cooperation between the two countries. But the virtual first summit of the Mexican and US Presidents reflects the growing importance that Mexico has gained for the United States in terms of the economy and the influence of the Hispanic community. President Bush visited Mexican President Vicente Fox first in 2001. The media named the meeting a "cowboy summit" due to the sympathy of both toward such lifestyle. But Fox and Bush have known each other since they were Governors of Guanajuato and Texas, respectively. Both are conservatives, and while Fox took office on December 1, 2000, Bush followed soon, on January 20, 2001. Indeed, Bush put high hopes on the deepening of relations with Mexico, especially on issues such as trade, immigration, and energy, but also on combating drug trafficking.

With this symbolic first visit to the southern neighbor, Bush demonstrated the willingness to overcome the attitude that Mexico (and Latin America) are just an afterthought of US foreign policy or the backyard of the US economy. Besides, US Republican politicians have identified Latino voters as the fastest-growing ethnic bloc with traditionally conservative values on family, work, religion, patriotism, abortion, and marriages. And by the summer of 2001, the US administration was very close to coming to an agreement with Mexico over a temporary work visa program for Mexicans. However, the terror attacks on the World Trade Center and the Pentagon on September 11, 2001, interrupted this process and stopped further negotiations. Security became the first priority in US foreign policy and the Bush administration neglected Latin America. The proposals for a Free Trade Area of the Americas were ineffectual and failed at the Summit of the Americas in Mar del Plata in November 2005 against the resistance of almost all Latin-American countries (except Mexico). These efforts were further neutralized by the initiatives of Venezuelan President Hugo Chavez who proposed the *Alternativa Bolivariana para las Américas* (ALBA) for economic cooperation among the South American states without US hegemony. In his exit interviews as US President, Bush regretted that he did not tackle immigration reform with the vigor he had intended at the beginning of his presidency.

For Fox, the failure of immigration reform was one of the important setbacks in his presidency. His politics failed due to the US Congress rejecting the setting up of a comprehensive migration reform. During the Iraq crisis, Mexico was a non-permanent member of the United Nations Security Council and had rejected the war initiatives of President Bush. It was felt this stance was necessary to improve the chances of the PAN to defend its majority in the Parliamentarian elections in 2003. In spite of the traditional neutrality and pacifism in foreign policy, the Mexican electorate did not honor this attitude, however, and voted in a majority for the PRI (36.7 percent versus 30.8 percent for the PAN).

During the early stages of the primaries, President Calderón visited the United States in February 2008.[20] He did not meet any running candidates, however. Instead, he traveled to New York, Boston, Chicago, Sacramento, and Los Angeles in order to talk with expatriate Mexican community leaders, academics, and figures in the financial sector. During his trip he did not really address the issues associated with deportation of undocumented Mexican migrants or guest-worker programs. Though he promoted a new perspective on Mexico and Latin America, argued in favor of migration reform and against the construction of a security fence along the border, he failed in giving answers to how Mexico might contribute to regional security and how it may share in the US efforts at fighting terrorism.

THE IMPLICATIONS OF
THE OBAMA ADMINISTRATION FOR MEXICO

President Bush treated Latin America as a low priority region with respect to US and global security interests. In the 2008 US election campaign, Latin America was seen only as a domestic issue and not as an external problem. Migration or free trade still depended largely on the US economic situation. Therefore, many Mexican analysts shared a moderate and unenthusiastic opinion about the future of US-Mexican relations.

Obama does not know Latin America. He selected several counselors as his advisors for Central and South America. The top counselor to be selected is Dan Restrepo, a lawyer with a Colombian mother and a Spanish father. He will have direct access to Obama and should prepare for a reinvigoration of the bilateral dialogue. In an interview he stated very clearly what could be the Mexican expectations from an Obama administration. Although he cautioned that "Obama does not want to overestimate the relationship with Mexico. He wants to put it in the proper context of cooperation, understanding and work that will benefit the people of the two countries." Still, Restrepo agreed that Obama does not know the priority subjects of this relationship in detail. However, he assured that, once [Obama] installs his cabinet, he wants "to work arm in arm" with the Mexican government on the economy and security. Restrepo maintains that Obama is concerned, and to a degree annoyed, that the Mexican people are facing the consequences for decisions made by the government of George W. Bush in the struggle against narcotics trafficking: abandoning programs that ensured a reduction in drug use and not allotting more personnel or resources in order to restrain illegal activities in the United States that help organized crime and narcotics trafficking from across the southern border. "Obama wants first to decrease the demand for drugs in the United States. He is firmly determined to do that which is necessary in order to revitalize the rehabilitation programs that, we well know, work, and that unfortunately have been abandoned in recent years," he emphasized.[21]

Another member of his team of advisors is Riordan Roett, Director of the Latin America Program at Johns Hopkins University. His recommendation to the President is to develop better communication with all Latin-American governments. That could be dangerous for the left populist leaders such as Chavez of Venezuela, but also for Mexico's self-declared "legitimate president," Andres Manuel Lopez Obrador, who lost the 2006 Mexican presidential election against Calderón and started a campaign of separatism against the neutral Federal Election Institute and the PAN. But due to his extreme positions and roadblocks, in the cities he lost dramatically in approbation of Mexican citizens, and he lost out even inside his PRD. However, the worsening of the Mexican economy could revitalize his line of politics and enable him to regain part of his former supporters. Nevertheless, Obama's campaign slogan "Yes, we can" is dangerous for the leftist populists, and it is motivating the opposition after the elimination of the odium image of President Bush. The Mexican government hopes that Obama would reestablish a united front against the domination of Brazil in Latin America and, thus, may increase Mexican influence in the region.

After the election was over, all Mexican parties confirmed the hope that Obama will turn toward Mexico and take on the many challenges in the region. President Calderón congratulated Obama for his convincing victory and continued the tradition of holding the first summit before the US president-elect took the oath of office. The Mexican President was the only foreigner who had the honor to talk with the US president-elect at the Mexican Culture Institute in Washington, DC on January 12, 2009.

Unlike Bush, however, Obama will not focus his activities on unilateral free trade agreements. His approach is much more in line with the tradition of the Democratic trade policy that leans to protectionism and is rather skeptical of economic liberalism. Because of the current global financial and economic crisis, Obama wants to renegotiate NAFTA in a way that would provide more protectionism for the US market and secure the jobs of millions of workers in the United States. This intention has alarmed Mexico and the topic was given top priority in the agenda of the first meeting between Obama and Calderón. Given the current situation, however, the Mexican President is under immense pressure to stabilize Mexico, which forced him to launch political initiatives toward the new US administration. A couple of days after the election, Calderón met with representatives of the Obama team, such as the former secretary of state Madeleine Albright and ex Congressman Jim Leach, to prepare a future summit with him and to emphasize that protectionism would diminish the opportunities available to Mexico to recover from the current economic crisis.

During the "summit" on January 12, 2009, Obama and Calderón agreed on the importance of NAFTA for the Mexican economy, the importance of the migration problem and its link to the issue of remittances to help the country stabilize its own economy, and the security challenge that grows from the problem of drug trafficking.[22] But they also agreed that real changes would not be happening so fast because of the economic crisis.

Obama suggested to update NAFTA and to strengthen bilateral cooperation in the areas of migration, economy, and security, especially against drug violence. His speaker, Robert Gibbs, stated that Obama wants to foster labor and environmental measures within NAFTA:

> On trade and the economy, President-elect Obama said that with both countries facing very difficult economic times, it's important to work together to maintain a constructive and comprehensive dialogue. He expressed his continued commitment to upgrading NAFTA to strengthen labor and environmental provisions to reflect the values that are widely shared in both of our countries, and proposed the creation of a consultative group to work on a host of issues important to the United States and Mexico, including NAFTA, energy and infrastructure.[23]

The group of advisers will elaborate the future agenda, mainly on NAFTA, energy, and infrastructure. In terms of security, the Merida Initiative could be the first step toward deeper relations, and Obama expressed his support to President Calderón with respect to the efforts to fight money laundering, and trafficking in drugs, humans, and arms.

According to data of the US Bureau of Alcohol, Tobacco, Firearms, and Explosives, 90 percent of all weapons confiscated by the Mexican authorities originated from the United States. This poses an enormous challenge to the "War on Drugs."[24] In fact, the coordinator of the PRD in the Mexican Senate, Carlos Navarrete, emphasized the necessity to stop arms proliferation from North America into Mexico. The weapons of the drug cartels came from the United States, where there are quite liberal rules regarding the possession of arms because of the strong lobby of the National Rifle Association. The Senator postulated that the US government should restrict the purchase of arms in order to halt the flow of weapons to the South.[25]

Regarding the migration issue, Obama promised to work with Congress in order to promote secure, legal, and ordinary migration with the common objective to reduce illegal migration.[26] But this is a real challenge for Mexican policymakers. According to Latin-American political tradition, the president is always the main decision-maker in foreign policy. But neglecting the US Congress has been the main reason that all reforms have failed, because the US Senate and the House of Representatives are the key players in the legislation process. Calderón classified the first summit as a new step into "constructive and constricting" US-Mexican relations.[27] He said that the safer Mexico is, the safer the United States will be. And the spiraling drug violence in Mexico has prompted the Department of US Homeland Security to develop even in the transition period a plan that permits a surge of civilian and military actions against the ongoing smuggling and killing at the border. The plan includes the deployment of aircrafts, armored vehicles, and military teams to halt the spillover of violence from Mexico to US territories. The most number of killings happened in Mexican border cities.[28]

In spite of the drug war, the mayor of Mexico City, Marcelo Ebrard from the left PRD, looks forward to establishing good relations with Obama without focusing always on security issues. Ebrard wants to become Mexican president in 2012 and could represent Mexico during a possible second term of Obama. He said that it would be necessary to enlarge the agenda beyond migration and drug trafficking and include, for example, the development of metropolitan areas, but also investments and exchange of technology. It would be a mistake if Mexico could not achieve any progress on the bilateral agenda in the next few years due to its refusal to be open to the security concerns of the United States. He stated that NAFTA had failed in terms of producing concrete results for Mexico and wished that Obama would be open to new ideas regarding new economic arrangements and a new society.[29]

The Mexican journalist Carlos Loret de Mola[30] classified Obama's victory as his own triumph of willingness to get the power. But he stated that Mexicans would have liked John McCain more than Obama if he had been a Democrat. McCain knows Mexico and he visited the country during his campaign. He is an expert in migration and foreign policy, and he favors free markets. As Senator he cosponsored the most progressive initiative on a migration reform with the most pro-Mexican legislator, Senator Edward Kennedy. Loret de Mola said that actually McCain would be a better fit for the Mexico-US bilateral agenda than Obama. The latter's victory would be the logical consequence from the fact that McCain was seen as too close to Bush, despite the fact that Obama defended, like McCain, the crucial issues of a security fence and the Merida Initiative.

Analysts like Ricardo Aleman hope that Obama may combat drug trafficking in Mexico because it is in many ways a US problem, since the main consumers live there. But the political journalist criticized Obama for not talking about drug addiction and drug crime in the United States and the connection of these issues to US relations with Mexico. He would only emphasize the security of the US border, but no one knows what his policy might actually be like.[31] Other Mexican authors believe that Obama will set the same initiatives as President Franklin D. Roosevelt did in 1932 with the New Deal to absorb the consequences of the Great Depression, which would have positive affects on the Mexican economy, too.[32] And the Mexican government certainly knows that it could use the option of cooperation in the Security Council of the United Nations better to support the foreign policy initiatives of the United States in international political developments like the war in Afghanistan, to defeat Al-Qaeda, and in the so-called War on Terror. Mexico has been elected as a non-permanent member starting in December 2010 and could become a diplomatic key player if it learned from its experience under the Fox administration. Such cooperation on the international level could also open new doors for progress on the bilateral agenda.

CONCLUSION

From the Mexican perspective, too, the US presidential election was indeed seen as a "global election." It impacted Mexico because of its geographic and economic closeness to the United States and the family ties of Latinos living—legally or illegally—there. The well-known Mexican intellectual Luis Rubio[33] recognized five main concluding drivers that defined Mexican interests on the US elections. The political analyst and president of the think tank CIDAC (Center of Research for Development) in Mexico City stated that, first, Mexicans have direct and private sources of information within the United States due to the fact that 50 percent of them have a relative living there, with whom they share their impressions and opinions. Second, he explained that Mexicans are, in general, conservative and tend to be uncomfortable with African-Americans or female candidates for political offices. But many Mexican Americans have voted for Obama instead of their traditional party preferences. The third driver was the war in Iraq and the fact that Mexicans in the US Army have been killed in that war and were buried in military uniforms. The Mexican press reported intensively on this. Fourth, the immigration reform and the construction of a security fence along the border have affected the Mexican public view. In general, the Mexican conviction is that the border with the United States should be open and all Mexicans should be allowed to cross it freely. Due to the fact that an estimated 12 million Mexicans live undocumented in the United States, any comprehensive immigration reform linked with a legalization process is necessary to overcome the main dispute in the bilateral agenda. In addition, Mexicans have a different attitude to laws and the rule of law, because of their experiences during the seventy years of one-party-rule by the PRI and the high corruption in politics and society. For Rubio, the fifth driver was NAFTA and how the trade agreement has opened up Mexican society. It forced the government to improve governance, accountability, and transparency in public policy, which went beyond the overwhelming benefits of trade and investment.

In Mexico, former presidents still have influence on political decisions. Therefore, they sometimes comment on current issues. The last president of the PRI, Ernesto Zedillo (1994–2000), suggested the issue of migration at a conference of the Brookings Institution in the United States as a crucial topic that must be addressed to improve the relations between the United States and Latin America. He emphasized that a comprehensive migration reform is necessary and that the construction of the security fence would be an offence to the friendship between the United States and Mexico. He pointed out that the United States benefits annually from US $15 billion through the labor of immigrants, and that the lure to move to the United States illegally is derived from the discrepancy between the need of cheap labor on the US side and the availability of this labor in Mexico to cater to this demand.

However, whether the new US administration will recognize this economic reality of the past years and act accordingly is questionable owing to the currently increasing number of unemployed people. Thus, the fear is growing that the economic crisis will hit Mexico also harshly. Officially, Mexico has an unemployment rate of 4 percent, but approximately 50 percent of the population aged between fourteen and sixty-four years works in the informal sector. The Mexican government is expecting a growth of zero percent of the GDP for the year 2009.

Economic stagnation in Mexico could stimulate further migration to the United States. Ex president Vicente Fox (2000–2006) likewise criticized the plan of Obama to renegotiate NAFTA, even though it has already brought many benefits to the United States. Fox said that Obama must "put his feet in reality, because he did not do this in his campaign."[34]

In contrast to many other countries in the world, Mexico has clearly shown major skepticism toward Obama. The election of the Mexican Parliament in July 2009 will pose challenges to the politics of the US administration, just as the challenges raised by the US presidential election in Mexico. A likely victory of the PRI would weaken the PAN-government of Calderón and could halt the democratization process. The escalation of drug crime; the discussion in the Parliament about the reintroduction of the death penalty for drug trafficking, murder, and kidnapping, which is supported by 75 percent of Mexican citizens; the growing corruption of the weak institutions; and the dispersion of violence inside the country could eventually transform Mexico into a narco-state, like Colombia was in the 1980s, or it could even get worse and become a failed state.[35] Different paramilitary groups in the north of the country have already proclaimed that they will in fact become vigilantes and arbitrarily take law into their hands to stop the drug cartels. A recently published report of the US Joint

Forces Command (JFCOM) entitled "The Joint Operating Environment (JOE)"[36] has predicted the collapse of Mexico (along with Pakistan). It has argued that politicians, police, and the judicial infrastructure are under sustained assault and pressure by criminal gangs and drug cartels. Due to the involvement of the Mexican army, the drug war could turn out into a civil war and this would imply serious consequences for US homeland security. A US military intervention is theoretically an option, perhaps even with the support of the Mexican government, if Mexico would not be able to cope with this challenge on its own. This scenario that is predicted for Mexico and the United States could become a tremendous challenge for security at the US-Mexican border, where the US Border Patrol is already monitoring cross-border drug violence:

> Less far-fetched is the extension of a Mexican failure into the borderlands of the United States. Street-level violence already has crossed the border. But a deeper, more systemic corruption—particularly on the local level—could easily extend into the United States, along with paramilitary operations between cartels and between the Mexican government and cartels....U.S. Secretary of Defense Robert Gates recently visited Mexico, and there are potential plans for U.S. aid in support of Mexican government operations. But if the Mexican government became paralyzed and couldn't carry out these operations, the U.S. government would face a stark and unpleasant choice. It could attempt to protect the United States from the violence defensively by sealing off Mexico or controlling the area north of the border more effectively. Or, as it did in the early 20th century, the United States could adopt a forward defense by sending U.S. troops south of the border to fight the battle in Mexico....Mexico's potential failure is important for three reasons. First, Mexico is a huge country, with a population of more than 100 million. Second, it has a large economy—the 14th-largest in the world. And third, it shares an extended border with the world's only global power, one that has assumed for most of the 20th century that its domination of North America and control of its borders is a foregone conclusion. If Mexico fails, there are serious geopolitical repercussions. This is not simply a criminal matter.[37]

Though rhetoric will change and politics will tend to be more pragmatic, the new US administration will face the same challenges, and the government will demonstrate its willingness to solve current problems. President Obama wants full-spectrum dominance of US hegemony, but in a multilateral context. This includes the continuation of US efforts to improve border security. Michael Chertoff, the former secretary of the Department of Homeland Security, advised his successor Janet Napolitano, formerly governor of Arizona, to go on with the construction of the security fence at the border.[38] Like Obama, she is in favor of the "high tech" wall. Therefore, Mexicans do not see any real change coming with regard to the number one topic in the bilateral agenda: immigration. They fear that in the long run the security fence will enlarge the gap between the poor and the rich, North America and Latin America, and the zones of security and instability—without actually solving the problems. Mexico still keeps trembling for its own sake between skepticism, hope, and disillusion.

Notes

1. United States Department of Homeland Security, Yearbook of Immigration Statistics: 2006, Washington, DC: US Department of Homeland Security, Office of Immigration Statistics (2007).
2. Thomas Cieslik, David Felsen, and Akis Kalaitzidis, *"Immigration," A Documentary and Reference Guide* (Westport : Greenwood Press, 2009).
3. See the 1823 Illegal Immigration Enforcement and Empowerment Act; also the 2049 Border Security and Modernization Act of 2005; H.R. 3704 Protecting America Together Act of 2005; H.R. 3622 Border Protecting Corps Act; H.R. 4099 Homeland Security Volunteerism Enhancement Act of 2005.
4. Access via Open Congress, http://www.opencongress.org/ (accessed January 25, 2009).
5. Data from "Secretaria de Economia," *Quezada, Sergio Aguayo: Almanaque Mexicano 2007* (Mexico City, 2007), 231.
6. World Bank, Mexico Country Brief, September 2008, http://go.worldbank.org/QM0CY5UNF0 (accessed December 29, 2008).
7. Council on Foreign Relations, "Building a North American Community," Independent Task Force Report No. 53, New York, 2005.
8. Günther Maihold and Claudia Zilla, "Geteilte Sicherheit in Lateinamerika," *Stiftung Wissenschaft und Politik. SWP-Aktuell* 36 (May 2008), 7.
9. Mark Potter, "Mexican Drug War 'Alarming' U.S. Officials," NBC-World Blog, June 25, 2008, http://worldblog.msnbc.msn.com/archive/2008/06/25/1166487.aspx. (accessed January 25, 2009).
10. Stephanie Hanson, "Mexico's Drug War," Council on Foreign Relations Backgrounder, November 20, 2008, http://www.cfr.org/publication/13689 (accessed December 29, 2008).
11. Freedom House, Mexico (2008), http://freedomhouse.org/template.cfm?page=22&year=2008&country=7447 (accessed January 26, 2009).
12. Transparency International, TI Corruption Perceptions Index 2008, http://www.transparency.org/policy_research/surveys_indices/cpi (accessed January 25, 2009).
13. RSF, Annual Report 2008, http://www.rsf.org/article.php3?id_article=25592 (accessed January 25, 2009).
14. Paul Taylor and Richard Fry, "Hispanics and the 2008 Election: A Swing Vote?" December 6, 2007, http://pewhispanic.org/reports/report.php?ReportID=83 (accessed January 25, 2009).

15. Susan Minushkin and Mark Hugo Lopez, "The Hispanic Vote in the 2008 Democratic Presidential Primaries," Pew Hispanic Center, June 3, 2008, www.pewhispanic.org.

16. Ibid., 12.

17. ITAM (ed.), *México en el mundo*, Vol. 5 (10), November 2008, 2.

18. See survey: Consulta Mitofsky, Los mexicanos y las elecciones EUA 2008 (June 2008), http://www.consulta.com.mx/interiores/99_pdfs/12_mexicanos_pdf/20080622_NA_EleccionesEUA.pdf (accessed December 29, 2008).

19. Ted Lewis, "Trade Deals' Effect on U.S. Immigration a Problem for McCain," *The Mercury News*, July 3, 2008.

20. The Raw Story, "Mexican President to Visit US Amid Immigration Debate," February 10, 2008, http://rawstory.com/news/afp/Mexican_president_to_visit_US_amid__02102008.html (accessed January 28, 2009).

21. Jesus Esquivel, "What Obama Wants in the U.S. Relationship with Mexico," Mexidata.info, November 17, 2008, http://www.mexidata.info/id2064.html (accessed December 29, 2009).

22. Frank James and Ken Ellingwood, "Obama, Calderon meet in Washington," *Los Angeles Times,* January 13, 2009, http://www.latimes.com/news/nationworld/world/la-fg-obama-calderon13-2009-jan13,0,3026293.story (accessed January 25, 2009).

23. Al Giordano, "Obama Meets Calderon, Takes Rahm With Him," Special to the Narco News Bulletin, January 14, 2009, http://www.narconews.com/Issue55/article3338.html (accessed January 21, 2009).

24. *El Universal*, "Pretende Barack Obama mejorar el TLCAN," January 12, 2009.

25. Jorge Ramos and Ricardo Gómez, "Confía PRD que Obama coopere en lucha anticrimen," *El Universal*, January 6, 2009.

26. *La Jornada* "Propone Obama a Calderon actualizar el TLCAN: vocero," January 12, 2009.

27. *La Jornada* "Calderon y Obama por nueva etapa y conjuncion anticrisis," January 12, 2009.

28. Dan Glaister, "US Surge Plan to Contain Mexico Drug Violence," *Guardian*, January 9, 2009.

29. Alberto Cuenca, "Buscará Ebrard cercania con gobierno de Obama," *El Universal*, November 17, 2008.

30. *El Universal,* "Loret de Mola, Carlos: Historias de reportero," November 4, 2008.

31. Ricardo Aleman, "Iternario Politico," *El Universal*, November 4, 2008.

32. Jose Luis Calva, "Primeros 100 dias de Obama," *El Universal*, November 6, 2008.

33. Luis Rubio, "The World's Vote, the View from Mexico," *The American Interest*, November/December 2008.

34. "Vicente Fox llama "burro" a Chávez y critica política de Obama hacia México," *La Tribuna*, December 12, 2008, http://www.latribuna.hn/

news/44/ARTICLE/51337/2008-12-12.html (accessed December 29, 2008). The original quotation is: "poner los pies en la realidad (...) porque en la campaña no lo hizo así."

35. Fund for Peace: Failed States Index 2008, http://www.fundforpeace. org (accessed January 8, 2009).

36. USJFCOM, "Challenges and Implications for the Future Joint Force," Suffolk (VA) 2008, http://www.globalsecurity.org/ military/library/report/2008/joe2008_jfcom.pdf (accessed January 5, 2009).

37. George Friedman, "Mexico: On the Road to a Failed State," Geopolitical Intelligence Report, May 13, 2008, http://www.stratfor.com/weekly/ mexico_road_failed_state (accessed January 2, 2009).

38. Randal Archibold, "Tiene EU plan militar contra narcoviolencia," *El Universal*, January 8, 2009.

2

THE 2008 PRESIDENTIAL ELECTION: THE VIEW FROM VENEZUELA

Lesley Martina Burns[1]

The 2008 US presidential election presented an important opportunity for change in contentious US-Venezuela relations. Neither of the US presidential candidates seemed to offer a complete redefinition of bilateral relations; Barack Obama's position on many of the issues of importance to Venezuela meant that his presidency brings hope for a more conciliatory relationship between Venezuela and the United States. Although this relationship is likely to be more amicable than a John McCain presidency would have been, signals from both countries have been mixed, and there is no certainty on the direction of future relations between the two countries. This chapter provides an analysis of the key factors that may define this relationship during the Obama administration.

Propelled to power on a wave of change, Hugo Chávez, Venezuela's president since 1999, has incited more turbulent relations between Venezuela and the United States by appealing to deeply entrenched historical divisions between the two nations. The George W. Bush administration, occupied with other regions, did not play a strong role in Latin America. This made the 2008 election an important and critical juncture. Chávez often invokes the legend of Latin America's liberator, Simon Bolivar, who sought to unify the modern day countries of Venezuela, Colombia, Ecuador, Peru, Bolivia, and Panama against the Spanish colonial powers. In so doing, Chávez has effectively cast the United States as a colonial power and an imperial enemy that has, according to his argument, successfully subjugated the population of Latin America. Appealing to powerful figures such as Che Guevara and Fidel Castro, Chávez leverages anti-American sentiment to create an "us versus them" dichotomy. Even as these historical heartstrings are pulled, Venezuela remains highly dependent on the United States as a market for the sale of its oil. Despite the anti-American rhetoric and attempts to diversify,

Venezuela receives over 90 percent of its export earnings from oil revenue and the United States remains Venezuelan's largest market.

This Chapter also explores Venezuelan perceptions of the 2008 US presidential election. The primary focus will be on the role of the Venezuelan government, because the government in Venezuela is the main player in regard to relations with other governments. In the national economy, the Venezuelan state is a powerful player since it wholly owns the oil monopoly Petróleos de Venezuela (PDVSA). Moreover, the state plays a strong role in driving private sector relations and, in turn, how the United States and Venezuela interact. In addition, government policies have had a clear impact on US businesses operating in Venezuela, most notably through a recent wave of nationalizations.

To explore how the government perceived the 2008 US presidential election, this chapter begins by briefly summarizing US-Venezuela relations during the Bush administration in order to show how the 2008 election had the potential to change relations between Venezuela and the United States. It then explains how the Republican candidate McCain's and the Democratic candidate Obama's campaign platforms were perceived in Venezuela in contrast to the performance of the Bush administration. It then addresses the issues that the Venezuelan government views as the main bilateral issues: The future of the United States as an empire, the US position on Cuba, drug control, and energy policy. An examination of these issues shows that the position of McCain was perceived to be an extension of the Bush administration's position. This analysis reveals that at times the Venezuelan perception was shaped by a Cold War lens, viewing the world as two opposing poles fighting for ideological supremacy. This chapter demonstrates how Chávez has attempted to develop global and regional institutions; this demonstrates that he sees the possibility for mutual benefit through cooperation. The final section of this chapter investigates the implications of Obama's election as the US president, given Venezuela's global and regional interests and aspirations.

THE VENEZUELAN PERSPECTIVE ON THE MCCAIN/ OBAMA CAMPAIGNS

As an important supplier of oil to the United States, on one hand, and a harsh critic of the US government, on the other, both candidates referred directly to President Chávez on the campaign trail. McCain, who took a stronger anti-Chávez stance than Obama, was critical of Obama's willingness to meet with Chávez. This only fed into Venezuela's ability to paint McCain's policies as an extension of Bush's. From the Venezuelan perspective, the most important issues were prospects for continued US imperialism, its policy on Cuba, and drug and energy policies.

The candidates were clear about their perceptions of Chávez. McCain, for example, stated that "Hugo Chávez has used the cloak of electoral legitimacy to establish a one party dictatorship in Venezuela, breathed new oxygen into the decaying Castro regime in Cuba, allied with Iran and other American enemies, and supported populist, anti-American forces throughout the hemisphere."[2] McCain recognized both the growing wave of anti-American rhetoric that had developed throughout the region and noted Chávez's ability to leverage this anti-Americanism to his advantage. More directly, McCain called Chávez a "dictator."[3] McCain went on to state: "If I am elected president, the United States will forge a new policy toward Latin America and the Caribbean Basin founded on peace and security, shared prosperity, democracy and freedom, and mutual respect."[4] Despite the claim that this was a new direction, McCain's potential policies toward Venezuela have been largely seen as an extension of the Bush administration's policies.

Whereas McCain was adversarial, Obama supported more active engagement abroad, as evidenced by his agreement to meet with leaders such as Chávez. The McCain camp criticized Obama, seeing his willingness to speak to such leaders, potentially with no "preconditions," as a sign of weakness in his foreign policy platform. Obama's official policy for Latin America was to "bolster U.S. interests in the region by pursuing policies that advance democracy, opportunity, and security, and will treat our hemispheric partners and neighbors with dignity and respect."[5] Nonetheless, Obama, like McCain, saw Chávez as problematic, referring to him as a "demagogue" who leads an "authoritarian government."[6]

There was little on the campaign trail to suggest that either a McCain presidency or an Obama presidency would drastically change how the United States viewed US-Venezuela relations. Both candidates sought to improve democracy, security, and respect between the countries. Despite similarities in their agendas toward Venezuela, the Venezuelan government expressed a clear preference for Obama, who was more open to dialogue. A McCain presidency was seen exclusively as a continuation of the Bush administration's policies, an undesirable scenario given US relations with Venezuela under Bush. Peter Hakim and Daniel Erikson of the Inter-American Dialogue both stated that McCain's policies were reminiscent of US policies during the Cold War.[7] Splitting Latin America into "adversaries and allies," McCain's stance oversimplified the relationship because the global system has become far more interdependent than it was during the Cold War.

Even during the campaign, it had become clear to Venezuela that an Obama presidency would offer greater opportunity for rapprochement in bilateral relations. To be sure, the Venezuelan government's preference for Obama stemmed in no small part from a few policies of the Obama campaign that touched issues important to Venezuela's perceived interests. These issues included the role of the United States as a superpower, a power Venezuela believed was used for imperial purposes, such as the subjugation of Cuba, by implementing the drug eradication policy and energy policy.

THE KEY ISSUES FOR VENEZUELA IN THE 2008 US PRESIDENTIAL ELECTION

1. *The Future of the United States as Empire*: The relations between Venezuela and the United States took a downturn under the Bush administration. Scholars and journalists have asserted that negative relations between Latin America, including Venezuela, and the United States stemmed from the fact that the United States has been preoccupied in other regions, including Iraq and Afghanistan.[8] Similarly, in an early speech, McCain attributed growing anti-Americanism to America's preoccupation with other regions.[9] Statistics suggest, however, that the anti-US sentiment in Venezuela is not as severe as it was often made out to be. In the answer to the question, "do you have a positive or a negative opinion of the United States?" asked in a 2007 Consortium of Market Research and Consulting (CIMA) survey, only 26 percent of Venezuelans reported having a negative opinion of the United States. In comparison, when the same question was asked with regard to China, 59 percent of Venezuelans reported a positive image of China; when asked about Russia, 50 percent reported having a positive opinion. Although the negative numbers were reported for the United States and positive numbers for China and Russia, from this information we can extrapolate that perhaps 41 percent view China in a negative light and 50 percent view Russia in a negative light. This poll suggests that the vehement anti-Americanism professed by Chávez is not an opinion shared by the majority of the Venezuelan population. This does not explain how the rhetoric has worked to build support for Chavez.

Moreover, the development of multilateral relations among Latin American countries has occurred in the absence of US leadership, thus showing that regional cooperation can occur without US initiation. Chávez has resisted a unipolar domination by the United States,[10] and has made no attempt to hide his personal disdain for President Bush, calling him the "devil" in a speech at the United Nations. This was one in a long list of personal insults of the American President that included calling him "ignorant," a "donkey," a "sick man," "immoral," a "coward," a "liar," a "genocide promoter," a "killer of children," a "drunkard," and a "ridiculous man."[11] Personal attacks against President Bush stem from the Venezuelan government's belief and repeated accusations that the US government is responsible for initiating coups against Chávez. To justify these claims, reference is made to the 2002 coup attempt that removed Chávez from power for nearly forty-eight hours. The United States' recognition of the new president, Pedro Carmona, was interpreted as direct support for the coup. Further evidence to support the argument that the United States seeks to overtly undermine the Chávez government comes predominantly from the US government funding of civil society organizations vocally opposed to the government's policies.

Adding further fuel to the fire are Chávez's repeated claims to have uncovered US plans to assassinate him. These allegations are reminiscent of the US Central Intelligence Agency's (CIA) plots to kill Cuba's Fidel Castro in the 1960s. Allegations of such plans helped to rally anti-imperial rhetoric and, in turn, support for Chávez. In addition, opposition groups are regularly accused of working for, or being agents of, the CIA. Though many of these allegations are difficult to sustain, it is known that the National Endowment for Democracy (NED) has provided funding for civil society groups associated with the Venezuelan opposition.

Various Venezuelan governments have for quite some time attempted to cast the United States as an "evil empire." Carlos Romero argues that when relations between the two countries have been mutually beneficial, Venezuelan attitudes toward the United States have been positive; when the United States is believed to be unilaterally imposing its hegemonic position, anti-Americanism rises, especially among the general public.[12]

Chávez has been accused of employing anti-American sentiment to detract the Venezuelans from domestic political problems, including a growing crime rate, high inflation, and widespread corruption. For example, Milos Alcalay stated that "President Chávez has used his anti-Americanism as a form of government policy, not only internationally but also when faced with a series of errors that he cannot explain."[13] By building the idea that the United States is threatening Venezuela's sovereignty, Chávez successfully appeals to centuries-old anti-imperial sentiments that have characterized US-Latin American relations.

The 2008 US presidential election came at a critical time in Venezuela-US relations. Diplomatic tension reached a high point when Venezuela expelled the US ambassador in September 2008. The expulsion was done in support of Bolivia's Evo Morales, whose motivation to expel the US ambassador to Bolivia was based on accusations that the US embassy played a role in supporting violent antigovernment protests. Chávez stated that he had no intention of reestablishing relations with the Bush administration. Given the tendency to associate McCain with the Bush administration, the prospect of an Obama presidency offered a stronger opportunity for cooperation. Notwithstanding this opportunity, the Venezuelan government has taken a strong anti-US stance and there is no direct evidence that attempts to alter the relationship will be made in the immediate future.

2. *Cuba*: The nearly half-century-old US trade embargo against Cuba, combined with the influence of the Cuban vote in the United States, has earned Cuba a special place in US foreign policy—especially in election years. Despite what would seem like an antiquated carryover from the Cold War, US-Cuban relations have an impact on US policy in general.[14] Cuba and Venezuela have flourished in recent years based not only on a shared disdain for US imperialism but also on an exchange of Venezuelan oil for Cuban health care and social development assistance through both personnel and know-how. These increasing relations have led Chávez to become a vocal advocate for Cuba. Although neither of the presidential candidates has stated that he would be willing to remove the embargo on Cuba, Obama professed that he would be willing to lessen restrictions on travel to Cuba and to reduce limits on remittances, thereby easing restrictions on how Cuban-Americans living in the United States could interact with Cuba.[15] McCain took a stronger anti-Cuba stance, and the Republican candidate even criticized Obama for his willingness to engage in dialogue with Raul Castro, Fidel Castro's younger brother and successor designate, and the current President of Cuba himself.

Chávez's concern for Cuba goes beyond ideological guidance driven by an anti-imperial stance that is shared with, and influenced by, Fidel Castro. Venezuela also provides major oil subsidies to Cuba. A large portion of the money that the Venezuelan opposition and nongovernmental organizations (NGOs) have accused Chávez of giving to other countries over the past ten years has reportedly gone toward these subsidies. Moreover, Venezuela sees the US embargo on Cuba as an intentional act of imperialism. In light of the importance of Cuba for Venezuela's interests, Chávez showed a clear preference for the candidate Obama. Viewing Obama as the candidate more open to changing the US policy toward Cuba, Chávez stated directly that if Obama became American President, he should remove the US-imposed embargo on Cuba. However, neither of the presidential candidates seemed willing to go this far. Nevertheless, Obama's willingness to engage Cuba was seen as a welcome change.

Venezuela was also critical of human rights abuses at Guantanamo Bay. The candidates' policies on Guantanamo were similar, with both McCain and Obama stating that they would close down Guantanamo. Since both candidates shared this view, it was not a divisive issue and did not become important in Venezuela's perception of the 2008 presidential election.

3. *Drug Policy*: How the presidential candidate planned to proceed with the war against drugs was important for Venezuela. The US government

implemented "Plan Colombia" in 2000 and put over 1.3 billion US dollars toward reducing drug production in Colombia and the surrounding region.[16] As a bordering country of Colombia, a portion of the initial funding was directed toward fighting drug trafficking in Venezuela. In 2005, Venezuela cut off cooperation with the US Drug Enforcement Administration (DEA), asserting that the DEA was involved in espionage—an accusation the United States denied. Chávez reassured international law enforcement agencies that he would continue to cooperate with them, however. Venezuela and the United States have since implemented new smaller-scale operations.[17] The Venezuelan government still remains suspicious of US involvement.

The United States continues to be concerned with drug trafficking in Venezuela, and the DEA argued that its expulsion led to an increase in drug trafficking through Venezuela. John Walters, the director of the US Office of National Drug Control Policy,[18] stated that Venezuela was not only a "safe haven" but also a "major facilitator" of drug trafficking. This same position was reiterated by Deputy Secretary of State James Steinberg, who stated that the ease of drug transit through Venezuela would be a major concern for the new administration.[19] Steinberg also noted that rampant corruption and a weak judicial system make Venezuela more difficult to deal with.

As a supporter of the fight against drugs in Colombia, the United States is concerned about Venezuela's control in the border region. The border between Colombia and Venezuela remains a dangerous corridor for drug trafficking. Insecurity is further exacerbated by the large number of refugees who cross the border from Colombia into Venezuela and by an increase in kidnappings associated with guerrilla and paramilitary groups. Furthermore, accusations that Chávez has funded the Revolutionary Armed Forces of Colombia (FARC) have heightened US concerns over Venezuelan motivations. Venezuela has been accused of not only harboring FARC rebels, but also of funding the group's insurgence against the Colombian government.[20] This relationship is believed to be enabled in part through the help of Venezuelan government officials. The nature of the relationship between the Venezuelan government and the FARC is unclear, but a more amicable relationship in the region, if not directly with Venezuela, will be the best way for FARC to combat the war on drugs. The probability of this occurring under the new administration will likely be linked to the Venezuelan government's perception of US imperial intentions. Obama's agenda promoting greater engagement suggests that the relationship under an Obama administration will change from what had been the policy under the Bush administration. For Venezuela, US policies regarding antidrug and antiterrorist programs were a concern during the 2008 election because Venezuelan government officials have often viewed US involvement in the region as imperially motivated. The wave of optimism that initially arose with Obama's election was mollified when Chavez likened the Obama administration to Bush's and stated in speeches following Obama's inauguration that relations were unlikely to change.

4. *Energy Policy*: Oil is the lifeblood of Venezuela's economy, so naturally, the government is concerned with the candidates' positions on energy policy. The Obama-Biden platform promoted a regional "Energy Partnership for the Americas" aimed at sustainable growth and clean energy.[21] Obama put greater emphasis on developing alternative renewable energy sources through greater research and development. McCain, on the other hand, sought to reduce foreign dependency on oil through greater domestic offshore exploration and drilling.

McCain's agenda threatened to reduce oil exports from Venezuela. However, according to the Department of Energy's *Energy Administration Initiative* (EIA), these attempts to increase production were unlikely to impact domestic production until 2030, and even then, would not have raised oil output by more than a few percent (Petroleum Economist). Therefore, the McCain policy would be unlikely to directly impact foreign suppliers in the near future.

In an effort to reduce dependence on exports to the United States, Chávez has attempted to establish relations with diverse business partners in the oil industry through closer relations with Iran, China, and Russia. Oil industry experts, however, have suggested that these attempts have not provided Venezuela with the necessary technical expertise to increase its oil production. To ensure that production levels remain high, Chávez has reportedly reopened contract bidding for Western counties.[22] This signifies a change in relations between the United States and Venezuela, considering that in 2007 the Venezuelan government nationalized several foreign-owned projects, including those from US-based Conoco Phillips and Exxon Mobile. Thus, the future of relations between Venezuela and the United States will be determined by both economic necessity and by political relations. Despite increasingly hostile political relations between the two governments, the economic interdependence driven by the necessity for oil has kept the two nations trading.

The importance of the oil issue and its impact on perceptions of the US election should not be underestimated. The Economist Intelligence Unit states that Venezuela has become much more dependent on oil under Chávez. Specifically, "in 1998 non-oil income accounted for about 30% of foreign exchanges, but now it is only about 7%."[23] The need to diversify into the production of goods in the non-oil sector remains high.[24] Fear of greater disruptions come from public support from both Iran and Venezuela to change the OPEC exchange currency from US dollars to Euros. This idea goes back at least as far as 2001, but this move would be met with a strong response from the United States, a move that is understood by OPEC members, which suggests that such a change in exchange currency is unlikely to occur in the immediate future.

According to the Energy Information Administration, "Venezuela contains some of the largest oil and natural gas reserves in the world. It consistently ranks as one the top suppliers of US oil imports and is among the top ten crude oil producers in the world."[25] The interdependent nature of US-Venezuela relations means that neither country is likely to dramatically change the terms of the relationship, at least in the immediate term.

This means that, in the short-term, threats and anti-America rhetoric are unlikely to translate into the disruption or closure of trade ties. The United States remains one of Venezuela's largest trading partners. In fact, Venezuela still sends to the United States more than 50 percent of the oil that it exports.[26] Despite turbulent relations, direct attempts to cut off economic relations would be extraordinarily damaging to Venezuela. This suggests that despite the movement toward "Bolivarian socialism" advanced by Chávez, there does not appear to be a current threat that Venezuela would close off economic relations even if diplomatic relations are turbulent.

VENEZUELA IN A POLYCENTRIC WORLD

Venezuela has been diversifying its global relationships. It is not only anti-Americanism that has caused Latin American countries to attempt to work more closely together, but also the fact that the United States' engagement in other regions has enabled Venezuela to take more concrete attempts to advocate for a polycentric world by building ties with a wide array of nations. Among the most notable relations that will be of relevance to the United States are Venezuela's relationships with Russia, China, and Iran. Not only has the United States had difficult relationships with these countries, but they, for the most part, share Venezuela's attempts to move toward a multilateral international system by reducing US hegemony. If such alliances are viewed through a *Realpolitik* lens, the prospects for greater future cooperation are daunting. Venezuela has attempted to increase its influence both within Latin America and on the world stage. The key motivating factor, as repeatedly stated by Chávez, is to decrease the United States' imperial influence through diversification of trade partners, stockpiling of weapons, and anti-US rhetoric. Whereas McCain was seen as more inclined to view such actions as a flash back to the Cold War, Obama was perceived to appreciate the "complex interdependence" that has developed. The greater integration with Russia, China, and Iran will be briefly explored prior to moving onto an analysis of Venezuela's increasing involvement in interhemispheric affairs.

Venezuela has been actively trying to improve its relations with Russia over the past years. In late 2008, the Russian military participated in military exercises in the Caribbean for the first time since the Cold War ended. The Russian military brought warships to Venezuela to conduct military exercises, which included training exercises for the Venezuelan navy. Chávez declared that these training exercises were not intended to provoke the United States. He also noted that they could be used to create a pluripolar world.[27] In his attempt to build such an international environment, "President Chávez insisted that South America, including the Caribbean, has to be one of the facets of world power."[28] He sees himself as a key mastermind of this strategy. Although this is of great strategic importance, it does little to actually threaten the balance of power in the region. The United States continues to command the world's largest military.

Venezuela has begun to stockpile weapons. Some argue that this has been done to increase protection, others assert that in buying weapons and increasing military alliance with counties such as Russia, Venezuela is preparing for an offensive. Venezuela has purchased "radars, fighter jets, helicopters, and tens of thousands of Kalashnikov rifles."[29] *Jane's Defence Weekly* has reported that Venezuela plans to boost its defense spending by 25 percent in 2009.[30]

To further strengthen trade ties and to help increase trade and industrial development in Venezuela, Russia has also contributed to offshore oil projects and to a Gazprom project intended to ensure that Venezuela could produce its own gas in the next several years. Such projects are of great importance for reducing Venezuela's dependence on the US markets to sell oil and on US companies for technical expertise. In addition, Venezuela has begun building a nuclear reactor with Russian assistance. It has stated that the purpose of this reactor is for energy and the intention is entirely peaceful, however.

In its relations with China, Venezuela has been paying particular attention to the economic and trade dimensions. The market with the highest economic capacity to replace the United States as a consumer of Venezuelan oil is China. Ideologically, Chávez has proclaimed that the "Bolivarian Revolution" was founded upon the ideology of Mao Zedong's revolution in China. Dominquez stated that Venezuela sought a political alliance with China in order to provide a "hard balance" against US power.[31] Dominquez notes that China has increased its relations with Venezuela, but argues that these have been less relevant than relations with other countries—and that these relations are driven by economics. China has not shown any great evidence of actively supporting Venezuela's ideological shift away from the United States. Since China has little interest in entrenching ideological beliefs, most experts believe that the relationship will be predominantly economic.[32]

Economically, China cannot quickly nor seamlessly replace the United States as a key market for Venezuela. High transportation costs as a result of geographically distant location still make trade with China more expensive. In addition, Venezuelan oil is not easily refined, and specialized equipment is required for this. Building the capacity to refine Venezuelan oil cannot be done overnight. To progress in the direction of enabling China to refine Venezuelan oil, China and Venezuela have solidified plans to build a refinery in Orinoco.[33] China joins a growing list of countries that are developing oil production partnerships with Venezuela, which include Belarus, Cuba, Russia, and Iran, according to Reuters reports.[34]

Venezuela's trade with China has also increased, but the increase in this relationship is not substantive if we consider the role that China has played throughout the entire hemisphere. Considering the proportion of Chinese trade, Venezuela remains a Latin American country of comparatively lesser importance from the Chinese perspective. China has set its priorities in Latin America almost entirely on economic relations, making Brazil China's most important partner in the region.[35] The economic relationship between China and Venezuela is still in its infancy, given the size and projected future demands of the Chinese market.

Moreover, Venezuela has strengthened its bilateral trade links with Iran. US tensions have been high with Iran and it remains under UN Security Council sanctions for its program to enrich uranium. For its part, Venezuela has been a vocal supporter of Iran's right to a nuclear program. In a move toward closer relations, Venezuela and Iran have reached a deal to sell Venezuelan oil in Iran. Although Iran is an oil-producing nation, it needs to import refined oil in order to meet its domestic demands. Other economic deals include a petrochemical plant, construction contracts, and factories to produce powdered milk throughout Venezuela. Peter DeShazo, in his capacity as the America's program Director at the Center for Strategic and International Studies, stated that "foreign investment in the entire hydrocarbons sector remains inhibited by the government of Venezuela's fiscal voracity and by political uncertainties."[36] Concern over operating with the Venezuelan government has impacted the extent to which other countries are willing to engage, according to the CSIS study.

The United States is concerned with Venezuela's close relations with Iran and its weapons purchases from Russia. The United States, according to the Economist Intelligence Unit, sees these factors as having the potential to destabilize relations in Latin America.[37] For its part, within Latin America, Venezuela has been actively cultivating closer relationships. This chapter will now turn to an examination of these relationships.

VENEZUELA'S CHANGING ROLE IN LATIN AMERICA

In the past decade Venezuela has sought to play a larger role in the western hemisphere. This means that Obama is inheriting a very different hemisphere than Bush did when he took power. Some have accused the Bush administration of not paying enough attention to the United States' backyard backyard, and others have qualified this by stating that the United States has been too preoccupied with the war in Iraq and the fight against global terrorism to solidify its influence in the region. During the Bush Presidency, Latin American countries forged closer economic and political relations with each other. Michael Shifter reported that neither McCain nor Obama put forth any "great new thinking on Latin America."[38] This suggests that it is unlikely for the new US administration under President Obama to drastically alter its policy toward Venezuela. Still, Obama's presidency could be an important determinant of future directions in US-Latin American relations.

Some important recent Western hemispheric trends have had an impact on how Venezuela has perceived the election and will no doubt have an impact on US-Venezuela relations under the Obama administration. Chávez has used this opportunity to develop his aspirations to become an influential leader throughout Latin America, if not globally. To support this bid, Chávez has initiated the creation of multilateral lending agencies reminiscent of the International Monetary Fund and the World Bank through the Banco Del Sur (Bank of the South). He has also backed the building of a trade agreement, the Bolivarian Alternative for the Americas (ALBA), largely to replace the failed US-led Free Trade Area of the Americas. ALBA seeks to include greater civil society participation and economic development that benefit the people over privatization.

Venezuela is looking toward decoupling regional economic development from American involvement. Chávez has argued that Latin America has fallen victim to an "imperial tool of economic domination," created by the regions reliance on structural adjustment programs and the "Washington Consensus" policies promoted by international organizations such as the International Monetary Fund. In response, he has taken a leadership role in setting up the Banco del Sur. The bank was created at the end of 2007 on Venezuela's initiative to counter the influence of the International Monetary Fund (IMF), the World Bank (IBRD), and the Inter-American Development Bank (IDB). In addition, its purpose is to provide greater monetary independence to counter the threat of US domination; the bank aims to promote infrastructure development and integration among Latin American countries. The main funders are Argentina, Brazil, and Venezuela; other member countries include Bolivia, Ecuador, Paraguay, and Uruguay. Other Latin American nations will also be eligible to receive the bank's funding.

Given that the bank's intention was, at least in part, to increase relations within Latin America, it is considered an organization to mitigate regional conflict. In fact, Brazil was motivated to join in large part to counterbalance

Venezuela's influence. The bank's role as a conflict mediator suggests that the bank could have some political weight. If it is able to increase its influence, the United States would face the possibility of dealing with these countries as a bloc instead of dealing with each country individually through bilateral diplomacy. Moreover, without the ability to insist that countries implement broad, sweeping structural adjustment programs in order to receive funding from the international financial institutions dominated by the United States, such as the IMF, IBRD, and IDB, the United States would lose significant influence over the direction of economic reform in the region.

Furthermore, Venezuela has expressed its interest in further regional integration, moving beyond economic integration. In addition to a bank to fund development in Latin America, regional integration has been reinforced through the Alternativa Bolivariana para las Americas (ALBA). This regional trading block includes Cuba, Venezuela, Nicaragua, Bolivia, Honduras, Dominica, Antigua and Bermuda, and San Vincent and the Grenadines (Ecuador has been granted observer status). The purpose of ALBA is to present an alternative to the US-led Free Trade Area of the Americas. The FTAA failed when several member countries banded together to object to the lack of transparency in the negotiation process, and to several policies seen as too neoliberal.

ALBA states that its intention is to overcome existing asymmetries in the region and to reduce inequality by reducing poverty, instead of focusing on trade liberalization. Since the organization is new, it is unclear how much of an impact ALBA will have. There is a general agreement that the previous wave of economic development that was based on the Washington Consensus largely failed to deliver on the promises of decreased inequality. It is important to mention this attempt by ALBA at regional integration as it is explicitly anti-status quo. The organization was established in large part based on the understanding that neoliberal economic relations had failed to deliver benefits to Latin American countries, and to adequately redistribute resources to the people who live in these countries. ALBA's success will be largely dependent on how good it is at maintaining economic stability—this will be put to the test as a global economic recession looms.

A larger trade union involving more countries in South America has been created, and is called the "Unión de Naciones Suramericanas" (UNASUR). Membership in UNASUR includes all South American countries (except French Guiana). It is modeled after the European Union both in its aspirations for political unification and because there has been talk of a common currency. This organization has often been deemed to be an inter-American NATO. However, Jane's Defence Weekly states that "Chávez's calls for creation of NATO-type alliance in South America have largely been ignored."[39] Yet, the organization, which is seen as a union of MERCOSUR and the Andean Community, has continued to push for economic development based on transparency and equality. The future of this organization is uncertain, but it is seen as significant because it is one among several attempts at regional integration that do not include the United States. The future of US involvement in the region will be impacted based on how Obama engages the region.

Even in the absence of the United States, Latin America is making concrete attempts to integrate and cooperate among themselves. Having taken a clear initiative in the establishment of these organizations, Chávez has been accused of projecting himself to a leadership position. There is, of course, one major notable difference: Chávez focuses on the ability of these organizations to bring greater wealth and equality to the people in these countries. Again, it is too soon to conclude whether UNASUR will be successful. Similar policies to reduce poverty have been implemented earlier in Venezuela, but a lack of transparency in the country makes it difficult to evaluate the true impact of these changes. Few argue that the programs have had no impact; however, several others argue that they have been motivated more by politics than by necessity.[40] Additionally, critics argue that this development model cannot be implemented in countries that do not benefit from oil windfalls like Venezuela does.

The Future of Venezuela-US Relations Under Obama

As previously discussed, throughout the presidential campaign, Obama's position on the issue of importance to Venezuela made him the preferred candidate. His election in no way promises to be a cure-all for US-Venezuela relations, but it provides an important opportunity to normalize relations between the two countries. Chávez rarely gives a speech without reference to the "imperial threat" that comes from the United States. The Bush administration did little to publically respond to his personal attacks. Obama's election, in what Gamarra has called a country that "is widely seen as racist and imperialist," is significant on many fronts. Chávez, who shares the perception of the United States as imperialist and racist, has used this image to bolster his "us versus them" policy.[41] This fear has been used to ensure that the military and militia are trained for an imminent imperial attack. This threat has helped to unite support behind Chavez. The support that Chavez gains from highlighting the potential threat of the United States helps explain why Obama was so quickly painted, by the Venezuelan administration, as an extension of the Bush administration, despite initial optimism.

Optimism for more cordial relations was found in the Venezuelan Foreign Affairs Minister Nicolas Maduro's comments. Maduro reflected on the significance of Obama's election, stating that "for the first time in history of humanity [Obama's election] opens up the possibility of a world without empires."[42] Nevertheless, optimistic views such as Maduro's notwithstanding, it appears unlikely that a marked difference in policy toward Latin America was on the horizon.[43]

Chávez noted on several occasions the significance of Obama's ethnicity: "The historic election of a man of African descent (Obama's father was Kenyan) to the head of the most powerful nation in the world is the symptom that the change of an epoch that has been developing from the South of the Americas could be touching the doors of the United States."[44] To be sure, this is a noteworthy accomplishment, as Obama himself noted in his inaugural speech on January 20, 2009: "A man whose father less than 60 years ago might not have been served at a local restaurant can now stand before you to take this sacred oath." This fact should certainly be celebrated by those within the Venezuelan administration who have tended to see the United States as racist and indeed see it as a triumph for racial equality globally.

Chávez has made statements to suggest that Obama's ethnicity may impact his presidency: "We don't ask him to be a revolutionary, we don't ask him to be a socialist, only that, as a black man about to become president of the United States, he take his place in history."[45] Riding this wave of optimism, Chávez stated that he would be willing to negotiate with the United States. Specifically, he stated in a speech that "I am willing to sit down and converse on equal footing and with respect."[46]

However, such optimism toward the incoming Obama administration was not long lived in Venezuela. Some critics have suggested that the demonization of the United States has been a necessary pillar to gain domestic support during a time of increasing economic hardship.[47] Chavez reverted to this approach when he called Obama the "new leader of the empire," accusing the United States of meddling in a referendum campaign held in February, 2009, in which Chávez won the right to eliminate presidential term limits. It remains unclear how the new White House will react to such accusations.

Obama was clear in his inaugural speech about the United States' role in the world: "We are ready to lead once more." He also addressed the growing anti-American sentiment. Although not necessarily directly aiming at Chávez, he stated: "To those who blame their societies' ills on the West, know that your people will judge you on what you can build not on what you destroy." Since Chávez has often relied on accusing the imperial power of holding down the people of Latin America, this message is of great relevance to the region. Moreover, this message warns that actors should not look to anti-Americanism as a means of bolstering domestic support. The warning against the use of the United States as a scapegoat is of particular relevance to Venezuela. The irony is that while arguing against unfair imperial actions, by some measures Venezuela has increased, not decreased, its reliance on the United States.

James Steinberg, speaking as the new deputy secretary of state, emphasized US willingness to engage with Venezuela, especially on issues of drug trafficking and on Venezuela's relationship with the FARC. For its part, Venezuela cannot do without economic ties to the United States. Trade relations are not likely to be impacted either way by Obama's election. The extent to which anti-American rhetoric continues will depend both on the domestic impact it has and on how the United States reacts. Further, the Obama administration would leverage little from a mudslinging fight with Venezuela. If the United States initiates a change in relations, this could fuel anti-American sentiment throughout Latin America, if not across the globe. For the United States, there does not seem to be any strategic advantage for such a shift. Should a swing occur, it would signify a remarkable change in global affairs.

The Obama presidency offers Venezuela a greater hope for rapprochement that would not have existed had McCain become president. As Obama begins his term in a time of global financial unrest, his administration faces far-reaching challenges, many of which cannot be anticipated in a fast changing globally integrated world.

NOTES

1. The author would like to thank Tessa Matsuzaki and Raul Pacheco-Vega for their support and assistance with this chapter. A special thanks is also extended to the Instituto de Estudios Superiores de Administración (IESA), which provided research support while the author was a visiting Research Fellow at Caracas, Venezuela in 2005–2008. Gerardo Gonzalez, Universidad Central de Venezuela, contributed valuable research and insight into this article.
2. CNN, "McCain's June 20, 2007 address on Latin America," http://edition.cnn.com/2007/POLITICS/12/21/mccain.trans.latinamerica/index.html?iref=newssearch (access on January 13, 2009).
3. Michael Shifter, "U.S.-Latin American Relations: Recommendations for the New Administration," University of Virginia Miller Center Forum, October 27, 2008, Transcript and audio/video recording available at http://www.thedialogue.org/page.cfm?pageID=32&pubID=1625 (accessed January 9, 2008).
4. CNN 2007.
5. Obama-Biden Plan, "Barack Obama and Joe Biden's Plan to Secure America and Restore our Standing," *Obama for America* (2008), http://origin.barackobama.com/issues/foreign_policy/#onlatinamerica (accessed on January 13, 2009).

6. James Suggett, "Chávez Hopes to Improve Venezuela-U.S. Relations if Obama Wins Presidency," 2008, http://www.venezuelanalysis.com/news/3925 (accessed on November 12, 2008).

7. Peter Hakim, "What Latin America Can Expect from the Next US President?" *Inter-American Dialogue*, October 22, 2008, http://www.thedialogue.org/page.cfm?pageID=32&pubID=1626 (accessed January 9, 2008).
   Daniel P. Erikson, "Will the American Elections Shake Up Washington's Cuba Policy?" *Inter-American Dialogue*, October 13, 2008, http://www.thedialogue.org/page.cfm?pageID=32&pubID=1624 (accessed January 9, 2008).

8. Michael Shifter, "U.S.-Latin American Relations: Recommendations for the New Administration," University of Virginia Miller Center Forum, October 27, 2008, Transcript and audio/video recording available at http://www.thedialogue.org/page.cfm?pageID=32&pubID=1625 (accessed January 9, 2008).

9. CNN 2007.

10. Daniel Hellinger, "Political Overview: The Breakdown of *Puntofijismo* and the Rise of *Chavismo*," in Steve Ellner and Daniel Hellinger, *Venezuelan Politics in the Chávez Era: Class, Polarization & Conflict* (2008).

11. Aporrea, "Presidente Chávez cataloga a Bush de ignorante, burro, hombre enfermo, inmoral, cobarde, mentiroso, genocida, matañiños, borracho y ridículo," March 19, 2006, http://www.aporrea.org/tiburon/n74802.html—*19/03/06* (accessed on January 13, 2009).

12. Carlos A. Romero, "Jugando con el Globo: La Política exterior de Hugo Chávez," Caracas: Ediciones B. (2006).

13. Inigo Guevara, "Socialism: Alive and well in the New Venezuela," *Jane's Defence Weekly*, October 3, 2007.

14. The United States is pressured to remove the Cuban Embargo every year through a vote in the General Assembly of the United Nations. In 2007, a total of 184 countries voted in favor of removing the embargo. However, the United States insisted that it was an issue of bilateral relations and that the true embargo was against the freedom that is denied to the Cuban people ("UN Once Again Calls for End to United States Embargo against Cuba," United Nations, October 30, 2007. http://www.un.org/apps/news/story.asp? NewsID=24471&Cr=Cuba&Cr1= [accessed December 18, 2008]).

15. Control over the remittances to Cuba are regulated by the Cuban Assets Control Regulations (CACR), which limits the amount that Cuban nationals can send and specifies to whom the remittances can be sent. The policy has changed considerably since the embargo on Cuba was initially implemented in 1962. For a more complete overview of the restriction, and the chronology of changes, see Mark Sullivan, "Cuba: US Restrictions on Travel and Remittances," CRS Report Prepared

for Members and Committees of Congress, RL 31139, January 21, 2009. Washington, DC: Congressional Research Services.

16. Raphael Perl, "Drug Control: International Policy and Approaches," in *Illegal Drugs and Government Policies*, Barton (ed.), (New York: Nova Publishers, 2007), 32.

17. Greg Morsbach, "US, Venezuela to seal drug accord. British Broadcast Corporation," Caracas Venezuela (2008).

18. The US Office of National Drug Control Policy is a component of the executive branch of the US government with the mandate of "establishing policies, priorities, and objectives for the Nation's drug control program," http://www.whitehousedrugpolicy.gov/about/index.html (accessed January 22, 2009).

19. Pedro M Burelli, "Obama's Policy toward Hugo Chavez," *Petroleum World*, January 23, 2009, www.petroleumworld.com/Lag09012301. htm (accessed on 23 January, 2009).

20. Rory Carroll, "Laptop emails link Venezuela to Colombian Guerrillas," May 16, 2008, guardian.co.uk (accessed January 19, 2009).

21. Obama-Biden Plan 2008.

22. Simon Romero, "Chavez Lets West to Make Oil Bids as Prices Plunge," *New York Times*, January 15, 2009, http://www.nytimes.com/2009/01/15/world/americas/15venez.html (accessed January 12, 2009).

23. Complicating any analysis of oil production in Venezuela is the discrepancy in statistics. The Venezuelan state-owned oil company (PDVSA) claims to have produced "3.3 million barrels a day throughout most of 2008. But other sources, like OPEC, of which Venezuela is a member, place the figure closer to 2.3 million and show a fall of about 100,000 barrels a day from a year earlier." See Juan Forero, "Post Foreign Service As Election Looms, Chávez Steps Up Rhetoric: Venezuelan Leader Warns of U.S. Plots Against the Country," *The Washington Post*, October 16, 2008.

24. Economist Intelligence Unit—Risk Briefing, "Venezuela Risk: Alert—Future of Chavismo at Stake as Cash Runs Low," Risk Briefing, January 22, 2009.

25. The Energy Information Administration provides the official statistics from the US government with the aim of providing policy neutral data, forecasts, and analysis. It is within the US Department of Energy but its analysis is independent of the Departments. For more information, see http://www.eia.doe.gov/.

26. Michael Shifter, "U.S.-Latin American Relations: Recommendations for the New Administration," University of Virginia Miller Center Forum, October 27, 2008. Transcript and audio/video recording available at http://www.thedialogue.org/page.cfm?pageID=32&pubID=1625 (accessed January 9, 2008), 10.

27. Prensa Presidencial, "South America Should be among the New Facets of World Power," Embassy of the Bolivarian Republic of Venezuela Press Office President Chavez, November 25, 2008, http://www.embavenez-us.org/news.php?nid=4560.

28. Ibid.
29. Nick Coleman, "Russian Leader ue in Venezuela for Show of Military Muscle," *Agence France Presse*, November 26, 2008.
30. Guevara, "Socialism: Alive And Well In The New Venezuela," October 3, 2007.
31. More information on Chavez's visits to China from the official Chinese news Agency Xinhua is available at http://www.news.xinhuanet.com/world/2004-12/22/content_2367821.htm. Additional information from Reuters is available at http://www.freerepublic.com/focus/f-news/1308798/posts; and from the Associated Press at http://www.boston.com/news/world/articles/2004/12/28/chavez_predicts_energy_deals_with_china_to_boost_trade_to_3b/. For an analysis of Sino-Latin American relations, see Dominquez 2006.
32. Jorge Domínguez, "China's Relations with Latin America: Shared Gains, Asymmetric Hopes," *Inter-America Dialogue*, Washington, DC (June 2006). NACLA, "Progressive Policy for the Americas? A NACLA Roundtable," Report: US Policy, January/February 2009.
33. Steven Bodzin and Wang Ying, "Venezuela, China to Build Refineries, Boost Sales," *Bloomberg*, http://www.bloomberg.com/apps/news?pid=20670001&refer=china&si.(accessed January 10, 2009).
34. Reuters News, "Venezuela Puts $12 billion Cost on New China Oil Deal," May 13, 2008.
35. Domínguez, "China's Relations with Latin America: Shared Gains, Asymmetric Hopes," 47.
36. Peter DeShazo, Center for Strategic and International Studies, "Venezuela Forum Conclusions and Future Implications: A Report of the CSIS Americas Program," ed. Center for Strategic and International Studies, *Policy Papers on the Americas*, Volume XIX: Study 1 (April 2008), 8.
37. Energy Information Administration, 2007, http://www.eia.doe.gov/emeu/cabs/Venezuela/Background.html (accessed January 30, 2009).
38. Shifter, "U.S.-Latin American Relations: Recommendations for the New Administration," 2008.
39. Inigo Guevara, "Venezuela Boosts Its Spending on defence by 25%." *Jane's Defence Weekly,* November 19, 2008, 10.
40. Michael Penfold, "Clientelism and Social Funds: Empirical Evidence from Chávez's 'Misiones' Programs In Venezuela," Caracas Venezuela (May 2006).
41. Eduardo Gamarra, "The 2008 Presidential Elections: Does (Did) Latin America Matter?" Latin American and Caribbean Center, Florida International University (2008), http://lacc.fiu.edu/ (accessed on January 22, 2009).
42. "Venezuela: No Haste to Arrange Chavez-Obama Meeting," EFE News Service, November 6, 2008.
43. Shifter, "U.S.-Latin American Relations: Recommendations for the New Administration," 2008.

44. Venezuela, 2008.

45. Ibid.

46. James Suggett, "Chávez Hopes to Improve Venezuela-U.S. Relations if Obama Wins Presidency," 2008, http://www.venezuelanalysis.com/news/3925 (accessed on November 12, 2008).

47. Francisco Toro, "For Chavez, Obama = Bush," *Huffington Post*, 2008, www.huffingtonpost.com/francisco-toro/ (accessed on January 22, 2009).

3

BRAZIL: BETWEEN CONTINUITY
AND CHANGE

João Pontes Nogueira and Kai Michael Kenkel

INTRODUCTION

US presidential elections have, in the past twenty years, received considerable attention from the Brazilian media, particularly given the importance of bilateral relations in the historical perspective. Currently, public opinion tends to concentrate its attention on issues directly affecting Brazilian interests, usually in the areas of finance and trade, as well as—to a lesser degree—on the global role of the United States as the sole military/strategic world power in the post-Cold War era.

Due to what is perceived as the limiting nature of the two-party system being practiced in the United States, presidential elections are viewed as highly dependent on the candidates' personalities and therefore as having limited potential to truly alter policy outcomes. However, this clearly was not the case with the 2008 presidential election. The long and intensely contested primary process in the Democratic Party in particular, with its added interest of a contest between an African-American and a well-known female candidate, generated, as in most of the world, a great deal of attention in Brazil. Additionally, the perceived declining prestige of the United States worldwide and widespread antagonism toward the incumbent Bush administration also increased Brazilian domestic interest in the outcome.

This chapter takes note of the unusual degree of space given in Brazilian mainstream media to the 2008 presidential election. The coverage in the national newspapers, in the major television and cable networks, the radio, and the Internet was unprecedented in both depth and breadth. Specifically, the coverage began early in 2008 during the primary campaigns and was maintained at a steady volume across all media throughout most of the year. This coverage notably included the posting of foreign correspondents at unprecedented levels, the production of several special news programs, separate recurring thematic sections in major newspapers, and other increased activity.

Put succinctly, it can be said that in Brazil the 2008 election produced the greatest volume of information and analysis of any US presidential contest in recent history. The characteristics of the Democratic candidates and the widespread rejection of the policies of the Bush Administration were the main variables that determined the content of the coverage. The analysis offered below is based on daily newspaper sources, news magazines, a number of academic journals, and the experience of one of the authors as a regular participant on television broadcasts.

The chapter is organized in six sections. We begin by contextualizing the different perspectives about the US election considering aspects of Brazilian history and its economic and social structure. In the second section we identify the key issue areas perceived as more relevant for Brazilian interests given the election's outcome. The factors that condition the local perceptions about the Republican and Democratic candidates are the subject of the third section, which is followed by a more detailed analysis of the critical political issues that informed the different perspectives of Brazilian public opinion toward Barack Obama and John McCain. The chapter concludes with two sections in which we discuss the potential impact of the electoral outcome for Brazilian domestic and foreign policies.

A Country Divided? Divergent Brazilian Viewpoints on the US Election

Brazil is in many ways a country whose political landscape is still beset by the legacy of colonial times. This results in a series of cleavages in the reading of political events within the country, two of which are particularly salient to perceptions of the 2008 presidential elections in the United States. These are, first, a division between powerful political and financial elites and a vast lower and smaller middle class; and, in a second cleavage that mirrors the first, a significant racial divide. In practical terms, this means that the reading of the elections by the country's economic and political elites has the potential to differ significantly from that of the greater public; importantly, however, the changes in the extent and nature of the gap that came to the fore during the course of the elections are also important indicators of changes and progress within Brazilian political culture. Accordingly, we focus here first on the viewpoints taken by the individuals and institutions that make up the Brazilian political establishment, before turning then to the impact of the elections on the middle and lower classes. This latter aspect, in light of the election of Obama as the first African-American president of the United States, is viewed through the lens of its implications for the community of Brazilians of African descent. It is worth bearing in mind that the mainstream media are, broadly speaking, in coverage and editorials, more likely to reflect the interpretations of the political and financial centers of power than of the general populace.

In terms of the country's political leadership, the majority of relevant reaction in the media came from two sources: the Presidency and the Ministry of External Relations (MRE or "Itamaraty"). Brazilian President Luís Inácio "Lula" da Silva of the Workers' Party (PT) is the country's first left-wing leader in the post-dictatorship era. A former machinist and union leader, he is also the first prominent politician whose origins are not only outside the country's traditional elites, but who also has a socially and economically modest background. This fact has shaped a number of policies introduced by Lula's administration, as well as his reception of the candidacy of Obama. Throughout the electoral campaign, Lula expressed his personal affinity for the Democratic candidate, based on what he perceived as common modest social origins: "The same way Brazil elected a metalworker and Bolivia an indio, the victory of a black man in the largest economy in the world will be a cultural advancement"[1]

Indeed, the evolution of Lula's preference among the candidates for the world's most powerful office seems to be more complex, and to have followed several determinants at once:

> Lula discreetly hoped for an Obama victory over (Hillary Clinton), and later for a McCain victory, based on the assumption that the Republicans are less protectionist than the Democrats. In fact, only McCain spoke favourably of Brazil's ethanol programme and of ending the subsidy to American producers. With the approaching end of the campaign, Lula declared himself openly in favour of Obama, with whom he feels a connection due to their common modest social origins.[2]

The above quote from *O Globo*, one of Brazil's most influential dailies, reveals not only the multiple and conflicting motives that come together to influence the Brazilian President's viewpoint, but also the association inherent in some quarters in Brazil between Obama's race and perceived poverty. In fact, Obama was faced with considerably less hardship than Lula da Silva during his childhood, but the article is emblematic of a tendency to identify Obama, due to his race, as the candidate of the disenfranchised and of those wishing to be "politically correct."

In sum, Lula's assessment of the American presidential candidates can be assumed to be influenced by at least three major factors: alongside his own personal social origins, Lula's viewpoint is guided by perceptions of which candidate would be best for Brazil as a whole, and considerations of left-of-center party-political affinities. Republican party candidates are traditionally seen as more favorable to Brazilian trade interests because their core constituencies are considered less likely to commit them to protectionist policies that would complicate the entry of Brazilian exports into the American market. This indicates an inherent foundation of elite support for the candidacy of McCain. However, as a result of affinities at the party-political level, Lula da Silva has increasingly strengthened ties with leaders involved in Latin America's recent upsurge in leftist-populist governments, such as Hugo Chávez of Venezuela, Evo Morales of Bolivia, and, to a lesser extent, Fidel and later Raúl Castro of Cuba. Lula thus viewed favorably Obama's repeated indication of a greater willingness to open a dialogue with these leaders whose relations with the Bush Administration were already severely strained.

The MRE is similarly torn "between reason and the heart," in the words of Foreign Minister Celso Amorim. Despite much admiration for the Democratic candidate and the ideals for which he stood, the diplomat's major concern once again was based on the perception that the Republican McCain would be best for Brazilian trade interests.[3] This rift also illustrates the relationship between the partisan priorities of a given administration and the long-term foreign policy interests elaborated by the MRE, which in Brazil tended generally to favor McCain.

Even within the purely rational calculus of interests, however, the candidates' platforms created a rift between two fundamental principles of Brazilian foreign policy: whereas trade interests dictated support for McCain, Obama was seen as much more likely to revive multilateralism— the fundamental tenet of Brazilian diplomacy—and to support Brazilian proposals to increase the global South's clout in decision-making in international fora, especially in the economic realm.[4] Admittedly, Brazil had escaped much of the nefarious effect of the Bush Administration on many of its neighbors, having been treated as a privileged partner and allowed to develop avenues for continental leadership.[5] In this sense, there was less of an impetus for the MRE to distance itself from the continuity with the Bush Administration that McCain embodied. In short, while institutional interests and the traditional reading of priorities with regard to the United States led the MRE somewhat to favor McCain, sympathy for Obama was such that the preference was not pronounced, especially moving further down the ranks of the foreign service hierarchy. The positions of Brazil's economic interest groups will become evident as this chapter discusses the major issues at stake in the Brazilian reading of the election.

Brazil has the largest population of African descent anywhere outside Africa, and this population continues to suffer the latent effects of colonialism and race discrimination. This discrimination takes on a different form in Brazil from that in the United States. While Brazil abolished slavery only in 1888—twenty-three years after the United States—the black population did not see discrimination in the letter of law as severe as that of Jim Crow and Southern segregation.[6] However, despite this seeming legal advantage for Afro-Brazilians, the United States has made far greater strides in integrating descendants of Africans into positions of influence and power, and in balancing out, particularly, income and educational discrimination. For example—though the situation has improved noticeably under the Lula government—United Nations Development Program (UNDP) data reveal that in 2000 Brazil's black population had a Human Development Index (HDI) equivalent to that of El Salvador (0,702), ranked 104th of 173 countries studied, while the white population enjoyed an HDI of 0,814, equivalent to that of Costa Rica, ranked 43rd.[7] In 2007 Brazil still possessed the world's tenth-worst Gini coefficient (57,0), an indicator of income distribution.[8] Obama's October 12 avowal that "I think that when you spread the wealth around, it's good for everybody" thus garnered strong support both from the large lower and middle class in Brazil and from its left-leaning government.

Alongside these gaps in income and standard of living, Afro-Brazilians "are only 3 percent of Brazil's college graduates. Only one senator among 81 is black.... Twelve of Brazil's lower house's 513 members are black, compared with 46 out of 435 U.S. house members."[9] To many Brazilians, Obama incarnated the notion of upward social mobility that had hitherto been impossible in Brazil, providing hope that his election to the most powerful office in the world might accelerate progress in their own country.[10] Many, including the country's (black) Minister for Racial Equality Edson Santos, proclaimed that a career such as Obama's would be impossible in Brazil today.[11] Furthermore, one black leader controversially pointed out that Obama's success was based on his *post-racial* discourse, a discourse that, according to the argument in question, is as yet premature in the Brazilian context.[12] In this sense it is critical to note that much of Obama's support can be attributed not only to purely racial factors but also to the attractiveness of his campaign message of hope and change, which fell on fertile ground not only with elites frustrated with the sitting Administration, but with a broader populace hungry and hopeful for change in its own conditions and position.

Perceived Relevance of the Election Outcome for Brazil

The Brazilian reaction to the 2008 contest displayed a break with past US presidential elections, which had been perceived by Brazilian public opinion with relative indifference concerning the relevance of the outcome for the country's foreign and domestic affairs. While relations with the United States have, due to the northern neighbor's predominant stature, historically been at the top of the country's foreign policy agenda, transitions of US presidential administrations have seldom produced significant shifts in bilateral relations. Since the beginning of the recent democratic era, for instance, relations with the United States have been dominated by economic issues. In the early 1980s, Brazil's negotiation of its foreign debt and protection of certain strategic elements of its industrial and service sectors produced continuous difficulties in the overall bilateral relationship. More recently, trade negotiations at the multilateral level (World Trade Organization, or WTO) as well as the Washington-led bid to create a free trade zone in the Americas (Free Trade Area of the Americas, or FTAA) have been at the top of the agenda.

The last presidential election to have a significant impact on Brazil was perhaps Jimmy Carter's, in 1976, which came at the height of the military regime that ruled the country from 1964 to 1985. Carter's more aggressive policy of monitoring human rights violations in Latin America met with a bitter reaction from the highest military authorities in Brazil and, according to most foreign policy analysts, produced a shift in orientation toward what was called "responsible pragmatism," a doctrine that defined national interests based on the desire for autonomy from US regional hegemony. While the ensuing US administrations abandoned Carter's high-minded foreign policy toward the region, returning to emphasizing the more familiar economic agenda; the issue of autonomy remained a doctrinal mantra in foreign policy and intellectual circles in Brazil.

To be sure, autonomy was not meant to stand for any kind of counter-hegemonic ambitions in the region; rather, it expressed Brazil's determination to define its national interests and foreign policy objectives without undue interference from external powers. The main goal of this doctrine has been, for some time, economic development and the continuous reduction of the country's dependence upon (and hence, vulnerability to) foreign financial investment (in the form of current account imbalances produced by foreign debt) and technology. As a result, Brazilian foreign policy emphasis in the past twenty years has fallen on regional integration (Mercosur) and the strengthening of multilateral trade regimes (WTO) as the preferred means to achieve "global player" status in world trade; this is joined by the cautious combination of the defense of democratic regimes in South America with the traditional regard for the principle of noninterference in the internal affairs of its neighbors.

In the perceived lengthy absence of a coherent US policy orientation toward the continent, Brazilian official concerns regarding the outcome of the 2008 election have been of a more specific nature, such as who will be guiding trade negotiations, whether a newly composed Congress will grant the incoming president "Trade Authority" to negotiate multilateral (or bilateral) agreements, as well as what ties the new Administration will have to protectionist sectors of the US economy such as agriculture, steel, cotton, and ethanol.

In sum, the relevance of US presidential elections for Brazilian public opinion, as well as for government officials, has been relative and mostly issue-oriented. Moreover, there is no single issue that would raise the stakes for the country that specifically depends on whether a Republican or Democratic candidate is elected. On the contrary, local preferences are usually fragmented according to sectors of the economy or the ideological orientation of social groups. The differences in the outcome of the election are evaluated based on nuances within specific issue areas rather than on generalized political preferences for either party or program; this is true of the 2008 elections as well. However, the present Brazilian government has diverged from its predecessors on a series of international and regional issues that could be affected, at least indirectly, by the results of the 2008 elections.

Brazil has been claiming for a permanent seat in the United Nations Security Council since the founding of the Organization. During the Cold War, Brazilian representatives would periodically bring up the issue of underrepresentation of developing countries in that body as a reminder of the need for more progressive UN reforms.[13] In the post-Cold War era, the issue of UN reform was brought to the global agenda by Secretaries-General Boutros-Ghali and Annan. While Security Council reform was never seriously considered, the climate was suited to the reintroduction of claims by countries such as Brazil, Germany, Japan, India, and South Africa, among others, for reform toward making the Security Council more representative. Amorim has taken this issue to heart since his first tenure in office, and also during the presidency of Itamar Franco (1993–1994), and more forcefully during the current Presidency of Lula da Silva, whose Workers' Party (PT) has long advocated the democratization of international institutions.

Amorim, with Lula's support, has pursued this issue relentlessly over the past six years; however, there is very little to show given the considerable political capital spent in this quest. While the Bush Administration, especially Amorim's personal friend, Secretary of State Condoleezza Rice, demonstrated guarded support for this goal, it has never backed the matter seriously at the UN. During the campaign, Obama and his staff did not speak on record about this issue. However, Obama has stated that he is committed to changing the US orientations toward multilateral organizations such as the UN, in an effort, inter alia, to recuperate America's international standing in the wake of the damage done by his predecessor. Brazilian officials are hence mildly optimistic about the prospects of Security Council reform and an eventual permanent seat for Brazil.

Brazil has invested politically and economically in a number of initiatives aimed at advancing South American regional integration according to a framework that hedges against US interference and strengthens its own position as regional power. After the failure of negotiations to create the FTAA, the current government has created a number of forums with the main goal of articulating a common political perspective for the integration of South America, overcoming the market-oriented logics of Mercosur, the Andean Pact, and the FTAA. This strategy has had mixed results.

While the expansion of Mercosur continues to be an important goal, its attainment is clearly more complex than expected, and it is unlikely to deliver the political results Lula desires. A more recent attempt has come in the shape of UNASUL (the Union of South American Nations), a project of political and economic integration of South America put in motion since 2004, inspired by the new ideological climate in the region. All of these initiatives have prospered in the context of unprecedented US neglect for South America and the disastrous support of the 1999 coup in Venezuela, which has enshrined Hugo Chavez as a regional champion of anti-American causes.

Obama has never set foot in South America, and he and his campaign team demonstrated little interest in or knowledge of the region. In other words, there are indications that the "benign" neglect of the Bush years might continue during the Obama Administration, practically leaving plenty of space for Brazil to develop its regional leadership further. However, his choice of Hillary Clinton as secretary of state could bring back contentious elements of the Clinton Administration's former agenda for the region, such as the FTAA, democracy promotion, militarized antidrug policies, and migration issues. It is the perception of many policymakers in Brazil that such a scenario, though unlikely, given the more urgent challenges at hand for the new Administration, would have a negative impact on Brazil's projects for the region.

Climate change was one of the main themes of the Obama campaign. The new president, moreover, has chosen a competent and high-profile team of policymakers and scientists to deal with the issue in his Administration. This is a clear break with his predecessor, who was notoriously opposed to international governance of climate change. While the Brazilian government has defended the Kyoto Protocol and supported additional conferences to reach a new framework for a regime to control carbon emissions in the immediate future, it has also continued to defend a differential treatment for developing countries vis-à-vis advanced economies. Brazil's position, along with other big polluters such as China and India, has come under intense pressure, not only from Europeans and Americans but from the environmentalist movement as well.

Behind Brazil's resistance to caps on emissions in developing countries is a more entrenched vision of the relationship between the environment and national sovereignty, specifically, the perception that limits on emissions would restrict Brazil's sovereign right to development. Considering that trade seems so far to be a difficult issue for the Obama team (see the difficulties mentioned below concerning the so-called Doha Round), it is possible that the environmental agenda may occupy a more central place than before in policies toward Latin America. In that case, depending on the strength of the environmental lobby's position in key Administration posts, the stakes for the Brazilian government might be quite high, especially if additional international pressure is applied regarding caps on emissions and a putative "international responsibility to protect" the Amazon biosphere.

In the late 1970s, Federal Reserve Chairman and recently appointed chair of the Economic Recovery Advisory Board in the Obama Administration, Paul Volcker, raised US interest rates to 20 percent in order to contain domestic inflation. However, this exacerbated the problems of the developing world, including those of big debtors such as Brazil and Mexico, which descended toward bankruptcy. These states needed more than a decade to recover from the chronic hyperinflation resulting from that crisis. It was a typical case of "the US sneezing and the developing world catching a cold." Paul Volcker is now again an adviser to a Democratic president. The question that concerns Brazilian policymakers is whether he will again risk "externalizing" the costs of US economic adjustment to more exposed economies down the now even more integrated global economic chain. The stakes are high for the Brazilian economy. For the first time in almost two decades, the country has had positive GDP growth rates for four consecutive years, and appears to be finding solutions to structural constraints to its development.

Lula da Silva (echoing French President Nicolas Sarkozy, who has expressed the wish to "redefine capitalism") has defended the call for reform of the institutional architecture of international financial regimes as a necessary step to provide stability to the world economy.[14] As illustrated below, this view considers a larger role for the G20, or a more inclusive G7, as urgent measures. It remains to be seen whether the Obama Administration will be sensitive to these claims, and what the impact of the recovery package for the US economy will be on the Bretton Woods institutions and the future regulation of the mechanisms necessary to promote equitable global economic growth.

PERCEPTIONS OF THE CANDIDATES

In what may be further testimony to the racial element in Brazilian perceptions of the elections, it is interesting to note that a public opinion poll taken less than a week before the vote revealed that, when confronted with a photograph of both candidates, 60 percent of Brazilians could not identify Obama, and 77 percent did not recognize McCain.

This did not prevent them from expressing a 66 percent to 9 percent ratio of preference for Obama.[15] Similarly, the October Latinobarometro poll revealed a bias among Brazilians toward the Democrat, with 41 percent favoring him to win.[16]

It is impossible to assess how the candidates—especially Republican frontrunner McCain—were perceived without discussing briefly the legacy of George W. Bush. Many of Bush's policies—the invasion of Iraq, the scuttling of a UN convention against racism, opposition to the Kyoto Accord, and a general disregard for the merits of multilateralism and consultation—led to a strong decline in American prestige and in equally strong increases in negative assessments of the United States as a whole. As such, by virtue of the greater distance of his policy positions from those of Bush, Obama enjoyed an advantage in Brazilians' perceptions from the beginning. This was helped by the content of those positions, such as his multilateralist stance and other more detailed positions, which will be outlined below. Thus, the United States is beginning to be again viewed as a potential partner and player in multilateral fora.[17] The feeling of relief and reconnection was summed up by Amorim who saw the bilateral relationship moving from "pragmatism and respect to affinity and cooperation."[18] The negative effect of the Bush legacy was felt most strongly by McCain, whose image suffered from his ideological association with the incumbent president. Although, as stated, the traditional reading of Brazil's foreign policy interests tends to give Republican candidates a boost in local support, this appears to have been cancelled out by the devastating effects of the Bush era, and any potential advantage was further evened out by the fact that both candidates, as shall be seen below, took policy stands on key issues that were favorable to Brazilian commercial and geostrategic interests.

Obama's racial identity and international background generated affinity within the Brazilian population, which is made up of equal parts white (92,014 million) and black/mixed-race population (together 91,126 million).[19] It is interesting to note that in Brazilian parlance Obama would not be referred to as "black" but rather as "mulatto," a term now in desuetude in the United States, but which is not derogatory in Brazilian usage. This enlarges even further the category of the population that sees its own problems and possibilities reflected in the Democrat. Such was the enthusiasm for Obama that six candidates in municipal elections throughout the country made use of a quirk in election laws to register themselves under the name "Barack Obama."[20] Obama further gained some profile among supporters of the Lula government through his connection with Roberto Mangabeira Unger, Lula's Minister for Strategic Affairs, who had been Obama's professor during his time as a student at Harvard Law School.[21] At least one analyst contends that Obama had already emerged with strengthened support of the government right from the Democratic primary elections, as some within the Workers' Party (PT) government may have been leery of strong connections built between the Clinton Administration and the government of Fernando Henrique Cardoso, whose party base was in the competing Social Democratic Party.[22] This perception turned in favor of Hillary Clinton, however, when she was nominated as secretary of state, as this association led to the view of her being ascribed with strong knowledge of Brazilian affairs and an affection for the country. Racial affinity and the Mangabeira connection were the primary factors differentiating perceptions of Obama and McCain as candidates per se. In general, other differences in perception between the candidates derived from the policy positions they espoused during the campaign.

CRITICAL POLITICAL ISSUES

In Brazil, there are three issues, all interrelated to some degree, that are seen as paramount in the perceptions of the effects of the American elections. These are foreign trade policy in general (as noted above); more specifically, biofuels, such as ethanol; and the future development of multilateral institutions and Brazil's role within them. Despite the strong impact of some of these issues on the Brazilian political agenda, there is a general consensus—despite the occasional overassessment by the MRE of Brazil's clout in Washington—that Latin America and Brazil will continue to rank low on the list of priorities for the next American President, remaining behind the wars in Iraq and Afghanistan, and the strong focus on domestic issues occasioned by the worldwide economic downturn of 2008, which began in the crucial US housing and derivative markets[23] Alongside these issues, there have been efforts to draft a bilateral treaty to avoid double taxation,[24] and Lula da Silva and Obama in a postelection telephone conversation spoke of renewing cooperation on the economy, social and education programs, and renewable energy (ethanol).[25]

As noted above, the degree to which candidates endorsed trade-protectionist measures was one of the most important issues to Brazilian observers. Brazil has the tenth-largest economy in the world by GDP,[26] and the United States is the largest recipient of Brazilian exports: in 2005 the balance was $22.7 billion of a total of $118.3 billion.[27] Many of these exports are primary goods such as soybeans, coffee, and iron ore, and are highly susceptible both to protectionist measures in recipient markets and to shifts in world commodity prices. As stated above, the export-driven nature of the economy leads Brazilian economic leaders to tend to favor Republican presidential candidates, who, due to their typical constituencies, are seen as less likely to implement such measures as are their Democratic counterparts.[28] Access to the US market for Brazilian exports was clearly, to Brazilian observers, the most important substantive issue at stake in the 2008 election.

Brazil has taken a leadership role in attempting to rekindle the frozen negotiations of the World Trade Organization's so-called Doha Round, which has stalled due to disagreements over agricultural trade between the United States and several other major producers such as India and China. Indeed, one of the fastest and strongest reactions to the election of Obama came from Foreign Minister Amorim, who criticized the United States' "lack of flexibility" and exhorted the new president to show commitment to finalizing the Doha Round rather than "hiding behind the formalities" of transition. Faced with a strong reaction from Washington, Amorim underscored that he had not wanted to take an accusatory tone, but rather had hoped to see a positive sign of commitment to the Doha Round from the president-elect.[29] The importance to Brazil of the Doha talks lies in that they unite the desire to establish free trade with the multilateral approach cherished by the nation's diplomatic establishment. With regard to the United States, however, one area of trade in particular is of paramount importance to Brazilian observers: fuel ethanol or biofuel, a source of renewable energy in which Brazil is undisputedly a world leader in innovation, production, and consumption.

In 2007, Brazil produced 5.1 billion gallons of fuel ethanol,[30] accounting for 42 percent of world production.[31] Despite being the only country to produce more ethanol than Brazil, during the same year the United States imported 188.8 million gallons of the fuel from Brazil.[32] Brazilian ethanol has a competitive advantage over its American counterpart in that it is seven times more efficient to produce,[33] and can call upon a domestic market in which 88.3 percent of new cars sold run on flex fuel,[34] thanks to a 1993 law mandating the use of this technology. Brazil and the United States have signed a 2007 memorandum of understanding designed to foster cooperation in ethanol research and production. Ethanol is not only one of Brazil's major exports but also a prestige issue for Brazil, as the country feels it can compete on even terms with the world's leading economies such as the United States and the European Union, and thus ethanol ranks very high on the MRE's agenda.

As a renewable resource that reduces dependence on Middle Eastern oil, ethanol was an important component of both US presidential candidates' energy policy platforms. Key to their deliberations was the dual support ethanol receives—despite the cooperation accord—from protectionist policies in the United States: Domestic ethanol producers receive a subsidy of fifty-one cents per gallon, while imports are subject to a fifty-four-cent-a-gallon tariff.[35] McCain's free-trade agenda led him to state as early as June 2008 that he favored the removal of both protectionist measures on ethanol, a position that was very well-received in Brazil.[36] Obama, as a Senator from the second-largest corn-producing American state, supported both the tariff and the subsidy, and analysts noted that, despite indications he would seek improved relations with Brazil over the subject in accordance with the "Energy Partnership for the Americas" proposed by Obama while a candidate, the new administration was unlikely to remove the tariff or the subsidy.[37]

Both candidates were quite closely aligned with Brazil's interests in the area of its interactions with multilateral institutions. Both supported Brazil's entry as a permanent member of a reformed United Nations Security Council, which, as noted above, has been a major long-term foreign policy goal of Lula da Silva's administration. Multilateralism has long been the MRE's preferred means of advancing the country's interests, and a further priority under Lula has been increasing Brazil's voice, and that of the global South, in various—particularly economic—fora. This has recently included plans to devolve more power to the developing countries within the global financial institutions and increase cooperation with emerging powers such as Russia, China, India, and South Africa, alongside a drive to enlarge participation in gatherings such as the G-8.

Obama benefited from a general perception of greater receptiveness to multilateralism because of his greater distance from the unilateralist stances taken by George W. Bush. Similarly, his greater openness to dialogue with Latin America's leftist-populist leaders aligned him with Lula's own policies, and this offered Brazil the prospect of retaining a role it had increasingly crafted as a mediator between Washington and those states.

McCain's specific substantive proposals both helped and damaged his image with Brazilian observers. His March 18 proposal for a "League of Democracies" at a low level of institutionalization[38] was seen by some as working directly counter to the desire for broader participation espoused by the Brazilian government.[39] Paradoxically, on March 26 McCain called for Brazil to replace Russia as a member of the G8; this position was more warmly received by the potential new member. The balance of perceptions appears to be that while Obama's general policy orientation and background gained a warm reception from Brazilians, McCain's specific trade policy positions may actually have objectively been more favorable to the country's interests. This seems to indicate that trade policy played a lesser role, and geopolitical aims a greater one, than they did previously in determining preferences between potential US presidents. This comes as a result of two factors: the strong rejection of policies associated with the incumbent US President, and the factors regarding Obama's personal background presented above.

Possible Impact of the Outcome for Domestic Politics

The interdependence between US politics and Brazilian politics at the domestic level is traditionally low. The predominance of the economic agenda in bilateral relations has, as mentioned before, created an attitude of relative ideological indifference regarding candidates from either party. At the level of party politics, there are few links between the Brazilian leftist parties and the Democratic Party. To the right of the spectrum, few relevant Brazilian political parties share any programmatic points with the Republican Party.

As derived from the above analysis, at the level of civil society one finds more defined preferences usually for Democratic candidates more oriented toward multilateralism and human rights. However, given the record of US interventionism in Latin America, both by Republican and (more often) Democratic administrations, broader public opinion as well as organized civil society generally tend not to distinguish between opposing candidates in party terms. This attitude can be understood as an inherent anti-Americanism that pervades Brazilian society and that varies in intensity in response to the relative hawkishness of US foreign policies. In the case of the Bush Administration there is an obviously clear exception that is displayed, with polls rating a preference higher than 60 percent for Obama and an almost universal rejection of the Bush administration.

While Lula did not publicly support any particular candidate (having enjoyed, by his own admission, good personal relations with Bush), he did, as mentioned above, offer an interpretation of Obama's election as parallel to his own, as expressions of a broader trend toward change in the Americas. Some of Lula's advisors have gone further in establishing similarities between both men's profiles in a rather opportunistic attempt to capitalize on the global wave of support for the new American President.

Two points, however, can be made out as to the more general effects of the outcome of the 2008 US election for Brazilian domestic politics. First, it can be expected that the pendulum of anti-Americanism in civil society and in the majority parties (particularly the Workers Party) will tilt toward a less virulent rhetoric. Depending on the extent of this shift, the reduction in anti-American positions may have an impact (even if indirect) on some issues of the broader foreign policy agenda. We may also see, as a consequence, a weakening of the more hard-line nationalistic agendas that have been used, when convenient, by the current government to gain internal legitimacy.

The second issue concerns the prospects for the 2010 presidential elections. The return of several Clinton staff to the Obama Administration will surely embolden their former preferred counterparts in Brazil, that is, the followers of former president Cardoso and his Social Democratic Party (PSDB). Current polls show the main PSDB presidential hopeful, São Paulo State Governor Jose Serra, leading all potential candidates. If Hillary Clinton succeeds in devising a coherent policy toward the subcontinent, or even towards Brazil, it may well help the opposition to Lula da Silva. It is, however, quite early to evaluate such trends, given Lula's exceptional skills in adapting to political shifts and maintaining working relations with leaders of all ideological stripes (to which his relationship with Bush attests).

PERCEIVED IMPLICATIONS FOR BRAZIL

The implications of the election outcome for Brazil are generally perceived as positive in much the same way as they are for most countries with close ties to the United States. The United States is still Brazil's largest individual trading partner and the hegemonic power in the region. In this sense, the return of a more rational foreign policy is welcomed by officials and public opinion alike. In the specific issue areas, perceptions are mixed. Most sectors of public opinion and government officials seem to expect more attention to be paid to regional matters but harbor no illusions that the first years of the Obama Administration will focus on the global economic crisis, Iraq, and Afghanistan. In this sense, the immediate impact of the election outcome might simply be neutral, as opposed to the long-term effects of a broader shift in American grand strategy.

Several matters of direct interest to the Brazilian government stand out. First, the expectation of a reprise for the Doha Round negotiations. As discussed above, this issue has been mentioned in several interviews by Brazilian officials and businessmen as potentially an important result of the election. All objective indicators, however, point in the opposite direction. Given the present vulnerability of the US economy and the growing rate of unemployment, the investment of political capital in another round of free trade agreements is highly unlikely. The failure of the Doha Round is a stiff blow to Brazilian diplomacy. In the absence of US leadership in the trade area, Brazil would most likely try to reestablish negotiations of a free trade agreement with the European Union (on hold because of the Doha Round) and pursue its aspirations for regional integration by investing in UNASUL.

In the case of UN reforms, Obama's election should encourage Brazilian diplomats to engage the United States again in negotiations to grant the Security Council greater representativeness. Again, the circumstances of the early Obama years might hamper such lofty projects, but an argument might be made that reforming international institutions is a step toward better global governance and a more stable international system and world economy. Indications on such issues from the Obama transition team have been vague, to say the least, but this agenda is clearly in line with changing US attitudes and standing in the international stage. A more concrete implication, given the new Administration's approach to multilateralism, would be a greater resolve in the peace-building efforts in Haiti, where Brazil has invested a great deal of political capital by leading the military component of the local UN peacekeeping mission. The successful outcome of that mission would encourage a change in attitude, in Brazil and in Latin America in general, toward UN peacekeeping operations, a subject usually faced with distrust by most countries in the region.

In recent statements Lula da Silva expressed his expectation that Obama's term in office would contribute to correcting "America's misguided policies towards Latin America." While our analysis points to a continuation of a subordinate role for the continent in US foreign policy, the above statement indicates what many leaders and intellectuals in the region do expect from the new Administration the ability to avoid the mistakes that under the previous Administration had compromised the potential for partnerships in several areas of common interest in US-Latin American relations. A rare but clearly positive expectation, which arose in the few weeks preceding the inauguration, concerns the relaxation of the restrictions on travel to and from Cuba and, perhaps, a gradual process toward normalization and an end to the embargo against that country, a policy widely considered as anachronistic and anomalous across the region.

Further, the new president and his diplomatic team seem to favor dialogue over confrontation with adversarial leaders such as Chávez and Morales. A change in attitude here would represent an important step forward for the normalization of the region's relationship with the United States, thus contributing to the stabilization of social conflicts and political unrest, particularly in the Andean region. In the economic arena, officials hope that more emphasis will be given to development aid and less to counterinsurgency and antidrug policies. Fears of more protectionism toward the region's commodities and manufactured goods are also a factor in every election of a Democratic American president.

Finally, the presence of approximately 900,000 Brazilian illegal immigrants in the United States has brought US immigration policies to the attention of the government and broad public opinion. It is expected that the new Administration's approach to the issue will not be overdetermined by the strategic considerations of the "War on Terror" or by anti-immigrant rhetoric fueled by labor protectionism.

Conclusion

The post-Cold War era has coincided with a historical period in Brazilian history in which the transition from military rule to democracy has taken place, its economy has stabilized and its institutions increasingly matured. On the basis of these important processes, Presidents Cardoso and Lula da Silva have pursued foreign policies that sought to improve the country's competitiveness in a globalizing economy as well as to raise its standing in the institutions of global governance. The changes effected within the international system by the Bush Administration, the invasion of Iraq and the "War on Terror," undermined US leadership in global affairs and stimulated trends to counterbalance American influence worldwide. Brazil was not impervious to these trends and in the recent years has sought to strengthen ties with other emerging powers, which was informed by a worldview that privileged South-South cooperation as a necessary strategy to face potential threats to its regional and global interests. Perhaps the impact of President Obama's election may be felt, more globally and in the medium term, in the opening of possibilities of partnerships around some specific issue areas and a reduction of the mistrust inspired by American foreign policy during the past eight years. Such a shift could well contribute to stimulating domestic debates in Brazil concerning the general orientations of the country's foreign policy.

Notes

1. All Portuguese texts quoted were freely translated by the authors. Paula Adamo Idoeta, "Obama deve ser melhor para o mundo e o Brasil, dizem especialistas," *G1*, November 5, 2008. Retrieved from http://g1.globo.com/Noticias/0,,MUL847933-15525,00-OBAMA+DEVE+SER+MELHOR+PARA+O+MUNDO+E+O+BRASIL+DIZEM+ESPECIALISTAS.html.

2. Merval Pereira, "O fator Clinton," *O Globo*, November 15, 2008. Retrieved from Factiva database (GLOBO00020081115e4bf00044).

3. Denise Chrispim Marin, "No Itamaraty, rivais opõem 'razão' e 'coração'," *O Estado de São Paulo*, November 2, 2008. Retrieved from Factiva database (ESTADO0020081102e4b20000a).

4. Lu Aiko Otta and Fernando Nakagawa, "Lula quer G-20 na solução da crise," *O Estado de São Paulo*, November 9, 2008. Retrieved from Factiva database (ESTADO0020081109e4b9000b6).

5. Eliane Cantanhêde, "Por multilateralismo, Brasil quer Obama" *Folha de São Paulo*, November 2, 2008. Retrieved from Factiva database (FOLHA00020081102e4b20005v).

6. Arthur Dapieve, "Coisas que nunca existiram," *O Globo*, November 14, 2008. Retrieved from Factiva database (GLOBO00020081114e4be0004a).

7. *United Nations Development Programme [UNDP]*, "Human Development Report 2002: Deepening democracy in a fragmented world" (New York: Oxford University Press, 2002), 149–151. *Programa das Nações*

Unidas para o Desenvolvimento [*PNUD*], "Relatório de Desenvolvimento Humano - Brasil 2005: Racismo, pobreza e violência" (Brasília: PNUD, 2005), 58.

8. *United Nations Development Programme* [*UNDP*], "Human Development Report 2007/2008: Human solidarity in a divided world" (New York: Oxford University Press, 2007), 281–284.

9. Bradley Brooks, "Obama Win Forces Brazil to Take a Tolerance Check," *Miami Herald*, December 12, 2008. Retrieved from http://miamiherald.com/news/americas/story/799923.html. Carlos Heitor Cony, "O presidente," *Folha de São Paulo*, November 9, 2008. Retrieved from Factiva database (FOLHA00020081109e4b90005u).

10. Roldao Arruda, "Integração do negro é nó até hoje não desatado," *O Estado de São Paulo*, November 9, 2008. Retrieved from Factiva database (ESTADO0020081108e4b90015x).

11. Gabriela Manzini, "Obama não conseguiria ser presidente no Brasil, dizem especialistas," *Folha de São Paulo*, November 6, 2008. Retrieved from http://www1.folha.uol.com.br/folha/mundo/ult94u464946.shtml.

12. Dojival Vieira, "As lições da vitória de Obama e a syndrome do puxadinho," November 6, 2008. Retrieved from http://www.afropress.com/editorialListLer.asp?ID=59. Dojival Vieira, "O furação Obama e o desafio dos negros brasileiros em 2008," January 6, 2008. Retrieved from http://www.viapolitica.com.br/comunidade_view.php?id_comunidade=70.

13. See Castro, A. Várias Conferências. Org. Rodrigo Amado Ed. UnB, 1982.

14. See Edward Cody, "Sarkozy Calls for Revamping of Capitalist System," *Washington Post Foreign Service*, October 17, 2008, A20.

15. Luís Ferrari, "Brasil desconhece rivais, mas "elege" foto de Obama," *Folha de São Paulo*, October 29, 2008. Retrieved from Factiva database (FOLHA00020081029e4at00061).

16. *The Economist*, "The more things change," October 25, 2008, 48–49.

17. Paulo Nogueira Batista Jr., "Vira-lata sem complexo," *O Globo*, November 15, 2008. Retrieved from Factiva database (GLOBO00020081115e4bf0000u).

18. Jamil Chade, "Amorim espera postura de parceria do novo governo," *O Estado de São Paulo*, November 6, 2008. Retrieved from Factiva database (ESTADO0020081106e4b6000bs).

19. Instituto Brasileiro de Geografia e Estatística [IBGE], "Pesquisa Nacional por Amostra de Domicílios," Volume 26, 2006. Retrieved from http://www.ibge.gov.br/home/estatistica/populacao/trabalhoerendimento/pnad2005/brasil/tabbr_1_1_e_1_2.pdf.

20. Tom Phillips, "Now for Brazil's Barack Obamas – all six of them," *The Guardian*, September 15, 2008. Retrieved from http://www.guardian.co.uk/world/2008/sep/15/brazil.barackobama.

21. Paolo Sotero, "Obama, McCain e o Brasil," June 29, 2008. Retrieved from http://acantus79.wordpress.com/?s=obama+mccain+e+o+brasil. Deborah Berlinck and Chico de Gois, "Lula: não se deve esperar muito do G-20," *O Globo*, November 12, 2008. Retrieved from Factiva database (GLOBO00020081112e4bc00031).

22. Merval Pereira, "O fator Clinton," *O Globo*, November 15, 2008. Retrieved from Factiva database (GLOBO00020081115e4bf00044).

23. Paolo Sotero, "Obama, McCain e o Brasil," June 29, 2008. Retrieved from http://acantus79.wordpress.com/?s=obama+mccain+e+o+brasil.   Luiz Felipe Lampreia, "Obama e a América Latina," *O Globo*, November 15, 2008. Retrieved from Factiva database (GLOBO00020081115e4bf0000v).

24. Paolo Sotero, "Obama, McCain e o Brasil," June 29, 2008. Retrieved from http://acantus79.wordpress.com/?s=obama+mccain+e+o+brasil.

25. Deborah Berlinck and Chico de Gois, "Lula: não se deve esperar muito do G-20," *O Globo*, November 12, 2008. Retrieved from Factiva database (GLOBO00020081112e4bc00031).

26. *United States of America Central Intelligence Agency*, "World Factbook–Brazil," 2008. Retrieved from http://www.cia.gov/library/publications/the-world-factbook/geos/br.html.

27. *The Europa Yearbook* (London: Europa Publications, 2007), 941.

28. Clovis Brigagão, "Realidade aproxima os dois países," *O Globo*, October 26, 2008. Retrieved from Factiva database (GLOBO00020081026e4aq000hb).

29. Paolo Sotero, "O que Lula e Obama podem fazer," *O Estado de São Paulo*, December 17, 2008. Retrieved from http://www.estadao.com.br/estadaodehoje/20081217/not_imp295080,0.php.

30. *Renewable Fuels Association [RFA]*, Statistics, 2008. Retrieved from http://www.ethanolrfa.org/industry/statistics/#E.

31. *World Bank*, "Biofuels: The Promise and the Risks," 2008. Retrieved from http://siteresources.worldbank.org/INTWDR2008/Resources/2795087-1192112387976/WDR08_05_Focus_B.pdf.

32. *Renewable Fuels Association [RFA]*, Statistics, 2008. Retrieved from http://www.ethanolrfa.org/industry/statistics/#E.

33. Larry Rohter, "With Big Boost from Sugar Cane, Brazil Is Satisfying Its Fuel Needs," *New York Times*, April 10, 2006. Retrieved from http://www.nytimes.com/2006/04/10/world/americas/10brazil.html?_r=1.

34. *Reuters*. "Vendas de veículos flex no Brasil sobem 31,1% em julho ant 2008," August 6, 2008. Retrieved from http://hojenoticias.com.br/negocios/vendas-de-veiculos-sobem-311-em-julho-ant-2008/.

35. *Wall Street Journal*, "Very, Very Big Corn," January 27, 2007. Retrieved from http://online.wsj.com/article/SB116985512034389563-search.html?KEYWORDS=ethanol&COLLECTION=wsjie/6month.

36. *Estado de São Paulo*, "Republicano pede fim de taxação a etanol brasileiro," October 16, 2008. Retrieved from Factiva database (ESTADO0020081016e4ag000gu).

37. *Biofuels Digest*, "US Ethanol Tariff Unlikely to be Eliminated by Obama Administration under 'Energy Partnership for the Americas,'" November 12, 2008. Retrieved from http://biofuelsdigest.com/blog2/2008/11/12/us-ethanol-tariff-unlikely-to-be-eliminated-by-obama-administration-under-energy-partnership-for-the-americas%E2%80%9D/.
38. John McCain, "America Must be a Good Role Model," *Financial Times*, March 18, 2008. Retrieved from http://www.ft.com/cms/s/0/c7e219e2-f4ea-11dc-a21b-000077b07658.html?nclick_check=1.
39. Eliane Cantanhêde, "Por multilateralismo, Brasil quer Obama," *Folha de São Paulo*, November 2, 2008. Retrieved from Factiva database (FOLHA00020081102e4b20005v).

4

ADMIRATION REBORN: THE BRITISH VIEW OF THE US PRESIDENTIAL ELECTION

Adam Quinn

INTRODUCTION

Listening in on Britain's national conversation on the US presidential election during 2008, one might have been forgiven for thinking that what approached was a referendum on Barack Obama rather than a contest between two candidates. Certainly Obama's photogenic visage and sweeping rhetoric in search of "change" won the lion's share of the British media coverage. Indeed, often coverage and debate seemed to slide close to tacitly assume Obama's coming victory, and minds turned regularly to asking whether and to what extent his rhetoric would be implemented once in office. To the extent that this presupposition of victory was challenged, it was through the prism of the debate on race, with a question mark suspended in British minds over the plausibility of America's election of a black man to the highest office in light of its tortured racial history. This latter factor ensured that at least some consideration was given to the possibility Obama might be denied victory, though at the expense of drawing attention away from specific features of the candidate himself and onto his meaning in the context of evolving social attitudes to race. Only a relatively small effort was put into weighing the qualities of his Republican opponent, John McCain, who was thoroughly overshadowed in the popular consciousness by the bulldozer of the Obama narrative. McCain's intriguing personal biography and his reputation as a hard-liner in foreign policy did garner a measure of attention. But as in the United States itself, the most effective attention-grabber in McCain's campaign proved to be vice presidential nominee Sarah Palin, thanks both to her "energizing" effect on the Republican base[1] and her extraordinary talent for generating gaffes and scandals.[2]

As in many other European nations, the British fascination with Obama's candidacy arguably had roots in the still-powerful sense of reaction against the outgoing president. George W. Bush similarly captivated British attention for extended periods of his presidency, but in his case the dominant sentiments were irritation and disdain, almost from the moment of his first appearance on the international stage. Where Bush embodied the panoply of negative stereotypes about Americans stashed in the depths of the British psyche, Obama appeared his opposite: suave, thoughtful, and cosmopolitan. More substantively, his election could be interpreted as symbolizing a successful counterrevolution in American politics, a rejection of the unilateralist and militarist thrust of the Bush administration's foreign policy ideology. Thanks in no small part to this, the substantial majority of the British population joined the rest of the world in simultaneously hoping for and expecting an Obama victory.[3] Its ultimate arrival seemed to offer the prospect of restoring the British public's regard for American leadership and society, and consequently reinvigorating the Anglo-American relationship.

For understandable reasons of political good sense, the broad popular embrace of Obama could not be shared, at least not with the same public intensity, by the British political leadership. Nevertheless, with Tony Blair, who had been Bush's strongest European ally, departing from the scene, no party leader had any great fondness for the outgoing administration. Obama's message, on the other hand, had a broad appeal that most politicians thought it wise to try and tap as best they could. But the issue was not entirely one of personality and mood: an Obama victory would present British leaders with concrete issues to mull, not least the consequences for joint military operations in Iraq and Afghanistan, and the direction of the broader campaign against international terrorism and weapons proliferation. On a more reflective note, it also presented British society with a spur to self-analysis: Was a "British Obama," that is, a successful political leader from an ethnic minority, a realistic prospect in the foreseeable future? If not, where did that leave British presumptions regarding the existence of equality in the UK? More generally, Obama's capacity to inspire huge crowds of loyal followers led Britons to take a hard look at their own leaders as the pain of severe national and international crises began to sink in. Could Britain find energizing new leadership in the way that the United States seemed to have done?

WAR, TERROR, AND FOREIGN POLICY

The preeminent issue in Anglo-American relations for the past seven years has been the conduct of the campaign against international terrorism—the "War on Terror" in its original, now disfavored, formulation—and the military commitments in the Greater Middle East that have flowed from it. Besides the United States itself, Britain was the only other power to devote significant military resources to the invasion and occupation of Iraq, taking control of post-invasion security and the transfer of power to Iraqis in the southern city of Basra and its environs. It has also, in recent years, played the lead role in NATO operations seeking to extend the writ of the Karzai government in Afghanistan in the face of an apparently strengthening Taliban insurgency. As of January 2009, British armed forces had sustained 178 casualties since the beginning of operations in Iraq and 141 in Afghanistan, placing the UK second only to the United States in terms of casualties in each theatre.[4] As a result of this entanglement of British and American military interventionism, the likely attitude of the victor in the American election toward these campaigns was a major issue for British security policy, perhaps the single greatest issue of importance at stake.

In the case of Iraq, Britain's presence has suffered from weakening domestic support for the operation for a considerable time. As long ago as 2005, polls showed creeping majorities in favor of withdrawal within a maximum of twelve months, despite—or perhaps because of—pessimism regarding the outlook for Iraqi security.[5] By 2008 a sizeable majority of Britons regretted that military action in Iraq had ever been undertaken and wanted it to end immediately.[6] British withdrawal at the earliest respectable opportunity has therefore been widely expected since the replacement of prime minister Tony Blair, a public architect of the Iraq intervention, with the less enthusiastic and less publicly committed Gordon Brown. For nearly a year before the US election, British operations in Iraq had already been restricted to a presence at an out-of-town base near Basra, which had succeeded in reducing the risk of casualties but at the cost of surrendering the hope that British forces might meaningfully influence events on the ground.[7] In December 2008, Brown announced his intention to withdraw all British troops from Iraq by July 2009, with a steady surrendering of responsibility to Iraqis during the intervening period.[8]

It is clear, then, that Obama's public opposition to the Iraq war before it began, and his support for an explicit withdrawal timetable during the election campaign, put him on the same side as the center of gravity in British opinion regarding both the initial wisdom of Anglo-American deployment there and the desirability of a prompt exit.[9] McCain, on the other hand, emphasized during the campaign his potentially open-ended commitment to US presence in Iraq pending the attainment of "victory."[10] This was not a position any British party, whether in government or opposition, would have felt comfortable advocating for fear of a severe public backlash. While the logistical realities of orderly withdrawal prohibit an overnight exit, Obama's electoral victory has evidently tilted the political scales toward a faster timetable for withdrawal.[11]

To the extent that Britain's desire was for a shrinking commitment to Iraq without the necessity for conflict with US policy, an Obama victory was helpful.

Whether the majority that followed the US election from Britain understood all the subtleties of the candidates' positions on Iraq is doubtful. Certainly there were efforts on the part of those offering reportage and analysis for the British audience to flag up the complex shades present in the candidates' positions.[12] McCain may have been a staunch defender of the American presence in Iraq, but he had been critical of the occupation as actually executed, lambasting the Bush administration for mismanagement and supporting deployment of additional troops before talk of a "surge" became fashionable. Obama, meanwhile, opposed the war in a more nuanced and less ideological way than many of his Democratic foot soldiers, and there was some awareness in British coverage of his campaign that his victory would not signal an immediate evaporation of American commitment to Iraq. Both campaigns were guided by the need for careful political positioning so as to allow ultimate reconciliation in office between principle and practicality. McCain sought to signal steadfast commitment to the war's objectives while also expressing horror at how it had been carried out in practice and optimism for its satisfactory end within the course of his own presidency. Obama, meanwhile, needed to be seen as opposed to the war itself, but also wanted to avoid being tied down later by an absolute commitment to a hasty withdrawal. Hence he advocated a sixteen-month withdrawal timetable, with some wiggle room, depending on facts on the ground. Defrocked of their rhetorical cloaks, these positions, while not altogether reconcilable with one another, both had moderate caveats that rendered the candidates less far apart than one might have thought based upon surface impressions alone. The broad public perception of the candidates abroad, however, was that one was "for" the war while the other was "against" it, a formulation that could only lead to overwhelming support for Obama in British popular opinion.

In Afghanistan, things were less straightforward. The British commitment there in recent years has been substantial. It has also been bloody, with British forces undertaking a concerted effort to defeat the Taliban militarily in its strongholds. This engagement is not terribly popular with the public, which increasingly harbors doubts about the underlying point of the operation and its efficacy. Those with a grounding in British military history perhaps also sense a creeping element of déjà vu in British efforts to control and civilize territory in that singularly rugged part of the world. Polling suggests that most Britons want to see an end to British commitment[13] and would oppose further deployment of British troops even at the request of President Obama.[14]

In this case, however, Obama appeared committed to a troop "surge" in Afghanistan, a policy reflecting both his conviction that America's conflict with al Qaeda is best fought in the Afghanistan/Pakistan theatre, and also his electoral need during 2008 for a hawkish counterpoint to balance out his desire for a swift drawdown of troop numbers in Iraq. Indeed one of his stated objectives in reducing the US presence in Iraq was the redeployment of troops to Afghanistan.[15] If, as it seems that it does, Obama's election heralds increased commitment to operations in Afghanistan, the most important practical question for Britain is whether pressure will now be applied to obtain a similar redeployment of those UK forces withdrawn from Iraq to the Afghan front. Such a move would not only be a hard sell to a disillusioned general public, but also to the British defense establishment, which reportedly considers the present deployment of 8,100 troops to be their preferred ceiling, and complains that the UK defense forces as a whole are overstretched.[16] Obama's victory therefore presents a continuing challenge to those in Britain who wish to see military commitments overseas reduced. On the other hand, an election is a choice, and McCain offered nothing that would have sat better with British sentiment. Given his commitment to Iraq and his strident support for the principles underlying the initiation of that conflict, Obama was undoubtedly the lesser of the two evils from a mainstream British perspective. Nevertheless, the issue remains: it was rare for British election coverage to steer observers toward Obama's emerging hawkishness on Afghanistan. Likewise, limited attention was paid to his posture toward Pakistan, where he argued that US military operations against the Taliban/al Qaeda would be justified even without the consent of the Pakistani government. Given the general popular impression of Obama as the dovish candidate, the British public's reaction to his intention to escalate an already fairly unpopular war, once discovered, will be interesting, to say the least.

Another important consideration was the campaign against international terrorism. As one of those countries allied to ongoing US interventions abroad, and one of those itself subjected to a major terrorist attack on home soil since 9/11, Britain had a stake in the future direction of that campaign. Though an early supporter of the "War on Terror" declared by Bush in 2001, the UK Government had by 2008 developed an aversion to that terminology and to the militarized American approach to the problem that it was seen to represent.[17] British society's need to contend with a disgruntled and increasingly politicized Muslim minority in its midst, vulnerable to radicalization, added an extra dimension to this challenge.[18] Of the two candidates, Obama was undoubtedly viewed as the likeliest to embrace the desired ideological reformulation of the fight against terrorism. By dint of his mixed race and previous residence as a child in Muslim Indonesia, he was also seen as equipped to build bridges with those communities least sympathetic to the United States and its policies.

During the campaign, Obama committed himself to the objective of directly confronting al Qaeda by means of military force and through use of the intelligence services, as well as stepping up pressure on key states such as Pakistan to cooperate with American efforts. In parallel with this, however, he drew sharp focus upon the counterproductive effects of the occupation of Iraq, and emphasized the importance of nonmilitary means of reducing the threat, chiefly by redefining America's global reputation in more attractive terms.[19] In making such declarations, Obama put himself in tune with British sensibilities regarding the issue. In the prevailing British discourse, the "war on terror" has long been regarded as a misdirected slogan, and the Bush Doctrine's approach to resolving terrorism condemned as dangerously insensitive to both friends' and allies' perceived grievances. With the exception of explicit opposition to torture, McCain's platform and rhetoric, on the other hand, seemed to offer close continuity with those of Bush.[20] That segment of the British population, Muslim and otherwise, offended by the rhetoric and policies stemming from the War on Terror construct were unlikely to feel particularly supportive toward the ideals of either presidential candidate, but from a negative perspective McCain was the one who seemed likeliest to continue to aggravate their feelings of grievance as Bush had done. For a British Government keen to prevent politicized anger in this latently dangerous group boiling over, an Obama victory would at least do something to improve their chances of success of keeping a lid on things, and perhaps cutting down on the numbers of individuals that would become fully radicalized and join terrorist groups.

The candidates' stances on terrorism overlapped with a hawk-dove split on the issue of nuclear proliferation. Over a period of years building up to the 2008 election, McCain emphasized his support for a confrontational posture toward Iran, determined to avert the threat of nuclear proliferation by a "rogue" state without being seen to reward bad behavior with bribes or unmerited political attention.[21] Obama, meanwhile, made some noises to underscore the seriousness with which he regarded the threat, but supported direct negotiation and appeared more optimistic regarding the prospect of a successful negotiated solution. In British politics in 2008, advocacy of a military strike against Iran was effectively beyond the pale as far as the leadership of the mainstream political parties were concerned, largely due to the public's resentful recollection of the WMD debate preceding the Iraq war. The popular consensus in Britain was that the nation had been willfully misled in that instance by the government's presentation of evidence, thus building a significant hurdle of skepticism in the way of any government contemplating military action against another Middle Eastern state on the ground of forbidden weapons development. The American public, of course, had its own resentments regarding Iraqi WMD and reservations regarding further military adventurism (a fact that may, in some part, have contributed to Obama's victory), but the breadth and depth of resistance was greater in Britain: several of McCain's statements regarding Iran would have been regarded as intolerably belligerent coming from any major British political figure.

In sum, the mood in British politics in 2008—both in parliament and the general population—was averse to any new military adventure or any avoidable confrontation. The nation was keen to get out of Iraq, redefine the fight against terrorism in more nuanced terms, and avoid the opening of new military fronts in the Middle East. Obama was widely and correctly viewed as the more dovish of the candidates, and thus more compatible with these aspirations. His victory, therefore, generated something of a collective sigh of relief from the political center field. As might be expected, those in the business of long-term foreign policy analysis offered due warning that the night-and-day change from warmonger to peacenik expected by some as Bush was replaced by Obama would prove rather more complex in reality. Familiar military and economic challenges would remain[22] and there would inevitably be elements of continuity between Obama and is unpopular predecessor.[23] Nevertheless, even if an Obama presidency did, as seemed certain, carry over certain foreign policy objectives from the old regime, there was much hope that the new president's tone would emphasize diplomatic means and add to, rather than subtract from, America's pool of "soft" and "smart" power.[24]

THE BLACK AND WHITE ISSUE

For all Obama's verbal attempts to play down its centrality, the topic of race hung without hope of dispersal over the presidential campaign. The British approach to the topic in essence boiled down to the posing of two questions. First, could America possibly elect a black man to the highest political office? And then the follow-up: if America can do it, could we?

Probably owing to Hollywood and other cultural exports from America than to historical education of the conventional sort, British awareness of racial division in the United States is pretty high. While the precise details of the Civil War, Jim Crow, and the Civil Rights Era are sketchy at best, Britons are nevertheless aware that America continues to contend with a legacy of slavery and discrimination that has repeatedly found expression in shrill political rhetoric and urban violence. The theme that many issues remain unresolved between African-Americans and Caucasians in America pervades America's most popular cultural output, from the rap and hip-hop enjoyed by British youth to the DVDs of *The Wire* and (with somewhat less sophistication) *The Shield* devoured by the British middle classes. International news coverage of events such as the Rodney King riots in Los Angeles in 1992 and the hype surrounding the 1995 O. J. Simpson trial have periodically projected America's deep racial divisions, especially between blacks and whites, onto a global canvas.

With all this as background, there was a good deal of interest in knowing whether a nation hitherto assumed to suffer from intractable racial strife could choose an African-American candidate for president in a national election, an outcome that would require substantial voting across racial lines by European Americans and Hispanics.[25] The prospect of the so-called Bradley effect, whereby polls supposedly overestimated the true support of African-American candidates due to closet racism among those polled, was much discussed, and it haunted those keen on an Obama victory up until the last minute.[26] Even with his strong lead in the polls and an unassailable lead in finances, there remained a residual suspicion that a silent section of the "white vote" in the swing states might balk at voting for an African-American candidate at the final moment.

When Obama's victory was confirmed, the British press embraced the moment with all gusto, pouring emphasis onto the racial significance of the occasion.[27] Amid the admiration, however, there was also time for some uncomfortable self-reflection. Having rather sniffily subjected America's credentials as a racially equal society to scrutiny, in the election's aftermath it swiftly dawned on Britons that their own country's claims to providing such equality, at least in terms of political representation, were rather thin. With only 15 out of 646 members of the House of Commons (the Lower House of Parliament) from the ethnic minorities, the representation of nonwhite population in parliament in 2008 was less than impressive, and the Cabinet had no Member of Parliament from any minority group.[28] In light of Obama's success in overthrowing preconceptions of racial exclusion in America, the reasons for Britain's rather dismal level of diversity in elected politics was subjected to renewed scrutiny, with the head of the Commission for Equalities and Human Rights, Trevor Phillips, previously a black Labor activist and deputy mayoral candidate, asserting that "bias" and "institutional racism" in the British party system made the rise of a "British Obama" unlikely.[29]

There are evident difficulties in making one-to-one comparisons between the United States and Britain when it comes to matters of race. In the UK, the nonwhite population totals only around 10 percent of the whole and, by comparison with the American case, arrived relatively recently.[30] Though the British Empire was, of course, involved in the business of slavery for a considerable time, nothing comparable to the American experience of a very large resident slave population occurred in

Britain itself. British nonwhite minorities instead arrived almost entirely by means of voluntary immigration in the mid-twentieth Century. As a result, the collective experience of British minorities has been substantially different from that of the cohesive and organized African-American community, and it does not have anything resembling that group's established and successful structures for channeling a shared agenda within the political process, or for successfully promoting group members as electoral candidates. The result is that no British minority possesses the political visibility or effectiveness of the African-American community in the United States. Perhaps reflecting this comparative political weakness, American-style "affirmative action" has never been adopted as official practice in Britain, though antidiscrimination laws purporting to guarantee racial neutrality have been put in place.

In the UK, as elsewhere, the issue of class is inextricably intertwined with that of race, a point raised in postelection analysis of the likelihood of a "British Obama." If such a candidate were to appear, it was noted by one analyst, he would almost certainly have to be the product of the elite wing of the British educational establishment.[31] Overall, Obama's candidacy and election stirred up intense interest in the relationship of race and political opportunity in Britain, but one sensed little clarity in the ensuing discussion as to what might be done. The implausibility of a black British Prime Minister within the foreseeable future seemed to be accepted across the board, but the reasons for its unlikelihood did not excite a great deal of engagement beyond those researchers professionally concerned with such issues, and concrete proposals for reform capable of generating a solution to the "problem" (if it is considered as one) were thin on the ground.

DOMESTIC POLITICS: WE LIKE YOU, BUT WE LIKE HIM BETTER

Obama did not start 2008 as the favored candidate of either of the main British parties. Gordon Brown, long a close follower of American politics and supporter of Labor's informal fraternity with the Democratic Party in the United States, most likely anticipated—and happily so—the return to the White House of the familiar figures of Hillary and Bill Clinton.[32] Indeed, at a time when Clinton's front-running status seemed assured, Brown reportedly refused a meeting with Obama, no doubt a source of some subsequent regret and embarrassment.[33] Brown could perhaps be forgiven for his attitude given that a Clinton victory—not only in the Democratic nomination battle but also in the election as a whole—was almost universally predicted by the British press and punditocracy in the run-up to the party primaries.[34] Britain having had relatively recent experience with female leadership in the form of

Margaret Thatcher, anticipation of a Hillary victory led to her occasional comparison with the Iron Lady in British publications. Perhaps significantly, however, that comparison emanated from Hillary's own camp in the United States rather than from British analysts,[35] and after her candidacy was rejected, the "Thatcher strategy" of seeking election by projecting steely determination rather than likeability was noted as one of the half-adopted component in a "flawed" and incoherent campaign plan.[36] The success with which Clinton managed to set likeability aside was reflected in the one major campaign story that broke in Britain: Obama advisor Samantha Power's ill-advised description of the candidate as a "monster" in an interview with *The Scotsman*, an indiscretion that forced her speedy resignation from the Obama team.[37]

On the other side of the political spectrum, David Cameron's Conservatives still had strong ties to the Republicans—though relations with George Bush had become strained[38]—and particularly to John McCain. Indeed, McCain spoke at the Conservative Party conference in 2006, offering strong support to Cameron's leadership at a strained moment.[39] In official terms, the party lines remained in this arrangement during the election campaign proper, even after Obama upset Brown's expectations by snatching the nomination from under Clinton's nose. Brown made noises favorable to Obama as political convention permitted, while Cameron and the Tories almost openly endorsed McCain.[40]

However, such was the force of Obama's rhetorical charisma that his international popularity complicated the picture as events progressed. While McCain, a regular visitor to events in Europe over the years, was well-known and well-liked in political circles, he was far less widely recognized among the British public and certainly less celebrated by the media. As such, association with McCain could contribute little to a British politician's stock, whereas there was advantage to be had by anyone who could hijack some of Obama's stardust for his own purposes. This desire for sparkle by association softened lines of party identification by pulling the whole political spectrum closer to Obama through necessity. In an effort to capitalize on public enthusiasm for the "mood" of the Obama campaign, both party leaders sought, one way or another, to portray either themselves or their agendas as the British political force corresponding to the Senator from Illinois.

In pursuit of this goal, Brown could seek to claim affinity between the values of Labor and those of the Democrats, and point to a shared faith in the capacity of government to provide stability and an element of social justice amid economic crisis. Thus he hoped to win over the voters, who were frightened by the collapse of economic prosperity, by chiming with Obama's ethos of collective action and benign government. His difficulty, however, was that while Obama was an outsider arriving to renew American politics and seek remedies to problems inherited from a previous generation, Brown had been in government for over a decade and was a highly visible architect of the presently collapsing economic order. Attempts to appear as a fresh, hopeful agent of change, and to deny complicity in the incubation of the present crisis, were thus in his case a high-wire act.

Cameron, on the other hand, could offer his youth and relative inexperience as evidence of his channeling Obama's spirit, as well as being able to generate a measure of believability in presenting himself as a force for change.[41] Unfortunately, the Thatcherite ideological legacy nurtured over three decades by his party ill-equipped him to mirror Obama's program for a new, wide-ranging array of government projects. In late 2008 the Conservatives set themselves up instead as moderate deficit hawks, opposed to major parts of Labor's plan for massive borrowing and "fiscal stimulus."[42] This put them out of step with the transatlantic mood in the Democratic Party. Further, while Obama's inspiring life story and ineffable air of coolness acted as a large part of his international appeal, Cameron's background as a millionaire and an attendee of the elitist school Eton made him vulnerable if biography became a factor in the campaign to speak for economically struggling British citizens.

As a result of the imperfect analogies available to connect either leader to the Obama phenomenon, a public wrestling match opened up, with both grappling to claim the Obama colors.[43] The contrast with Obama's opponent was striking: even when McCain led briefly in the American opinion polls in September, the battle to be recognized as a British incarnation of McCain was signalled by its absence. No doubt there was a conservative column within British politics that admired McCain for his war service, his hawkish views, and the contrast between him and a slick, multicultural opponent, and no doubt such people hoped for a McCain victory. But they were decidedly in the minority and found it impossible to convert others to their views.

The British public, meanwhile, was left somewhat envious of the Americans' acquisition of an inspiring new leader. Accustomed over eight long years to being able to land cheap shots on American political culture due to the verbal inelegance and intellectual shortcomings of Bush, Britons now faced a depressing contrast between Obama's engaging persona and the options before them in the House of Commons. Brown, whatever his virtues as a hardworking politician and a policy expert, became infamous for his inability to develop much charisma as part of his political personality and showcase it in his public performances.[44] David Cameron, meanwhile, possesses elements of the tested Blair formula of youth and slickness, but comes across as too upper class and, increasingly, too irritable to easily appeal to the same demographic group that Obama has managed to charm.

As a result of this gap, citizens of the UK find that Obama's triumph has a bittersweet quality. They are impressed at the capacity of the United States, not for the first time, to reinvent itself in the face of enormous and growing challenges. In the face of two wars, a crumbling economy, and shattered morale, the American political system has managed to generate a new leadership capable of mobilizing a broad popular majority behind the project of national reconstruction. Britain, meanwhile, heading into what looks to be a long and painful economic depression, is led by politicians less capable of lifting hearts. A nation with a just reputation in the modern era for a certain phlegmatic cynicism in the face of efforts at political inspiration, Britain now finds itself rather jealous of the enthusiasm generated across the Atlantic. To be robbed of an established sense of superiority over Americans in matters of politics will be uncomfortable for Britons, and they will require some psychological adjustment. No doubt this sense of loss will be added to the list of popular grievances, conscious and subconscious, held against the nation's "political class," for whom public dislike is deep-rooted.

CONCLUSIONS

It was probably a good thing for Britain that Obama won the presidential election of 2008, if only because his victory was so widely assumed before it actually occurred that it would have required an enormous mental readjustment to cope with it if McCain was elected in his place. The antipathy felt by most Britons toward the outgoing Bush made them at least as susceptible to Obama's call for change as the Americans, and they not only expected but also favored by a significant majority Obama's emergence as the US President. In this, of course, the British were far from alone, as Obama was preferred in most countries across the globe. Part of this was attributable to recognition, thanks to the disproportionate scale of the media coverage provided to Obama. Even when he was not actually in Europe delivering speeches to cheering German throngs, far more energy was expended on covering events based on him than on his rival. This was to some extent attributable to his charisma and the sense that his candidacy as an African-American had a historic quality. But it was also a self-reinforcing cycle, since the extent of media coverage of Obama itself became a story, and reportage on that fact again contributed to the cycle.

McCain, in contrast, was a bit-part player in the British narrative. He was portrayed as a man with an interesting backstory who might be there to pick up the prize should Obama stumble or be denied victory by the "Bradley Effect." Then again, President George W. Bush was enormously well-known in Britain and heavily reported on, but also

fervently disliked. Name recognition alone cannot explain British preferences entirely; clearly most Britons also found Obama to be the more
appealing figure.

The most concrete sense in which Britain had a stake in the election's outcome was in regard to its shared ownership of the "War on
Terror" and the military interventions in Iraq and Afghanistan. Being
keen to be free from these latter entanglements and to retire the militarized paradigm of a "war" against international terrorism, Britons were
instinctively sympathetic to Obama. McCain insisted on cleaving to the
perceived verities of the Bush era, and therefore a victory for him would
risk deepening the problem of Western relations with the Muslim world.
Perhaps most ominously for the future, he seemed as bellicose in his
attitude to Iran as he was unapologetic for the idea (if not the execution)
of the Iraq war.

Obama seemed by comparison to be a diplomat, and his presidency a
potential escape from the confrontational tone of recent years. Few with
the knowledge of the realities expected that Obama could or would
want to turn American policy around 180 degrees, but he seemed the
more reassuring among the available candidates. One question yet to
be explored is how the British public will react when they become more
widely aware of Obama's intention to escalate the war in Afghanistan
even as he draws down forces in Iraq. Given the British polity's wea-
riness with that campaign, an American request for renewed British
commitment is unlikely to be greeted with enthusiasm. When the real-
ization dawns that Obama wants more and not less war in Afghanistan
in the short term, it will be interesting to witness its effect on the
British public mood.

America's capacity as a society to overcome the legacy of racism by
electing an African-American to the highest office has been deeply and
genuinely admired in Britain. At the same time, the event did prompt a
flurry of self-doubt regarding British race-relations. Most could agree
that a similar spectacle in Britain seemed implausible, yet few had clear or
encouraging answers as to how the political prospects of ethnic minorities might be improved. Like class immobility, the issue of racial disadvantage seemed to be one that the British were well aware of, at least
when prodded, but it seemed that this issue did not hold mass attention
long enough in the UK to generate solutions.

By the end of the election campaign, Obama appeared to have won
the hearts of those at the top of the British political system, and both
major parties began a scrabble to be associated with his winning personal attributes and themes. Meanwhile, voters were left gazing somewhat enviously westward, unimpressed with the comparison between the
inspiring leadership America had found and that on offer at Westminster.
Britons had secretly been rather comfortable for eight years in regarding

the American President as a simpleton and the polity that produced him as dysfunctional. Such a state of affairs did, after all, offer ample potential for implicit flattery by comparison. Confronted with a less cheerful contrast today, Britons may feel the need for inspirational leadership more keenly, but they seem to have little chance of receiving it. Of course, just how the British temperament—insistent on self-deprecation and dismissive of things that consciously are set out to be grand—would actually react to the Obama-style leadership is an interesting open question.

Perhaps the greatest of the broad thematic consequences of the 2008 election, though this is not uniquely relevant to Britain, has been its restoration of the American "brand" in foreign eyes. The capacity of a great—and, in comparison, a giant—democratic society to regenerate itself and to peacefully oust a tired and distrusted government in favor of a brand new alternative, moving in the process from despair to renewed hope, has been remarkable to witness. During eight years of trial, war, and an increasingly unpopular government, it has been easy to forget what a resilient society the United States is, and the potential its institutions possessed to harness popular will for change when that will is mobilized. As they watched Barack Obama being inaugurated as the 44th American President on January 20, 2009, most British viewers felt anew the sense that the United States is, after all, a place that they rather like, and one they can admire without embarrassment when it returns to its good days. For those who wished to see ties renewed and deepened between these two nations, with so much shared culture and history between them, the rekindling of such sentiments has been elusive, and though these feelings may yet prove fragile, for now the feeling is quite priceless.

Notes

1. Toby Harnden, "Hillary Clinton's Failed Strategy Inspired by Margaret Thatcher," *Daily Telegraph*, August 12, 2008, http://www.telegraph. co.uk/news/newstopics/uselection2008/democrats/2548253/Hillary-Clintons-failed-strategy-inspired-by-Margaret-Thatcher.html (accessed January 19, 2009).
2. Paul Harris, "Winner or Loser, Sarah Palin Will Never Again be an Obscure Politician from an Obscure State," *The Guardian*, October 26, 2008, http://www.guardian.co.uk/world/2008/oct/26/sarah-palin-republican (accessed January 19, 2009).
3. James Kirkup, "Barack Obama Wins over anti-Bush Britain," *Daily Telegraph*, May 29, 2008, http://www.telegraph.co.uk/news/ newstopics/uselection2008/2049487/Barack-Obama-wins-over-anti-Bush-Britain-US-election-2008.html (accessed January 19, 2009). Julian Glover, "Foreign Poll Favours Democrat but Shows Hostility to US," *The Guardian*, October 17, 2008, http://www.guardian.co.uk/world/2008/ oct/17/uselections2008-barackobama1 (accessed January 19, 2009).

BBC World Service, "All Countries in BBC Poll Prefer Obama to McCain," September 10, 2008, http://news.bbc.co.uk/1/shared/bsp/hi/pdfs/10_09_08_ws_us_poll.pdf (accessed January 19, 2009).

4. UK Ministry of Defence "Defence Factsheet: Operations in Afghanistan: British fatalities," January 15, 2009, http://www.mod.uk/DefenceInternet/FactSheets/OperationsFactsheets/OperationsInAfghanistanBritishFatalities.htm (accessed January 19, 2009). UK Ministry of Defence, "Defence Factsheet: Operations in Iraq: British fatalities," December 12, 2008, http://www.mod.uk/DefenceInternet/FactSheets/OperationsFactsheets/OperationsInIraqBritishFatalities.htm (accessed January 19, 2009).

5. Clay Ramsay and Angela Stephens, "Among Key Iraq Partners, Weak Public Support for Troop Presence," WorldPublicOpinion.org, October 14, 2005, http://www.worldpublicopinion.org/pipa/articles/breuropera/74.php?nid=&id=&pnt=74&lb=breu (accessed January 19, 2009).

6. Angus Reid Global Monitor, "Britons Object to More Troops in Afghanistan," December 1, 2008, http://www.angus-reid.com/polls/view/32337/britons_object_to_more_troops_in_afghanistan (accessed January 19, 2009).

7. BBC News, "UK Troops Return Basra to Iraqis," December 17, 2007, http://news.bbc.co.uk/1/hi/uk_politics/7787103.stm (accessed January 19, 2009).

8. BBC News, "Bias would Hamper British Obama," November 8, 2008, http://news.bbc.co.uk/1/hi/uk_politics/7717149.stm (accessed January 19, 2009). BBC News, "UK Troops Hand Back Basra Airport," January 1, 2009, http://news.bbc.co.uk/1/hi/uk/7807482.stm (accessed January 19, 2009).

9. Barack Obama, Speech in Chicago, October 2, 2002, full text at http://en.wikisource.org/wiki/Barack_Obama's_Iraq_Speech (accessed January 19, 2009). Barack Obama, Speech in Washington DC, July 15, 2008, full text at http://tpmelectioncentral.talkingpoints-memo.com/2008/07/full_text_of_obamas_iraq_speec.php (accessed January 19, 2009).

10. John McCain, "An Enduring Peace Built on Freedom: Securing America's Future," *Foreign Affairs*, Nov/Dec 2007, http://www.foreignaffairs.org/20071101faessay86602/john-mccain/an-enduring-peace-built-on-freedom.html (accessed January 19, 2009).

11. Elizabeth Bumiller and Thomas Shanker, "Military Planners, in Nod to Obama, Are Preparing for a Faster Iraq Withdrawal," *New York Times*, January 14, 2009, http://www.nytimes.com/2009/01/15/us/politics/15policy.html?_r=1 (accessed January 19, 2009).

12. Tom Raum, "Campaigns Vie over Whether McCain is Bush Clone," *Guardian*, August 21, 2009, http://www.guardian.co.uk/uslatest/story/0,,-7742929,00.html?gusrc=gpd (accessed January 19, 2009). Andrew Sullivan, "Just be Ready for John McCain and Barack Obama to Swap Sides over Iraq," *Sunday Times*, February 17, 2008,

http://www.timesonline.co.uk/tol/comment/columnists/andrew_sullivan/article3382291.ece (accessed January 19, 2009).

13. AFP, "Most Britons Want Troops out of Afghanistan: Poll," November 12, 2008, http://afp.google.com/article/ALeqM5iDAlDVoYEb9h6trvlwYV55GKVVSA, (accessed January 19, 2009).

14. Angus Reid Global Monitor, "Britons Object to More Troops in Afghanistan," December 1, 2008, http://www.angus-reid.com/polls/view/32337/britons_object_to_more_troops_in_afghanistan (accessed January 19, 2009).

15. Alex Spillius, and Damien McElroy, "Barack Obama: Redeploy Troops to Afghanistan from Iraq," *Daily Telegraph*, July 21, 2008, http://www.telegraph.co.uk/news/worldnews/northamerica/usa/barackobama/2437883/Barack-Obama-Redeploy-troops-to-Afghanistan-from-Iraq.html (accessed January 19, 2009).

16. Richard Beeston and Mark Evans, "Pentagon Wants British Iraq Forces Redeployed in Afghanist 'Surge,'" *The Times*, November 21, 2008, http://www.timesonline.co.uk/tol/news/uk/article5197096.ece (accessed January 19, 2009).

17. David Rieff, "Brown Drops 'War on Terror,' Redefining the Fight," *International Herald Tribune*, July 22, 2008, http://www.iht.com/articles/2007/07/22/news/terror.php (accessed January 19, 2009).

18. Richard Norton-Taylor, "Counter-terrorism Officials Rethink Stance on Muslims," *The Guardian*, November 20, 2007, http://www.guardian.co.uk/uk/2007/nov/20/terrorism.religion (accessed January 19, 2009).

19. Barack Obama, "The War We Need to Win," Washington DC, August 1, 2007, http://www.barackobama.com/2007/08/01/the_war_we_need_to_win.php (accessed January 19, 2009).

20. John McCain, "An Enduring Peace Built on Freedom: Securing America's Future," *Foreign Affairs*, Nov/Dec 2007, http://www.foreignaffairs.org/20071101faessay86602/john-mccain/an-enduring-peace-built-on-freedom.html (accessed January 19, 2009).

21. Tim Reid and Tom Baldwin, "Nuclear Iran Must be Stopped at All Costs, Says McCain," *The* Times, January 26, 2008, http://www.timesonline.co.uk/tol/news/world/us_and_americas/article720690.ece (accessed January 19, 2009).

22. Paul Kennedy, "Soft Power is on the Up. But It Can Always be Outmuscled," *The Guardian*, November 18, 2008 http://www.guardian.co.uk/commentisfree/2008/nov/18/usa-obama-economy-military (accessed January 19, 2009).

23. Con Coughlin, "No Sign of Change in Barack Obama's Foreign Policy," *Daily Telegraph*, Nov 24, 2008, http://blogs.telegraph.co.uk/con_coughlin/blog/2008/11/24/no_sign_of_change_in_barack_obamas_foreign_policy (accessed January 19, 2009).

24. Paul Harris, "Hawks Depart as Clinton Ushers in New Era of US 'Soft Power,'" January 11, 2009, http://www.guardian.co.uk/world/2009/jan/11/obama-white-house-clinton (accessed January 19, 2009).

25. Haroon Siddique, "Racism Would Block British Barack Obama, Says Trevor Phillips," *The Guardian*, November 8, 2008, http://www.guardian.co.uk/world/2008/nov/08/race-barack-obama-britain (accessed January 19, 2009).

26. Jonathan Freedland, "All Sides are Behaving as if Obama has It in the Bag. And Yet, and Yet...," *The Guardian*, October 22, 2008, http://www.guardian.co.uk/commentisfree/2008/oct/22/obama-mccain-kerry-clinton (accessed January 19, 2009).

27. Nick Bryant, "How Barack Obama Defied History," BBC News, 2008, http://news.bbc.co.uk/1/hi/world/americas/us_elections_2008/7710449.stm (accessed January 19, 2009).

28. David Matthews, "Is there a British Obama?" *New Statesman*, February 7, 2008, http://www.newstatesman.com/society/2008/02/black-prime-obama-britain (accessed January 19, 2009).

29. B BBC News, "Bias Would Hamper British Obama," November 8, 2008, http://news.bbc.co.uk/1/hi/uk_politics/7717149.stm (accessed January 19, 2009).

30. Office for National Statistics, KS06 Ethnic group: Census 2001, http://www.statistics.gov.uk/statbase/ssdataset.asp?vlnk=6561   (accessed January 19, 2009).

31. Lee Elliot Major, "A British Obama Would Need an Elite Education," *The Independent*, November 27, 2008, http://www.independent.co.uk/news/education/higher/lee-elliot-major-a-british-obama-would-need-an-elite-education-1035966.html (accessed January 19, 2009).

32. Toby Harnden, "Brown's Secret Meeting With Clinton," August 2, 2007, http://blogs.telegraph.co.uk/toby_harnden/blog/2007/08/02/browns_secret_meeting_with_clinton (accessed January 19, 2009).

33. Tim Reid and Tom Baldwin, "Nuclear Iran Must be Stopped at All Costs, Says McCain," *The Times*, January 26, 2008, http://www.timesonline.co.uk/tol/news/world/us_and_americas/article720690.ece (accessed January 19, 2009).

34. Telegraph, "President Hillary Clinton? UK Experts Weigh in," *Telegraph*, January 23, 2008, http://www.telegraph.co.uk/news/worldnews/northamerica/usa/1576276/President-Hillary-Clinton-UK-experts-weigh-in.html (accessed January 19, 2009).

35. Sarah Baxter, "Hillary Runs for the White House as 'New Thatcher,'" *Sunday Times*, January 21, 2007 http://www.timesonline.co.uk/tol/news/world/article1294961.ece (accessed January 19, 2009).

36. Toby Harnden, "Hillary Clinton's Failed Strategy Inspired by Margaret Thatcher," *Daily Telegraph*, August 12, 2008, http://www.telegraph.co.uk/news/newstopics/uselection2008/democrats/2548253/

Hillary-Clintons-failed-strategy-inspired-by-Margaret-Thatcher.html (accessed January 19, 2009).

37. Gerri Peev, " 'Hillary Clinton's a Monster': Obama Aide Blurts out Attack in Scotsman Interview," *Scotsman*, March 7, 2008, http://thescotsman.scotsman.com/latestnews/Inside-US-poll-battle-as.3854371.jp (accessed January 19, 2009).

38. Francis Elliot and Rupert Cornwell, "Howard Fury over White House Ban," *The Independent*, August 29, 2008 http://www.independent.co.uk/news/uk/politics/howard-fury-over-white-house-ban-558204.html (accessed January 19, 2009).

39. Rosa Prince, "David Cameron Backs John McCain in US race," *Telegraph*, January 28, 2008, http://www.telegraph.co.uk/news/worldnews/1576478/David-Cameron-backs-John-McCain-in-US-race.html (accessed January 19, 2009).

40. Ibid.

41. Fraser Nelson, "The British Obama?" *Spectator*, March 2, 2008, http://www.spectator.co.uk/coffeehouse/533416/the-british-obama.thtml (accessed January 19, 2009).

42. David Cameron, "A Borrowing Binge: Brown Clearly Doesn't Read His Own Speeches. Unfunded Tax Cuts Would be Reckless and Wrong," *The Guardian*, November 18, 2008, http://www.guardian.co.uk/commentisfree/2008/nov/18/comment-labour-conservatives-tax-cuts (accessed January 19, 2009).

43. BBC News, "Brown and Cameron in Obama Clash," November 5, 2008, http://news.bbc.co.uk/1/hi/uk_politics/7710034.stm (accessed January 19, 2009).

44. Jane Wardell, "UK's Brown Cuts Charisma-free Figure," USA Today, January 26, 2008, http://www.usatoday.com/news/world/2008-01-26-288165123_x.htm (accessed January 19, 2009).

5

OH LA LA: OBAMANIA À LA FRANÇAISE

Ruchi Anand[1]

INTRODUCTION

What happens in the United States of America has inevitable consequences for the rest of the world. Obviously then, presidential elections
in the United States, the candidates, their agendas, and their foreign
and domestic policies are bound to raise interest in various countries
and their peoples across the world. Once every four years, the world
watches American democracy in action with a renewed chance for hope
and change.

Often quoted as one of the "world's greatest democracies," the United
States in its past conduct of foreign policy has created for itself many
friends and allies but also many adversaries and enemies. Some of these
adversaries stand for democracy but not for the lofty and war-prone ideals of American global "*l'hyperpuissance*"[2] and "*capitalisme sauvage*" at
the expense of justice.

France joined the club of countries that were seen opposed to the
US hegemonic policies under George W. Bush, particularly after France
decided, under the leadership of President Jacques Chirac, in 2003,
not to support the US invasion of Iraq. This US-French political fall-
out has marked the way US-French relations proceeded ever since. The
election of French President Nicolas Sarkozy, who was perceived to be
"the healer-elect" of the transatlantic friendship damaged by the Iraq
war, mended some of the wounds, however. While Sarkozy took office
hoping to restore positive, mutually beneficial relationships with the
United States, the alienation of Europe caused by brash Bush policies on
Iraq, Guantanamo, and Global Warming continued to surface in transatlantic discussions regardless.[3] Not just at the governmental level, but
at the level of ordinary citizens in France, too, an apprehension of the
United States, perceived as an "arm twisting bully nation" seems to be
accompanied by a certain disdain and disillusionment toward America.

Charlotte Lepri, in her book on fifty preconceived ideas the French hold of America, says, "The problem here is the French mix up Bush and Americans in general."[4] And Dominique Moisi, a French political scientist, boldly states, "The French are anti-American, it's not simplistic to say that."[5] Since the French simplistically started equating America to George Bush in the Bush years, being anti-Bush typically meant being anti-American.[6]

This disdain and disillusionment started to change with the US Elections in 2008. The entire world, including a typically anti-American France, held its breath as Barack Obama was elected to the highest seat of power in the United States. The celebration continued in anticipation of change into 2009, as Obama got ready to take over office as the 44th President of the United States of America. "From Tokyo to Paris, from Stockholm to Pretoria, never has the world been so passionate about a US election, never has the world participated with such conviction," said Pierre Rousselin in Le Figaro.[7] Having obtained 349 electoral votes, 79 more than the 270 required to win, Obama, admiringly described by some French newspapers as a cross between John F. Kennedy and Martin Luther King Jr., won by a landslide in a historic American election with the highest voter turnout in 100 years, with 136.6 million Americans having voted.

Newspaper headlines all over the world speculated about the kind of changes an Obama presidency might bring to the world. In his acceptance speech at Chicago's Grant Park on November 5, 2009, Obama acknowledged the international impact of his victory and all that brewed before. He referred to "all those watching tonight from beyond our shores, from parliaments and palaces [and] those who are huddled around radios in the forgotten corners of our world." People cheering his victory included a large international audience. Surveys carried out during the campaign illustrated that if non-Americans were allowed to vote in the US election, Obama would win in all but a few countries."[8]

In Europe, the celebration of the new hero Obama had its own term and was referred to as "*Obamania*." It was noticeable all over, particularly in France, Germany, and the UK. A poll by TNS Sofres, Angus Reid conducted on September 2 and 3, 2008 that asked the question "Who would you prefer as the next president of the United States?" using telephone interviews with 1000 French adults, showed that a large majority of 80 percent of the French people wanted the Democratic candidate Obama to win the US presidential race. In contrast, only 8 percent wanted McCain to win.[9] France has not been this strongly behind America since they shipped over the Statue of Liberty in 1885[10] or since John Kennedy's days in the early 1960s.

This widespread enthusiasm, the *Obamania à la française*, across the political spectrum owes it to two main reasons. First, an Obama victory promises an end to the Bush era that was characterized by a foreign policy loathed and rejected by the French. The loathing that had become *en vogue* in France during the eight long years of the two terms of the Bush White House was now giving way to a renewed optimism resulting from the election of an African American to its highest political office. In the eyes of the French, the United States now has a chance to renew and reestablish its place as a world exemplar of democracy. Second, France happens to be the home of the world's largest community of African immigrants and their descendants.[11] In the French suburbs, the Obama victory is being seen as a push for North African minorities to do the same in France as Obama achieved in the United States. Irrespective of political leanings, the *Obamania* in France can be documented at various levels of the political strata, that is, the media, the politicians, and the average French citizen.

The focus of this chapter will be on President Obama. Other presidential candidates, John McCain and Hillary Clinton will be discussed briefly but will not be the prominent figures of discussion and analysis. The French media in general focused primarily on Obama. It clearly supported the Democratic candidates, as they did in the past two presidential races. According to Eleanor Bradley, a Paris-based American freelance journalist "the public's focus on the duel between Barack Obama and Hillary Clinton is not surprising, and is directly linked to media coverage." She goes on to highlight that in the newspapers *Le Monde, Le Figaro,* and *Liberation,* as also on French television shows, Obama got center stage while McCain and Hillary got the back seat.[12]

THE FRENCH VIEWS OF THE CANDIDATES

McCain was portrayed as a war mongering neoconservative; old, violent, and trigger-happy. Republican nominee McCain's popular image suffered due to his shared party affiliation with President Bush, who was miserably unpopular in France. Although the French did not have much knowledge about what McCain stood for, owing to the lack of adequate media coverage, they nonetheless decided he would not be the candidate of their choice. The media bias in the coverage of the US election further perpetuated the stereotypes of a Republican politician that French people shared. Nothing exceptional was expected from McCain except a "continuation of Bush."[13]

Compared to McCain, Hillary Clinton saw a more positive and a more intensive coverage in French media. This was true in particular during the early primaries.[14] Then came Obama and everything changed, the *Obamania* started. The French in general were excited about the possibility of either a woman or an African-American to become US President. But between the two candidates, Obama clearly outshone

Clinton. Hillary Clinton, widely referred to by her first name, which was pronounced "EE-la-rrhee" by the French, was identified as the "wife of Bill," "the former First Lady," and someone who had "already had her time in the White House" rather than being viewed as a senator of New York. The French media and public had a hard time separating her from her familial ties, something not surprising for the way women are defined in French society. Hillary Clinton was viewed through the lens of the Monica Lewinsky scandal and generated a response that bordered on pity and sympathy and a bit of admiration for her strong character and her bid for power.[15] Christine Ockrent, a French television journalist, in Clinton's biography describes Hillary as having a "double face" with "one side turned toward her family and the other toward her thirst for power."[16]

Obama was portrayed all throughout as the epitome of change, youth, and revival; he was presented as charming and handsome, ambitious and charismatic, energetic and as a self-made man. Clearly, the French media had taken a strong position on which of the candidates they wanted as president of the United States early on. It was as if, in France, the media had already decided the results of the elections long before they took place. However, despite biased coverage and little reporting in terms of real agendas of candidates, the French people seemed unbothered and sure of their standpoint to support Obama's candidacy.

OBAMANIA IN FRENCH MEDIA

Almost every French newspaper hailed the historic Obama victory in the election, welcomed it, and connected it with hopes of change. Most were rather optimistic about the change to come. Right after the election of Obama was confirmed, some headlines that were rather optimistic in their tone were: "Victoire écrasante de Barack Obama, premier président noir des États-Unis" (Crushing Victory by Barack Obama, First African-American President of the United States) –AFP, "Elections US—Barack Obama, la renaissance du rêve américain" (US Elections—Barack Obama, the Renaissance of the American Dream)—France Soir, "La lame de fond démocrate a emporté des bastions républicains" (Substantive Democratic Tsunami Cuts Through Republican Strongholds)—Le Monde, "La victoire d'Obama marque la réconciliation de l'Amérique avec le monde" (Obama Victory Marks the Reconciliation of America with the World)—L'Express, Obama incarne le rêve de Martin Luther King. (Obama incarnates the dream of MLK)—Ouest France, "Quarante-cinq ans après 'I have a dream'" (45 Years Later—"I have a Dream")—Ouest France, "La victoire d'Obama montre les progrès d'un pays marqué par le racisme" (Obama's victory demonstrates Progress in a country marked by racism)—L'express, "Obama, l'homme qui peut changer le monde" (Obama, the man that can change the world)—*L'express* , "Cette fois le monde dit merci l'Amerique" (This time the world says thank you to America)—*Rue 89*,[17] "Quelle intelligence, quelle maestria, quel sang-froid" (What intelligence, what mastery, what sangfroid)—*Le Monde*[18] [All translations in this chapter by the author].

However, some voices could be heard that warned and advised a more cautious approach and to balance the optimism with a dose of realism. Headlines that were skeptical of the mass euphoria of this landslide victory were just a few, however. One for example stated: "La victoire de Barack Obama "n'est pas un raz-de-marée" (Barack Obama's victory "Not a Tsunami"—*20minutes.fr*).[19]

The French passion for Obama's candidacy seemed curious to Obama himself, who said to a group of tourists in Florida, "It's strange that I am so popular in France...I hear that you have problems in the *banlieues* (poor suburbs) and that the blacks are demonstrating...yet I hear that all the French, even the whites, would vote for me" (*Le Canard Enchaîné* reported the exchange). Obama then jokingly asked "You have socialists in France. Tell me, is it a serious disease?" He was referring to his rival McCain's comment in which he accused Obama of being a "most un-American animal, a socialist."[20]

In France, the *Obamania* started after the Iowa primaries when three French newspapers (*Le Monde, Liberation*, and *Le Figaro*) gave Obama's candidacy front-page coverage. What makes this even more striking is that this spotlight on Obama came in the midst of news about French President Sarkozy's rather rocky love life. Obama was so attractive to the French mainstream media, topping news about the country's own president and his private affairs, because the US presidential candidate of the Democrats presented the candidature that divorced itself from everything President Bush meant to France. Bush was seen as arrogant, ignorant, violence-prone, dismissive of the rest of the world, and not admiring enough of France, its status, and prestige. An Obama win in the 2008 elections would mean the end of the Bush legacy. *Le Monde* stated, "Obama is the man of and for this era, well-suited to introduce America to the 21st century." *Le Figaro* wrote, "After him, things can only get better." *The Liberation*, however, was more cautious and more skeptical, arguing that "although a Citizen of the world, Obama is still an American...he supports the sale of arms, the death penalty, free enterprise, he wants to intensify the war in Afghanistan...America's interests will always be top priority...he has raised hopes so high that he risks falling short from day one." The worldwide importance and coverage that the US elections had in 2008 could easily make one forget the fact that the main purpose of the American elections was primarily American. Despite all these reminders and words of caution, Europe, including France, seems to have been seduced by *Obamania*.

During the 2008 US presidential elections, there existed the Comité Français de Soutien à Barack Obama ("The French support committee for Barack Obama"),[21] whose chairman Samuel Sovit said that for the French, "Obama gives America a human face again. His political program is consistent, pragmatic and effective and his foreign policy is internationalist rather than being based on the concept of a fortress America as the world's policeman." He further said: "The French polls are all favorable to Barack Obama (e.g., Liberation, CSA)...the most remarkable thing is the level of mobilization behind him here in France, and he is the only candidate who has prompted such enthusiasm."[22]

This Committee gathered the support of many eminent French politicians, on both the left and the right, particularly those with an interest in foreign affairs. Some notable examples are Axel Poniatowski, MP, chairman of the Foreign Affairs Committee and chairman of the French-US Friendship Committee; Renaud Muselier, MP, vice-chairman of the Foreign Affairs Committee and former secretary of state for foreign affairs (2002–2005); Pierre Lelloche, MP, former president of NATO's Parliamentary Assembly; Jack Lang, former secretary of education; Bertrand Delanoé, Mayor of Paris and potential candidate for the Presidency in 2012; and other important Members of Parliament such as Charles de Courson, Marie-George Buffet, Dominique Bussereau, Nathalie Kosciusko-Morizet, Martine Aubry, Claude Goasguen, Yves Jégo, Louis Giscard d'Estaing, Jean-Louis Bianco, Jean-François Copé, Jean Leonett, Maxime Gremetz, and Marie-Jo Zimmermann.

Not only did politicians get involved, but entrepreneurs, intellectuals, and artists also gave their open support for Obama. Some names include Pierre Bergé, cofounder of Yves Saint-Laurent and leading HIV/AIDS campaigner; Bernard Henry Levy, Philosopher and author of "American Vertigo: Traveling America in the Footsteps of Tocqueville"; Sonia Rykiel, fashion designer; Olivier Duhamel, leading constitutional lawyer and political scientist; Françoise Gaillard, one of France's most prominent literary critics; and Frédérique Mitterrand, filmmaker. On top of all this, over a dozen Facebook groups supporting Obama sprang up: France for Barack Obama, Les Socialistes avec Barack Obama, Pour Un Ticket Obama/Edwards, J'aimerais top que Barack Obama soit President, Etudiants Français Pour Barack Obama, Comité francais de soutien à Barack Obama, France endorses Obama, We love too Barack Obama in France, Pour que Barack Obama se presente en France, La France derrière Barack Hussein Obama, Obama Appreciation Society in France, Barack Obama Fan Club in France, Obama President-France Support.[23] Nothing of this kind existed for McCain or for Hillary Clinton in the primaries.

The immense support for Barack Obama and the disproportionate coverage of his candidacy in the French media demonstrates a definite bias during US election coverage in favor of Obama. Pierre Drai, a researcher at the Transatlantic Studies Center, said, "The French media tends to observe closely what is going on in America politics but then analyze it through a French point of view. This can lead to confusion. American political life is not a left/right opposition in the French sense of these terms. The Democrats are often economically more to the right than the French right, but their social values are progressive..." Charlotte Lepri, a researcher at the International and Strategic Relations Institute, added a further line of criticism and charged the French media of being similar to its American counterparts in that "they are both more focused on personalities than genuine political issues."[24]

The same two experts were asked if they thought that most French are pro-Democrats or pro-Republicans. To this, Drai said, "Economically speaking, many French are closer to the American extreme left that is to say in favor of active, interventionist government. But socially speaking, they would be on the liberal side of the Democratic Party (pro-choice, in favor of gun control), and at the same time on the liberal side of the Republican Party." Lepri said she thought the French are pro-Democrat. She explains, "It can be explained by the fact that the United States is more on the right side on the political chessboard, including the Democratic Party."[25] Given the overall leaning of the US political spectrum, French *Obamania* reflects in some ways the overall French political attitude and how it corresponds with the one across the Atlantic.

FRANCE RESPONDS TO THE ELECTION

On November 4, 2008, France got the president it wanted—for the United States of America. French politicians, from extreme left to right, all applauded the Obama victory by showering celebratory words on him and the event itself and hoping for change. They all, irrespective of the political spectrum, alluded to the hope and change Obama, as the new US president, would bring to the White House. And more than that, the expectation was that he would also improve the American image abroad. They were, however, not so naive as to believe that just one man could drastically change transatlantic relations, race and minority relations, and US foreign policy, to name just a few key issues that needed to be addressed as far as the French were concerned. Statements by French leaders that follow are all reflective of this larger trend of hope and joy and the overall lack of any sentiments of caution. There were no expressions of disappointment, to be sure.

Nicolas Sarkozy, the French president, congratulated Obama on a "brilliant victory." He said, "It also crowns an exceptional campaign whose inspiration and exaltation have proved to the entire world the vitality of American democracy. By choosing you, the American people have chosen change, openness and optimism."[26] Nicolas Sarkozy added,[27] "At a time when we must face huge challenges together, your election has raised enormous hope in France, in Europe and beyond."[28] In a written communication to the president-elect, Obama, French Prime Minister François Fillon said, "I want to assure you of the importance my government attaches to transatlantic relations. France will stand by your side to meet these challenges, as it has always done throughout the long history that fraternally unites our two countries."[29]

French Foreign Minister, Bernard Kouchner, who was also holding the rotating EU presidency, stressed that the EU and France are ready to work closely with him "within the framework of a renewed transatlantic partnership." He said about Obama, "France, Europe and the international community need his energy, his rejection of injustice and his determination to go forward to build a safer, fairer and more stable world." He went on to say: "France and Europe need the dynamism of Obama and his will to move ahead for a more just world."

François Bayou, French centrist politician and President of the Union for French Democracy, made the following statement: "The world can breathe better. After the disastrous Bush years...the election of Barack Obama makes the world breathe better...This election represents equally a personal message to the millions of black men and women, boys and girls who have lived through discrimination."

Christine Lagarde, the Economic Minister, said, "Sarkozy also represents a minority." She hailed the victory of Obama as "symbolically extraordinary" and said that a representative of a minority group "already sort of happened in France." She was referring to President Nicolas Sarkozy, who was born in France to a Hungarian father and French mother of Greek Jewish origins,[30] Delanoé, the Mayor of Paris, called the Obama victory "a formidable message of hope," and said, "On behalf of Paris and myself, I salute this magnificent victory and I wish that his Presidency will echo a hope for peace, progress and justice that his name and image are associated with." Jack Lang, a Deputé of the Socialist Party (Partie Socialiste [PS]), said that the day Obama was elected was "a big and beautiful day for the world. The America we love is back. Barack Obama will have a huge effect and will bring a revolution of spirit and political practice. Then this example will incite European countries to take the path of real change. In this new context the metamorphoses of the French left will dominate more than ever." Devedjian, the secretary general of the UMP, said, "The Americans have voted for the American Dream...in a few hours, the US will again become what they stood for the beginning—a country of youth and equality, a nation where anything is possible, a model for democratic people and those that wish to become so."[31] Even Jean-Marie Le Pen (Front National) praised the election of Barack Obama.[32]

Commenting on the election of Obama, José Bové, the famous French farmer, trade unionist, and anti globalization activist, said: "My wish for the President focuses on two key issues: To finally arrange for the withdrawal of troops from Iraq and a clear and decisive commitment to climate and the environment...an area in which the United States has a lot of catching up to do."[33] These two issues were already vociferously mentioned in Obama's election agenda, and action in the direction of José's wishes is already underway.

Dominique de Villepin, the ex-Prime Minister of France, adopted a cautious approach toward the Obama victory. He said, "Obama is indeed seductive, but we are not going to reinvent Trans-Atlantic Relations if he is elected! America is not any more the center of the West nor is the West the center of the world. Obama, like McCain, will defend the interests of his country, which will not exactly be our interests. He has developed social themes that resonate Roosevelt's agenda. But he is also supported by powerful financial lobbies: half of the Obama financing comes from these big groups, the dollars come from Goldman Sachs..."[34] Villepin's caution was shared by many other leaders and political commentators. However, the cautionary notes typically flowered into optimistic ones at the turn on the page. If not optimistic, the caution was dampened by the sigh of relief and excitement that George Bush was leaving office. The caution expressed by Villepin, which was not easily found in the mass media, was, without a doubt, overshadowed by the Obamania that had bowled France over.

REASONS FOR FRENCH OBAMANIA

It is quite clear from the discussion above that France was elated by the Obama victory. In the following sections, this chapter will explore more details about "Why do the French love Obama."[35] "In France, they love him because he is breaking the stereotype that America is a superpower that wants to impose its will on the rest of the world, promoting a wild capitalism, and disgusting food," says Lepri.[36] What are the real issues? How were the presidential candidates perceived? How does France perceive the impact of the new president on international politics, bilateral politics, and domestic politics?

A transatlantic trends survey of September 2008 clearly showed the optimism that Europeans share, concerning how President Obama would improve transatlantic relations. Of those surveyed, 47 percent believed that under an Obama Presidency, US-European relations would improve, while 29 percent believed they would stay the same, and 5 percent believed that they would deteriorate. In contrast, only 11 percent believed transatlantic relations would improve if McCain was elected president, with 49 percent predicting no change, and 13 percent expecting relations to worsen if the Republican candidate won the election.[37]

Lepri says an Obama Presidency would strengthen ties between Europe and the United States. However, she could also see European governments being pressured by an Obama White House to play a greater role in the world's hotspots: "The French have adopted him, they have many hopes in his candidature, they are expecting big changes, that he ratifies the Kyoto Protocol, that he takes troops out of Iraq, that there is more dialogue between the two cultures. In the end, he will be asking a lot from us, that we engage more on the international stage, to be more present in conflict zones; that might be a bit surprising to the French."[38]

A NEW ERA FOR TRANSATLANTICISM?

The factors shaping French foreign policy, namely, a global perspective, multilateralism, faith in international institutions, reducing the prevalence of poverty in the less developed world, encouraging and endorsing the spread of literacy, democracy, and human rights, supporting only UN authorized uses of force and condemning the unleashed use of unilateral or preventive force, all seem to further the self-image of France on the international stage as having a "civilizing mission" (*la mission civilisatrice*).[39]

After the Bush era that consistently violated all the above ideals of what the French stand for in their foreign policy, the election of Obama opened up "a window of opportunity to restore transatlantic co-operation on key security issues. The list of common challenges includes, but is not limited to, Afghanistan, Iran and Russia."[40] The probability of his success vis-à-vis his transatlantic allies will depend largely on how innovative and different the new president is willing to be in real policy terms. Europe, according to Tomas Valasek, the Director of Foreign Policy and Defense at the Centre for European Reform, "will expect the next president to change the substance of US foreign policy as much as its style. On some issues like Iran and Afghanistan, Obama plans changes; on other like Russia he offered few new ideas during the campaign. He will have to think creatively on all fronts."[41]

In his foreign policy agenda, Obama clearly emphasized the need for a renewed transatlantic alliance in order to effectively counter the challenges facing the world. In his major speech on July 24, 2008 in Berlin he said, "We cannot afford to be divided....No one nation, no matter how large or powerful, can defeat such challenges alone....America has no better partner than Europe...Partnership and cooperation among nations is not a choice; it is the one way, the only way, to protect our common security and advance our common humanity...that is why the greatest danger of all is to allow new walls to divide us from one another."[42] Obama modestly acknowledged the shortcomings of his country's foreign policy record in recent years and also acknowledged that in the future, too, differences between America and Europe will occur. He said, "no doubt there will be differences in the future. But the burdens of global citizenship bind us together...America cannot turn inward...Europe cannot turn inward."[43] Emphasizing the need to work together, Obama shunned the puerile antagonism between Europe and the United States, saying, "In Europe, the view that America is part of what has gone wrong in our world, rather than a force to help make it right, has become all too common. In America, there are voices that deride and deny the importance of Europe's role in our security and our future. Both views miss the truth...The truth being the need to work together."[44]

This is not easy considering the deeper basis of confrontation between the two countries aggravated by the fact that France and the United States have a certain "attitude" about their roles on the international scene. "But while such characteristics come naturally with the power status that the US enjoys, they are the result of a permanent struggle for France, which can hardly pretend that it possesses the assets that would naturally give it a global vision or a global role."[45] France views its "soft power" as a determinant for its crucial role in world affairs and its reasoning to avoid falling in the sphere of influence of the United States.

In an article published in 1998, Dominique Moisi, Deputy Director of the French Institute for International Relations and Editor in Chief of *Politique Etrangere* (Foreign Policy), asked, "Why is France so difficult to deal with? It is, quite simply, in a bad mood, unsure of its place and status in a new world. The French are jealous of America, which seems to run the world; afraid of globalization, which threatens to erode their culture; and ambivalent about European unification, which might drown out their voice. France must meet these challenges while struggling with a cumbersome statist economy and a rising extreme right. To do it all, France must transcend itself."[46] This may be the case under a US-friendly French President Sarkozy and a Europe-friendly Obama. In terms of foreign policies too, the two countries are bound to come closer under an Obama leadership. Ushering in a changed image for the United States throughout the world, Obama's foreign policies that are expected to bring the United States closer to France are his position on the closure of Guantanamo, his acceptance of the need for the United States to participate in the race to save the planet, and his plans to withdraw US troops from Iraq.

Obama's policy toward Iran, that of talking to and negotiating with Iran, if followed through, will be a change in the right direction for US-European relations, and in particular with respect to how France feels this issue needs to be approached. The EU has had an ongoing dialogue with Iran since 2003 and have ever since wanted the United States to join in for the talks to be more effective. Whether or not the talks alone can generate a solution to the suspected designs of Teheran to acquire nuclear weapon is questionable, but what a "transatlantic consensus" certainly could generate is a tighter, more efficient embargo.[47] France, specifically, endorsed the rethinking of approach on Iran and Afghanistan by the Obama administration. Kouchner said to journalists in Washington recently, "I believe that the presidency of Obama will make a difference with Iran. You know the Iranians wish to talk to the United States. If you want to solve Iraq, you have to talk to the Iranians, if you want to solve Afghanistan, you have to talk to the Iranians."[48] Obama argued that Iraqi lessons should be applied to the Afghanistan strategy. However, Obama has spoken of sending more troops to the Afghanistan, which in turn would also mean that Europe will most likely be expected to do the same, one of the implications of multilateralism. In return, European governments will then expect a less black-and-white approach than the Bush administration had used in its effort to defeat the Taliban. To address the situation in Afghanistan, a Pakistan strategy will have to be worked out.

The change in the White House did not change a thing for how negatively the Russian President Dmitry Medvedev views the United States "aggression" and "unilateralism." With regard to the EU, Russia is trying to cause a divide amongst the EU member-states. President Obama needs to "strengthen the EU consensus on Russia," and to "bring Europe's and America's policies closer to one another." This need for a stronger transatlantic relationship between the EU and the United States is something that President Obama has never stopped emphasizing in his discourses. Be it with regard to Turkey or Bosnia or the Israeli-Palestinian conflict or any other international issue, the Europeans (and by implication the French) are open to discussing and possibly working things out with their new transatlantic friend, Barack Obama.

The initial skepticism, if any, about Obama's high ideals and big promises was buried with President Obama's first day in office when he put forward an Executive Order to close Guantanamo in 100 days, something the entire world was waiting to witness. Obama continued with his modest and realistic tone that impressed the entire world in his Inaugural Speech. Painted with strokes of modesty and hope, Obama in his Inaugural Speech on January 20, 2009, said:

> We remain a young nation, but in the words of Scripture, the time has come to set aside childish things...in reaffirming the greatness of our nation, we understand that greatness is never a given. It must be earned...and so to all other peoples and governments who are watching today, from the grandest capitals to the small village where my father was born: Know that America is a friend of each nation and every man, woman and child who seeks a future of peace and dignity,

and that we are ready to lead once more ... For the world has changed, and we must change with it.[49]

OBAMA EN FRANCAISE

Since the entry of Obama into the US presidential race, the French have been fascinated by and supportive of Obama, the black candidate, and Clinton, the women candidate. Throughout the primaries, the image of these two Democrat candidates was painted by an intrigue of the America the French loved to hate. All of a sudden, the United States had become the dream democracy that sparked minority candidates to the top and the country that made France question its own record in the area of minority politics. The question, "A quand un Obama français?" ("When will there be a French Obama?") is one that is on everyone's lips in France.[50] Lepri affirms, "In France, ethnic minorities are not well represented. The only exception is jobs where you are not elected but appointed. The Sarkozy administration appointed Rachida Dati (Justice Minister) and Rama Yade (State Secretary in Charge of Foreign Affairs and Human Rights)." Both are France's only black government officials.

However, Lepri also expressed serious skepticism about the US political system early in the campaign. In March of 2008, with a pinch of disbelief about the possibility of Obama or Clinton getting elected president, she said, "We have to wait before saying that United States are more open-minded than France. Neither Obama nor Clinton has been elected yet."[51] Ever since the election of President Obama, black voters in France vowed that "nothing will be the same" after Obama's victory. A racial shake-up of French politics was bound to happen. Secretary of State for Human Rights Rama Yade under the Minister of Foreign and European Affairs, Bernard Kouchner, said Obama's victory marked "the end of one world and the start of another," and a challenge to France's "conservative" elite to pave the way for change. Christiane Taubira, a black left-wing deputy from French Guiana was less optimistic about an immediate impact on France, however. She said she was "exhausted but happy" by Obama's triumph but was under no illusions on the immediate prospects for diversity in France. She said that the election of a French Obama was still inconceivable considering that neither of France's main political parties "has really come to terms with the colonial heritage, and neither has a clear stance on ethnic diversity." Speaking of France she stated that "We still need to unlock our society, to end the old boy's networks, the discrimination, the exclusion."[52]

The election of Barack Obama represents the equality of opportunity that the French do not have. Although France is home to Europe's largest black and Muslim communities, political integration based on race has been a failure since the political elite in France is still primarily white.

Part of the problem is that France is trying to be a color-blind nation. It wants to and claims to treat all French citizens in the same way without any special treatment for minorities through quotas or affirmative action. Promoting minority representation in French politics, then, quite obviously remains in the realm of an unfulfilled dream. A country with relatively new experience with non-European immigrants, France needs to quickly figure out a way to politically integrate its non-European citizens. While the prospects of a French Obama still remain bleak, an Obama victory has opened up the Pandora's box of questions regarding real equal opportunity for the millions of African and Arab French citizens.[53]

The French first lady, Carla Bruni, said it was now "high time for France to stamp out racism and shake up a white political and social elite that smacks of colonial times."[54] The Representative Council of Black Associations (CRAN), France's main advocacy organization for colored minority groups, has been fighting for exactly this.

At the domestic level of French politics, the strongest message that the Obama win has left behind echoes in the slogan "*Oui, nous pouvons!*" the French translation of Obama's campaign slogan "Yes, we can!" France now needs to reconsider its stand on affirmative action and convert the French ideals of equality for its alienated minorities into reality.[55]

CONCLUSION

In light of the French reactions to the Obama victory in the US presidential elections, one could safely argue that France perceives his presidency to be potentially positive for the United States and transatlantic ties in general and international relations in particular. Following the phase of ecstatic celebrations all across Europe, including in France, this more "socialist" president[56] has generated very high expectations from himself and from and *Obamamerica*.

There are three changes that France hopes to see with an Obama Presidency. First, France longs for a substantial change from the administration of President Bush who was immensely disliked not just by France but by Europeans in general, particularly after his war on Iraq that was seen as a unilateral, illegal, and bullish exercise at reasserting the American primacy in the international system. Any incumbent president would be preferred to Bush, but Obama seemed to have been the favorite replacement. Second, President Obama's victory was seen as a symbolic change of tide in transatlantic relations that had been strained during the Bush Presidency owing to his brash, dismissive attitude toward what Europe said, thought, or wanted during the Bush years. The strained transatlantic ties now can see a shift in many issue areas including Iran, Iraq, Afghanistan, Guantanamo,

War on Terror, Climate Change, the Middle East, Human Rights and international diplomacy based in "soft power," respect, and dialogue rather than hegemonic, primacy-seeking, and threatening means. The French would like to see an *Obamamerica* that views the world as round rather than flat, a la Thomas Friedman.[57] Even if the ends of US foreign policy do not see a drastic change under President Obama, more tactful and diplomatic means will repair a bruised relationship between the two transatlantic allies. Third, France, like many parts of the world, is ecstatic to see a nonwhite person of culturally eclectic upbringing taking over the highest office in the world. That President Obama is respected and recognized for his brilliance, academic excellence, political experience, and charismatic personality does not make the French admire less his potential to add a new and unconventional dimension to international politics due to his being the first black president of the United States. His victory has opened a Pandora's box of hopes and questions in the minds and aspirations of the blacks and minorities in France. A similar change in France would be welcome, even warranted.

President Obama brings with him a culture of hope rather than fear and a new image of America that promises not to repeat the "American century." Obama promises to give the world what it needs—a more modest and open America—and to France, the American president the French love.[58] Michael Freedman asks, "Have you noticed that Barack Obama sounds more like the president of France everyday?" He's referring to a steady and sure shift to a "European model of governance, regulation and paternalism."[59]

NOTES

1. I would like to acknowledge and thank my graduate student research assistant Christiane Peuker for researching the French print media database for articles that dealt with the US elections. Since March 2008 to January, Ms. Peuker was able to compile 1000 articles from a broad spectrum of French newspapers and magazines. I would also like to acknowledge the contribution of Stéphane Monrocq who helped me with some French translations and for productive discussions about the French political system.

2. A disparaging term used by former French foreign minister Hubert Védrine.

3. Bruce Crumley/Paris, "A 'Pro-American' French President?" *time.com*, May 8, 2007,   http://www.time.com/time/world/article/0,8599,1618506,00. html (accessed February 2,2009); J. F. O. McAllister, "Drifting Apart," October 1, 2006, *time.com*, http://www.time.com/time/magazine/ article/0,9171,1541243-3,00.html (accessed February 4, 2009).

4. Pascal Boniface and Charlotte Lepri, 50 idées reçues sur les Etats-Unis (50 ideas received on the United States), Hachette Littératures (October 1, 2008).

5. Political Scientist Dominique Moisi said this when he discussed how President Sarkozy was bold to break out of this mould that has represented France much before the anti-Bush years. As early as Charles de Gaulle, he based his foreign policy on independence from America, built his nuclear arsenal without its help, and kept France out of Nato's integrated command structure, even if the two cooperated closely in many areas. French-American relations hit a low point in 2003, when former President Jacques Chirac led opposition to the US-led invasion of Iraq. Capitol Hill ordered French fries be renamed freedom fries, but Mr. Chirac enjoyed massive public support back home. "Sarkozy the American Fails to Convert France: US Elections 2008," Henry Samuel in Paris, May 29, 2008, www.telegraph.co.uk.

6. "Sarkozy the American Fails to support France: US elections 2008," Henry Samuel in Paris, May 29, 2008, www.telegraph.co.uk. Polls from PEW Global Attitudes Survey show that less than half the French population have a favorable view of the United States as a political actor, while American people are viewed in more positive light than their country. This separation is particularly visible in Western European polls. Gallup polls echo the conclusions of the Pew Surveys.

7. Julien Bisson, "American Election Special," francetoday.com, November 10, 2008, http://www.francetoday.com/articles/2008/11/10/american-election-special.html (accessed February 4, 2009).

8. Catherine Mayer, "The World Sees Obama's Victory As a New Beginning for America," time.com, November 5, 2008, http://www.time.com/time/world/article/0,8599,1856668,00.html?cnn=yes (accessed February 8, 2009).

9. Angus Reid Global Monitor, "Obama Would Win Ten-to-One in France," September 17, 2008, http://www.angus-reid.com/polls/view/31768/obama_would_win_ten_to_one_in_france/ (accessed February 8, 2009).

10. Samuel Solvit, president of France's support committee for Barack Obama.

11. Katrin Bennhold, "Excitement in France over Obama victory," International Herald Tribune, June 6, 2008, http://pour-barack-obama.over-blog.fr/article-20280960.html (accessed February 4, 2009).

12. Institut Français de Presse, Paris, "French media Coverage: Low Marks for French media of US elections," http://afrencheyeonuselections.hautetfort.com/archive/2008/03/06/us-british-journalists-on-french-coverage.html (accessed February 5, 2009).

13. Institut Français de Presse, Paris, "The French Popular Image of John McCain. John McCain: The Devil We Don't Know," http://afrencheyeonuselections.hautetfort.com/archive/2008/03/05/john-mc-cain.html (accessed February 5, 2009).

14. Angus Reid Global Monitor, "Germans, French Want Hillary as U.S. President," August 29, 2007, http://www.angus-reid.com/polls/view/17033/germans_french_want_hillary_as_us_president (accessed February 3, 2009).

15. Pew Attitudes Global Survey July 2008 showed that Obama was more popular than Clinton in Western Europe. Respondents in France who said that they followed elections very or somewhat closely showed 84 percent supporting Obama and 60 percent supporting Clinton.

16. Christine Ockrent, The Double Life of Hillary Clinton (La Double Vie de Hillary Clinton), R. Laffont, January 2001.

17. *Rue 89*, November 5, 2008.

18. Eric Fottorino, "Le Monde, L'homme qu'il faut," *lemonade.fr*, November 5, 2008, http://www.lemonde.fr/cgi-bin/ACHATS/acheter.cgi?offre=ARCHIVES&type_item=ART_ARCH_30J&objet_id=1057846&clef=ARC-TRK-D_01 (accessed February 5, 2009).

19. 20 Minutes, "La victoire de Barack Obama «n'est pas un raz-de-marée»," http://www.20minutes.fr/article/269874/election-usa-La-victoire-de-Barack-Obama-n-est-pas-un-raz-de-maree.php (accessed February 10, 2009).

20. Charles Bremner, "Bonjour 'Barak'—France Loves America Again," *TimesOnline*, November 5, 2008, http://timescorrespondents.type-pad.com/charles_bremner/2008/11/post.html (accessed February 10, 2009).

21. http://Pour-Obama.fr [Translation by the author]

22. The World Wants Obama Coalition, "La France Avec Obama!" http://www.theworldwantsobama.org/2008/04/la-france-avec-obama.html (accessed February 12, 2009).

23. Ibid.

24. Institut Français de Presse, Paris, "A French Eye on US Elections," http://afrencheyeonuselections.hautetfort.com/archive/2008/03/06/experts-interviews.html (accessed February 12, 2009). Pierre Drai is a researcher at the Transatlantic Studies Center. Charlotte Lepri is a researcher at the International and Strategic Relations Institute.

25. Ibid.

26. Aljazeera, "World Reacts to Obama's Victory," November 6, 2008, http://english.aljazeera.net/news/americas/2008/11/20081155293464248.html (accessed February 2, 2009).

27. Barack Obama: les réactions en France, November 5, 2008, 05h48.

28. Gulf News, "World Leader's Reactions to Obama's Win," November 5, 2008, http://www.gulfnews.com/world/U.S._Election/10257136.html (accessed February 9, 2009).

29. Embassy of France in Washington, "US Presidential Election: Statements by F. Fillon, Prime Minister," November 5, 2008, http://www.ambafrance-us.org/spip.php?article1172 (accessed February 8, 2009).

30. European Jewish Press, "France's Extreme-right Candidate Evokes Sarkozy's Immigrant Roots," April 10, 2007, http://www.ejpress.org/article/15764 (accessed February 12, 2009).
31. LeParisien.fr, "Barack Obama: les réactions en France," November 5, 2008, http://www.leparisien.fr/international/barack-obama-les-reactions-en-france-05-11-2008-300100.php (accessed February 15, 2009).
32. LePost.fr, "Le Pen salue ironiquement le nouveau président Obama," November 5, 2008, http://www.lepost.fr/article/2008/11/05/1317341_le-pen-salue-ironiquement-le-nouveau-president-obama.html (accessed February 18, 2009).
33. Spiegel Online, "Good Morning Mr. President: What Europe Wants from America," November 5, 2008, http://www.stwr.org/united-states-of-america/good-morning-mr-president-what-europe-wants-from-obama.html (accessed February 20, 2009).
34. Pierre Rousselin, "Obama : un défi pour l'Europe" November 5, 2008, *LeFigaro.fr*, http://blog.lefigaro.fr/geopolitique/2008/11/obama-un-defi-pour-leurope.html (accessed February 19, 2009). "Obama est séduisant, mais n'allons pas réinventer l'atlantisme s'il était élu! L'Amérique n'est plus le centre de l'Occident qui n'est plus le centre du monde. Obama, comme McCain, défendra les intérêts de son pays, qui ne seront pas exactement les nôtres. Il développe des thèmes sociaux qui renvoient à Roosevelt. Mais il est aussi choisi par des lobbies financiers: la moitié du financement d'Obama vient des grands groupes, de dollars venus de Goldman Sachs...," (Original text).
35. Institut Français de Presse, Paris, "The French Popular Image of Barack Obama: Charisma of Kennedy, faith of Martin Luther King," http://afrencheyeonuselections.hautetfort.com/archive/2008/03/05/barack-obama.html (accessed February 18, 2009).
36. Jędrzej Bielecki and Jaromir Kamiński, "Europe is Betting on Obama," *watchingamerica.com*, May 31, 2008, http://watchingamerica.com/News/1527/europe-is-betting-on-obama/ (accessed February 20, 2009). Charlotte Lepri is a researcher at the International and Strategic Relations Institute
37. Transatlantic Trends, "Survey: Europeans Optimistic Obama Presidency Improves Transatlantic Relations, Think McCain brings Status Quo," September 10, 2008, http://www.transatlantictrends.org/trends/index.cfm?id=124 (accessed February 25, 2009).
38. Sauveur Anziano and Charlotte Lepri, "Paris Prepares to Welcome Obama," *Reuters.com*, July 24, 2008, http://reuters.viewdle.com/video/Paris%20prepares%20to%20welcome%20Obama.?vid=reuters-444-FRANCE-OBAMA_PREVIEW-1216926314.mpg&pid=fbbeca19a1a47bf9c7cba422820296e0 (accessed February 26, 2009).
39. Paul Gallis, "France: Factors Shaping Foreign Policy, and Issues in U.S.-French Relations," (Prepared for the members and committee's of Congress, Congressional Research Service, updated May 21, 2008), 9–11, 1–32. Paul Gallis is a Specialist in European Affairs, Foreign Affairs, Defense, and Trade Division, Congressional Research Service.

40. Tomas Valasek, "What 'Obama Effect' for Transatlantic Relations?" *Centre for European Reform*, November 10, 2008, http://centreforeuropean-reform.blogspot.com/2008/11/what-obama-effect-for-transatlantic.html (accessed February 15, 2009). Tomas Valasek is director of foreign policy and defense at the Centre for European Reform.

41. Ibid.

42. The Huffington Post, "Obama Berlin Speed: See Video, Photos, Full Speech Transcript," July 24, 2008, http://www.huffingtonpost.com/2008/07/24/obama-in-berlin-video-of_n_114771.html(accessed February 21, 2009).

43. Ibid.

44. Remarks of Senator Barack Obama (as prepared for delivery), "A World that Stands as One," July 24, 2008, Berlin, Germany, http://www.telegraph.co.uk/news/worldnews/northamerica/usa/barackobama/2455385/Barack-Obama-admits-Europe-and-America-view-each-other-with-suspicion.html (accessed February 27, 2009).

45. Thiery Tardy, "France and the US," *International Journal Winter* (2003–2004), 2, 1–22.

46. Dominique Moisi, "The Trouble with France," *Foreign Affairs*, May/June 1998, http://www.foreignaffairs.org/19980501faessay1392/dominique-moisi/the-trouble-with-france.html (accessed February 7, 2009).

47. See note 43 above.

48. Daniel Dombey and Demetri Sevastopulo, "France Backs Obama's Foreign Policy," Financial Times, November 14, 2008, http://www.ft.com/cms/s/0/9d1bc764-b1ee-11dd-b97a-0000779fd18c.html?nclick_check=1 (accessed February 16, 2009).

49. CNN, "Obama's Inaugural Speech," http://edition.cnn.com/2009/POLITICS/01/20/obama.politics/index.html (accessed January 30, 2009).

50. See note 9 above.

51. See note 27 above.

52. Agence France-Presse, "French Blacks Fired up by Obama Wind of Change," Khaleej Times, November 5, 2008, http://www.khalee-jtimes.com/uselections/inside.asp?xfile=/data/uselection/2008/November/uselection_November170.xml&section=uselections (accessed February 21, 2009).

53. Anne-Laure Piganeau de Chammard, "With Obama's Help, France, Too, Can Shatter the Glass Ceiling for Blacks," Christian Science Monitor, December 5, 2008, http://www.csmonitor.com/2008/1205/p09s01-coop.html (accessed February 12, 2009). With Obama's help, France, too, can shatter the glass ceiling for blacks, The 'Obama Effect' should now be harnessed to call for equal opportunity for French minorities.

54. Associated Press, "French, too, Say 'Yes, We Can!' End Racism, Carla Bruni-Sarkozy Hopes the 'Obama Effect' Will Reshape French Society," msnbc.com, November 9, 2008, http://www.msnbc.msn.com/id/27632400/ (accessed February 27, 2009).

55. Ibid.
56. John Meakam, "We are All Socialists Now," *Newsweek*, February 16, 2009, 14.
57. Thomas Friedman. *The World is Flat 3.0* (New York: Picador, 2007).
58. Michael Freedman, "Obama, Le Francais," *Newsweek*, February 16, 2009, 16.
59. Michael Freedman, "Big Government is Back-Big Time," *Newsweek*, February 16, 2008, 17, 16–19.

6

Russian Perceptions of the 2008 US Presidential Election: A Case for General Optimism or "Russian" Optimism?

Jeremy Dwyer and Peter Lentini

Q. What's the difference between Russian optimism and Russian pessimism?
A. A Russian pessimist believes, "It could never get any worse than this." A Russian optimist believes, "Oh yes, it can."

Soviet anecdote

Introduction

As the United States is the only country with greater military capacities than its own, and with which its predecessor the USSR was engaged in a global ideological struggle for nearly a half century, Russia's leaders and citizens are inherently concerned about America's political developments, and the prospects for establishing and enhancing the opportunities to foster smoother relationships between the two states. Indeed, the Russian Ministry of Foreign Affairs has indicated that, "Relations with the USA are one of Russia's foreign policy priorities, and an important factor of international stability." Moreover, the relationship between the Russian and American presidents is significant, as they are frequently in contact. There were twenty-four meetings between them during 2001–2008.[1] In these respects, who occupies the White House is of interest to Russians, largely because it will have a potential impact upon Russia's foreign and domestic policy.

We address several themes in this chapter. This includes engaging with the factors that make the US presidential elections of importance for Russia. In particular, we identify why it is possible to consider

Russia a potential stakeholder in the outcome of US presidential elections. In addition, we also query about the issues that were considered by the Russian press, public, and politicians to be most important in the campaign. The chapter also discusses about which candidates the Russians favored and why. We also examine how Russians felt the elections would impact upon the country's domestic and foreign policy agendas. Finally, we consider what implications the elections could have on Russo-US relations.

A BRIEF NOTE ON SOURCES

For our discussion of the campaign we utilize the online versions of three major Russian newspapers: Russia's largest-circulation weekly newspaper, *Argumenty i fakty*; Russia's largest-circulation daily newspaper, *Komsomol'skaia pravda*; and *Nezavisimaia gazeta*, which is perhaps the most highbrow among Russia's newspapers.[2] As with all major Russian media sources, the three newspapers are at present more or less pro-Kremlin in orientation. These newspapers have been selected for study because of their audience reach, including the diverse audiences for which they cater: *Komsomol'skaia pravda*, for example, is a tabloid aimed at broad tastes, whereas *Nezavisimaia gazeta* targets professionals. They have also been selected because they reflect Russian thought on the US elections. That is to say, across the three newspapers there were occasional news items on the US elections reproduced from international sources, but the overwhelming majority of commentary and analysis was written by Russian journalists for a Russian audience. In addition, we also include results from public opinion polls from the All-Russia Centre for the Study of Public Opinion (hereafter VTsIOM).

THE SIGNIFICANCE OF THE ELECTIONS

The 2008 US presidential elections can be considered important for Russia primarily for two main reasons: security and economics. Despite the fact that Russia is considered largely a major European power—a continent being separated by an ocean from America—Russians and Americans are in fact the closest of neighbors. The Alaskan Department of Commerce and Economic Development notes that,

> Alaska and Russia are less than 3 miles apart at their closest point in the Bering Strait where two islands, Russia's Big Diomede Island and Alaska's Little Diomede Island are located. In winter it is possible to walk across the frozen Bering Strait border between these two islands. At its closest the American mainland and Russian mainland are

55 miles apart where Alaska's Seward Peninsula and Russia's Chukotka Peninsula reach out to each other.[3]

The US comedian Tina Fey's statement, "I can see Russia from my house" may have been intended to parody Republican vice presidential candidate Alaska Governor Sarah Palin's defense of her diplomatic credentials in the interview the latter had with CBS reporter Katie Couric. However, this point would not have been far from the thoughts of Russian leaders who place a strong emphasis on geopolitics. Hence, the geographic proximity between Russia and the United States would have made the elections of significance to Russians.

Russia views the security relationship between the two countries to occupy "the centre of attention" of its bilateral diplomacy. This includes such issues as nuclear disarmament and arms proliferation. For Russia, establishing positive relations with the United States on nuclear issues is of crucial importance, as the United States has approximately 10,600 nuclear warheads and bombs, including nearly 8,000 of which are deployed and the rest in stockpiles.[4] In addition, Russia seeks to have positive relations with the United States as a member of the North Atlantic Treaty Organization (NATO), and participates in discussions with America and its NATO partners in the joint Russia-NATO Council.

The Russian Foreign Ministry has indicated that cooperation in countering terrorism "is one of the central themes of Russian-American relations at all levels." Like the United States, Russia has had to confront terrorism within its borders, largely from Chechen groups and international terrorists who have flocked to Chechnya and the North Caucasus to fight against Russian forces and civilians, including participating in "terrorist spectacular attacks" in the Dubrovka Theatre in Moscow (2002) and the siege of Beslan, North Ossetia (2004). Russians and Americans have had significant cooperation on countering terrorism since 2000, when both countries established the Russian-American Working Group for Combating Terrorism, which concentrates on a broad range of antiterrorism measures, including interdicting potential nuclear and WMD terrorist attacks, countering terrorist financing and support through narco-business, joint contributions to aviation security, and developing strategies to counter terrorist ideologies and propaganda. Indeed, Russian-American cooperation in combating terrorism has the highest priority as Presidents Bush and Putin signed a joint statement on antiterrorist cooperation in 2002, and both countries' diplomats coauthored documents such as the Global Initiative on Combating Acts of Nuclear Terrorism, to which there are more than sixty signatories.[5]

There are also significant economic and trade relations between the two countries. According to recent Russian official data, the United States is one of Russia's leading trade partners. Trade between the two countries grew from US $24.5 billion in 2006 to US $27.6 billion in 2007 (12.7 percent). This included a growth in Russian exports to US$ 20.2 billion (2 percent) and imports by US$ 7.4 billion (57 per cent). Well over half of Russia's exports to the United States are in petroleum and related products (US$ 11.5 billion or 57 percent), metals and metallurgy (over US$ 3 billion or 15 percent), and chemicals (US$ 1.9 billion or 9.4 percent). The United States signed documents endorsing Russia's accession to the World Trade Organization in 2006. By 2007 the United States had invested US$ 8.5 billion (3.9 percent of all foreign investment) in the Russian economy, making it one of Russia's leading sources of foreign investment (following Cyprus, the UK, Netherlands, Germany, Luxembourg, France, and the British Virgin Islands), and it occupied the third spot in direct foreign investment in Russia. Russian investment in the US economy during the same period was approximately US$ 10 billion.[6]

THE 2008 US PRESIDENTIAL ELECTIONS IN THE CONTEXT OF RECENT US-RUSSIA RELATIONS

The 2008 US presidential elections were perhaps of greater significance than other US election cycles for Russians because both countries were (at least notionally) experiencing leadership transitions during that year: a new president would be elected and take office (Russia) or be chosen by their electorate (US). In 2008 Russian President Vladimir Putin stood down after serving his constitutionally mandated two successive terms as the country's chief executive (Article 81.3).[7] Russians elected Dmitrii Medvedev as the Russian Federation's third president in elections on March 2, 2008 in which he garnered nearly 70.3 percent of the vote beating Communist Party of Russia Chairman Gennadii Ziuganov (17.7 percent), Liberal Democratic Party of Russia Chair and State Duma Vice Speaker Vladimir Zhirinovskii (9.35 percent), and Democratic Party of Russia Chair Andrei Bogdanov (1.3 percent).[8] Thereafter, Medvedev appointed Putin as Russia's Prime Minister. Like Putin, US President George W. Bush would be unable to run for a third term and the US electorate would elect a new president at the end of that year. Therefore, the prospects that both superpowers would be led by new chief executives provided the countries with the opportunities for new directions in Russo-American relations.

That Bush was vacating the White House offered some hopes that the often very frosty tone of interactions between the two countries might be warmed somewhat. Indeed, throughout Putin's presidency, which overlapped parts of the Clinton administration's tenure as well as most of Bush's period in office, there had been varying levels of affection and cooperation between the leaderships. Clinton welcomed Putin as

Yeltsin's successor, but it was clear that he had a great deal of affection for Yeltsin. On Putin's accession to the presidency after Yeltsin resigned and appointed Prime Minister Putin as Acting President, he wrote, "It was both a wise and shrewd move, but I was going to miss Yeltsin. For all his physical problems and occasional unpredictability, he had been a courageous and visionary leader. We trusted each other and had accomplished a lot together." Shortly after Putin became president, he and Clinton achieved successes in arms control. Clinton remarked favorably that it was not very long after the Putin Administration took charge that Russia's lower house, the State Duma, had approved the Comprehensive Nuclear Test Ban Treaty and START II, and that both presidents had "agreed to destroy another thirty-four metric tons each of weapons grade plutonium." However, he noted with some regret that they "could not reach accord on amending the ABM Treaty to enable the United States to deploy a national missile defense system."[9] Nevertheless, although there were positive personal relations between Presidents Clinton and Yeltsin during their respective leaderships, they still had several areas of sharp disagreement, including how to implement and then manage the peace in former Yugoslavia,[10] and the conflict in Chechnya, especially in respect to reports of Russian human rights violations. It would therefore be mistaken to claim that relations between the two countries were very friendly during this period. Such issues would have an impact upon the relationship between Presidents Putin and Bush, and Russo-Americans more broadly.

Nevertheless, in the aftermath of the 9/11 attacks there appeared to be a great outpouring of Russian sympathy for the United States.

President Putin was the first world leader to offer condolences through telephone calls and telegrams to US President, George W. Bush. Russia also officially expressed its sympathy through telegrams from the Russian State Duma, a joint statement from the Russia-NATO Council and by holding a nationwide minute of silence on 13 September 2001. In an official statement, Putin declared that Russia shares experiences confronting terrorist acts. Additionally, the Russian Security Council issued a statement urging the creation of a united international front against terrorism.[11]

Indeed, Russia's influence helped the United States to begin establishing bases within Central Asia to assist in the campaign in Afghanistan against the Taliban and Al Qaeda.[12]

However, there were noticeable declines in the relationships between these countries during both presidents' second terms. Russia was strongly opposed to US unilateral action in Iraq. There were more than seventy Russian enterprises that had contracts totaling more than US$ 5 billion operating in Iraq by 2001. In addition, Russia also had significant oil interests in the country and stood to lose from military conflict. In March 2003, before the US-led Coalition of the Willing invaded Iraq, well over 90 percent of Russians opposed the move. In addition, the Duma passed a nonbinding resolution condemning the war. Nevertheless, Russian officials also declared that they would prosecute anyone who sought to travel to Iraq to fight against US and other coalition forces.[13]

In addition, Russia expressed its disfavor and security concerns following US support for the so-called colored revolutions in the former Soviet states of Ukraine (Orange Revolution), Georgia (Rose Revolution), and Kyrgyzstan (Tulip Revolution) during 2004–2005. Bush's personal visits to these countries, very shortly after leaders who were well entrenched and at least somewhat favorably disposed toward Russia were replaced, greatly angered Moscow. Subsequently, relations between the two superpowers declined considerably.

In addition, the United States and Russia disagreed sharply over the proposed US establishment of an antimissile defense system based primarily in the Czech Republic and Poland, and other security issues. The United States and its NATO allies argued consistently that the aim of the antimissile shield would be to protect countries from a prospective Iranian missile attack, and that it was therefore defensive. Russia, on the other hand, viewed this as a system with potentially offensive capacities and felt that it was too much of a threat that would be set up too close to Russian territory. Additionally, tensions between the two countries heightened when Putin refused to renew Russia's commitment to the Conventional Forces in Europe Treaty (2007). Both countries also increased tensions with each other as the United States and NATO were engaging in discussions with Russia's neighbors Georgia and Ukraine on joining NATO and Russia established closer economic and military ties with US regional foes Venezuela and Cuba. On some points the two countries differed sharply over how to address Iran's desire to acquire nuclear technology.

The United States was also highly critical of the decreasing space for political competition within Russia. Putin and the party that supported him, United Russia, developed a stranglehold within Russian politics, especially within the Duma. The Kremlin was actively supporting the development of a multiparty system from above. Russia passed election laws that outlawed independent candidates from standing for election and greatly favored those parties affiliated with the Kremlin. Moreover, the Kremlin launched an assault on nongovernmental organizations, a kernel of civil society from 2004 onward.

Two events from 2008 highlighted the negative relationship between the two countries. In February 2008 the United States officially recognized Kosovo as an independent state. This greatly angered the Russians who considered it to be historically a part of their ally Serbia. Thereafter, in August 2008 Russia and Georgia engaged in a brief military confrontation (discussed in greater detail below). This resulted following armed clashes in South Ossetia—a part of Georgia that had for over a decade been seeking greater autonomy and independence from Tbilisi—between Georgian and separatist forces. For a time, Russia occupied Ossetia and parts of Georgia. As a result of this conflict, and following Russian forces' withdrawal, South Ossetia and Abkhazia, another Georgian region that had been seeking to break from Georgia, declared independence. Russia recognized these two countries as sovereign states, a move over which Washington protested vigorously.

These events had an impact on the Russian perceptions of Russo-American relations. Moreover, Russia now considered prospects for reestablishing previous goodwill between the two countries pessimistically. Indeed in a VTsIOM poll conducted in September 2008 some 65 percent of Russians felt that US-Russia relations were bad. Some 11 percent considered it adversarial and only 14 percent believed the relationship was friendly and normal. Despite these attitudes, a majority of those polled (55 percent) felt that the US presidential elections would be important for Russia.[14]

In these respects then, although there would be a new man in the White House—after Barack Obama won the democratic nomination it was clear that Hillary Clinton would not become the first woman president, and that in case of a Republican victory Sarah Palin could only achieve that post pending a disaster to John McCain—Russians were concerned whether the transition would be an opportunity for change between the two countries, or whether it would be the continuation of much of the same—ironically, similar to how many of the Americans and Westerners view Medvedev's succession of Putin.

Early Coverage of the Election Campaign

Relations between Russia and the United States have never been any more than lukewarm since the USSR's collapse, even at the height of cooperation in the so-called war on terror. But the months leading up to the 2008 US presidential elections saw the relationship between the two powers undergo a particularly notable deterioration, with robust, combative public exchanges and talk of a new Cold War. It is not surprising then that well before the Democrat and Republican Party conventions, Russian media commentators were already focusing on the links between the upcoming election and Russia-US relations.

In this early (and relatively sparse) coverage, Republican presumptive nominee McCain was singled out repeatedly for his perceived hostility toward Russia, including his calls to eject Russia from the G8 and admit

Ukraine and Georgia into NATO,[15] whereas the Democrats' presumptive nominee Obama was identified as supporting Russia's G8 membership.[16] Eduard Lozanskii cautioned, though, that Obama would by no means therefore be a better candidate from the Russian perspective, as he has "practically no experience in international affairs" and his advisers include people such as former Carter Administration National Security Advisor Zbigniew Brzezinski and Clinton's former secretary of state, Madeleine Albright, who are "not Russia's best friends."[17] A similar warning came from Artur Blinov, who argued that despite differences over issues such as Russia's membership of the G8, whichever candidate won would aim to "protect America's hegemony in the world," pursuing the expansion of NATO and other policies believed to be anti-Russian in nature—such as the missile shield—to achieve this.[18]

THE CONFLICT OVER SOUTH OSSETIA

In early August 2008, a month before the Republican and Democrat Party conventions, the Georgian government attempted to retake the separatist region of South Ossetia by force. The Russian government intervened militarily, repulsing the Georgian forces and briefly occupying parts of Georgia proper and humiliating Georgian president Mikheil Saakashvili. The Republican Bush Administration, strong supporters of Saakashvili and his putative democracy, retaliated by leading a public relations war against Russia over who was to blame for the conflict and what actually happened. It is in this context that Russian interest toward and coverage of the US election increased dramatically, and Russia-US relations were cemented as the central focus of this coverage.

Overwhelmingly, McCain received the most negative attention relating to the South Ossetia conflict. His links with the Republican Party, his widely publicized denunciation of Russian actions, and his curious statement on August 12 that "today, we are all Georgians," meant that commentators repeatedly singled him out as the candidate who opposed Russian interests.[19]

Among the more paranoid voices denouncing McCain, Aleksandr Dugin in *Argumenty i fakty* argued that the conflict was part of a US plot to destroy Russia's zone of influence, and this plot was being carried out at the insistence of the Republicans, who "are attempting to raise McCain's profile" to secure victory in the election.[20] Several others made similar claims about links between the Georgian conflict and the Republican campaign;[21] and in an August 29, 2008 interview with CNN's Matthew Chance, Prime Minister Putin proposed that there may be "grounds to suspect that some people in the United States created this conflict deliberately in order to aggravate the situation and create a competitive advantage for one of the candidates for the US presidency," clearly referring to McCain.[22] Artur Blinov offered a somewhat less conspiracy-laden version of this link between the conflict and the Republicans, noting that McCain's combative stance toward Russia over Georgia (as well as over the missile shield and NATO expansion into Ukraine) contributed to his popularity because "international crises as a rule strengthen the authority of conservatives in the eyes of voters."[23]

In addition to their persistent criticism of McCain, commentators also focused on Obama's position with respect to the conflict, and certainly did not promote him as a positive alternative who might heed Russia's interests in the region. Obama's criticism of Russian actions, albeit less trenchant than his opponent's, led Andrei Terekhov to lament that McCain and Obama "are competing in anti-Russian rhetoric" over Georgia;[24] Aleksei Vlasov and Andrei Parshev declared that no matter who won the election, tension between Russia and the United States over Georgia would continue.[25] And Obama's running mate Joseph Biden—who has a history of publicly criticizing Russia, and who visited Tbilisi after the conflict—was singled out for particular attention as an anti-Russian figure.[26]

A Choice Between Bad and Worse?

The portrayal of McCain as a fervently anti-Russian candidate, whose election would definitely lead to continuing poor relations between Russia and the United States, became entrenched in the general coverage of the US elections across all three newspapers during the two months between the party conventions and November 4, 2008.

Capturing the general consensus, Vladimir Vorsobin described McCain as "America's chief Russophobe" and blamed this on McCain's experience as a prisoner of war, which left him "fighting with an imaginary enemy" all his life.[27] And, on a related theme, Sergei Vladimirov wrote that McCain's attitude toward Russia is a holdover from the era of McCarthyism and the Cold War.[28] Sarah Palin, his running mate, was also skewered over her combative position with respect to Russia;[29] and even when McCain mentioned in a speech his desire to cooperate with Russia over various issues and challenges, this was dismissed as "merely a preamble to McCain's familiar 'song' about Russian aggression, international lawlessness, the threat [posed by Russia] to world stability and the security of the American people."[30]

A number of commentators directed similar criticisms at Obama, and lumped him together with McCain as a candidate whose election would in no way improve Russia-US relations. Nikolai Zlobin, for example, wrote that Obama and McCain are both mainstream US politicians, and "the American establishment has formed a clear, negative attitude towards Russia,"[31] so the electoral outcome will in no way change confrontational

US policy toward Russia. And Elena Chinkova and Aleksandr Dugin both declared that the two candidates play off US anti-Russian prejudices in their campaigns.[32] There was also much made of Obama's advisers, particularly the aforementioned Brzezinski, having a strong track record of advocating aggressive policies toward Russia.[33]

But together with these commentators who provided negative assessments of Obama, there was also a significant group that was somewhat more ambivalent about what his candidacy might mean for Russia-US relations, and identified at least the potential for an improvement on the way relations had been between the two countries during the Bush administration.

Dar'ia Aslamova typified this cautious position, carefully qualifying any optimism over an Obama presidency. She wrote that there are no "radical differences" between the Republicans and Democrats, "neither of them likes us." But whereas the election of McCain would guarantee continued tension between Russia and the United States, she proposed that the election of Obama "could mean a change of direction for America towards a more flexible attitude towards Russia."[34] Dmitrii Saims agreed that a McCain presidency would compound existing tensions between the United States and Russia because McCain's closest advisers are neoconservatives who believe Russia is "a new incarnation of the USSR, if not Nazi Germany." Obama, on the other hand, is perhaps less driven by ideology—Saims suggested that he may have criticized Russia during the election campaign mainly because he does not want to lose political advantage to McCain; "there are no American votes to be gained by supporting Russia"—and might potentially seek better relations once elected.[35] Several others offered similar comments on the possibility of an improvement in relations under Obama,[36] with Nikolai Zlobin capturing the general consensus when he warned that any "thaw" will be slow because there is a lot of momentum from the Bush years to overcome.[37]

A third main position enunciated with respect to Obama and Russia-US relations focused on the uncertainties and unknowns surrounding the candidate. Zlobin, for example, wrote that for Russians, McCain is the simpler and comprehensible choice in the election: he is the representative of a familiar way of American thinking about Russia. Obama presents a more complex case: he is not weighed down by Cold War stereotypes and "wants to build a new world order," but nobody is sure what this will look like.[38] Aleksei Malashenko embellished on this argument to defend the highly unusual position that McCain is the best candidate for Russia because he is a familiar and comprehensible figure who will merely follow Bush's well-worn path in international affairs, whereas Obama, on the other hand, is more risky as he represents a new way of doing things.[39]

This general pattern of uniformly negative assessments of what a McCain presidency would mean for Russia-US relations, accompanied at times by slightly more varied—though never enthusiastic—assessments regarding Obama, was repeated in Russian discussions of several other specific issues that emerged during the period. For example, McCain was consistently identified as the champion of building US missile shield infrastructure in Eastern Europe, which Russia strongly objects to, but Evgenii Grigor'ev and Sergei Rogov both noted that Obama might potentially rethink the shield plan if he were to win office.[40] McCain continued to be associated with ejecting Russia from the G8, but Obama's position on this issue was rarely if ever mentioned.[41] With regard to lifting the Jackson-Vanik amendment and admitting Russia to the WTO, there was a general skepticism that either candidate would pursue this course with any haste at all,[42] and indeed Obama's running mate Biden was singled out as a stumbling block because of the threats he made to block trade liberalization with Russia in the aftermath of the Georgian conflict.[43]

PERCEIVED IMPLICATIONS OF THE US ELECTIONS FOR RUSSIAN DOMESTIC POLITICS

While Russia-US relations absolutely dominated coverage of the election in *Argumenty i fakty* and *Komsomol'skaia pravda*, and was a mainstay of *Nezavisimaia gazeta* also, there was very little consideration of what domestic political implications the election might have for Russia. Perhaps this can be attributed to the heightened tensions between the two countries at the time: every word uttered by either candidate concerning Russia was reported and analyzed, and all other electoral issues were pushed to the side.

The single major domestic Russian political issue raised by all three newspapers was that of Chechnya. Specifically, McCain's ill-advised declaration, that if Russia was going to support South Ossetian secession from Georgia then the West should revisit the status of Chechnya within Russia, drew attention and a fair degree of scorn from commentators across the spectrum.[44] However, there were no serious, detailed discussions on how the election of McCain might actually lead to problems arising in Chechnya's status.

One domestic political issue that Zlobin flagged was that traditionally the Democrats have been more focused than the Republicans on Russia's internal political situation, freedoms, human rights, and so on. He proposed that this was partly why the relationship between the Kremlin and an Obama administration might be more promising, but also more complex.[45] A similar point was raised by Artur Blinov, who noted that the Democrats focused more than the Republicans on issues of democracy and human rights.[46]

Finally, Iurii Gromyko expressed concern that the election of Obama might have an indirect negative impact on Russia's energy security. He argued that speculatively high prices for oil and gas and energy distribution generally find more support in the Republican Party apparatus. But, on the other hand, Obama's supporters are in the high-tech manufacturing and other sectors that desire a drop in the inflated prices for oil and gas.[47] Given Russia's energy-driven economy, an Obama victory could see greater uncertainty.

After the Election

Russia-US relations remained at the forefront of Russian commentators' interest right up to the election day itself, and the Obama victory was initially greeted with a similar range of reactions to that his candidacy had attracted: from downright hostility and rejection of any suggestion that the relationship between Russia and the United States would improve under his presidency, to uncertainty, and to guarded hope that the relationship could now begin to be mended.

The central point made by those who regarded Obama's election as not improving Russia-US relations was the same as that made in the run-up to November 4: that there was no substantive difference between him and the Republicans who had held power for the past eight years. Aleksei Mukhin, for example, pointed out that relations would not improve because the Democrats are as hostile toward Russia as the Republicans,[48] and Viktor Kremeniuk agreed that things would stay as they were because Obama clearly despises Russia's domestic and international policies as much as his opponent does.[49] Dmitrii Iazov put forward a somewhat Soviet point of view, that there would be no change because the United States is "ruled by capital" and only does things in the interests of capital.[50] Another variation on this theme, presented by Dmitrii Gornostaev, was that America's foreign policy always has unfolded on a bipartisan basis, and this is why we should not await any big changes in foreign policy under Obama; Gornostaev added that one of Obama's major advisers is Brzezinski, a person who dedicated his life to the destruction of the USSR and who "up until this moment still believes this goal has not been achieved."[51]

Even the commentators who argued it was still too early to tell whether Obama would be good or bad for the US-Russia relationship had a decidedly negative bent to their positions. For example, Vladimir Kvint—who reasoned that we could not work out how Obama might approach Russia because he has no experience with Russia and no experience in relevant government organs—pointed out that Democrats focus on Human Rights, free media, and other liberal values that may cause tension with Russia.[52] Iuliia Petrovskaia noted that while it is still too early to know exactly what Obama's policy toward Russia would be, he has criticized Russia's internal political situation and actions in Georgia.[53] On a related point, some commentators expressed the fear that perhaps Russia-US relations would simply not be a major priority for the Obama administration.[54]

A number of Russian politicians, including Medvedev, Vladimir Zhirinovskii, and Gennadii Ziuganov, were among those reported to have greeted Obama's election with (very) cautious optimism and general statements of hope for better relations between the two countries.[55] Some commentators who echoed these sentiments expressed concern about who his advisors might be, though. For example, Dmitrii Saims welcomed Obama as a global and analytical thinker who might pursue better Russia-US relations, but warned that while Robert Gates and Clinton-era advisers would be good, Richard Holbrook would be bad for Russia-US relations.[56] Andrei Terekhov too was concerned that US foreign policy will not change appreciably while Obama is being advised by liberal interventionists such as Holbrook, though he saw some signs that in the longer term Obama had a record of wanting to cooperate with Russia.[57]

Moving to specific issues, there was some cautious optimism that under Obama the tensions caused by the conflict over South Ossetia will recede. Andrei Terekhov wrote that despite Obama's criticisms of Russian aggression and regional destabilization, in the longer term he has a record of wanting to cooperate with Russia, so things should smooth over.[58] Vladimir Kozhemiakin argued that Obama has far more important problems to deal with than Georgia, so Saakashvili might lose US support.[59] Iurii Simonian proposed that the defeat of Saakashvili's "patron" McCain might lead to new elections to remove Saakashvili, thus increasing stability.[60]

Similarly cautious, heavily qualified but nonetheless broad-based optimism was expressed for the resolution of the missile shield issue, despite Medvedev's threats (later withdrawn) straight after the election to deploy nuclear missiles to Kaliningrad to counter the shield's effectiveness. Several commentators reported that Obama was not a great supporter of the missile shield in the first place and has not given any guarantee that it will go ahead;[61] and Sergei Rogov expressed the hope that Russia could "become one of the USA's main global partners in peace" so long as the missile shield plan is abandoned, because otherwise Obama is likely to get caught up in a Cold War mentality.[62]

More generally with respect to arms control, there was hope that Obama would work productively with Russia to renegotiate treaties due to expire and support disarmament initiatives;[63] though Dmitrii Gornostaev, who believed that Obama would continue with the missile shield, claimed that Obama's ideas on nuclear arms reduction were for the most part a game, in that he wants the removal of a warhead from a rocket to be counted as the destruction of a nuclear weapon.[64]

The optimism over Georgia and the missile shield stood perhaps at odds, though, with widespread concern over what Aleksei Bogaturov has called the issue of "third countries";[65] that is, how relations between Russia and the United States might be shaped by their dealings with other nations where they both have interests, particularly the former USSR countries of the "near abroad."

A major concern among commentators was the further expansion of NATO into the former USSR, which Obama was seen to support. Gornostaev and Petrovskaia expressed worry that Obama appeared still committed to the NATO expansion into places such as Georgia and the Ukraine because of possible confrontations that could be sparked,[66] and Ekaterina Kuznetsova argued that NATO expansion into Eastern Europe had the potential to drive a wedge between Russia and Western Europe.[67] Tat'iana Ivzhenko, in a somewhat paranoid article, proposed that the US administration might provoke conflict to its own ends between Russia and Ukraine over the Black Sea Fleet.[68] Mukhin saw US interest in the former USSR as an aggressive step, writing that "from the outset Obama's team has supported the building of a strict 'security zone' around Russia comprised of new 'coloured democracies.' "[69] In this he found support from Aleksei Bogaturov, who claimed that under Obama "the ideal situation for Washington strategists is still that the former USSR states retain an anti-Russian orientation."[70]

Leaving aside Russia-US relations, the only other topic that received sustained attention across the Russian press was how Obama would deal with the rapidly unfolding global economic crisis. Stanislav Belkovskii and Boris Kagarlitskii emphasized that relations between Russia and the United States will be shaped far more by the unfolding economic crisis than by the personalities of Medvedev and Obama,[71] and several other commentators emphasized that it was a major challenge facing Obama as well as Medvedev.[72] There was very little discussion beyond this, though, as to exactly what needed to be done and exactly what concrete effect Obama's approach to the financial crisis would have on Russia-US relations.

THE ELECTIONS AND THE RUSSIAN PUBLIC

Throughout 2008, results from public opinion polls indicated that the percentage of Russians who considered the US elections important for Russia gradually increased. In March 2008 the All-Russia Centre for the Study of Public Opinion released data that indicated that 48 percent of those surveyed felt that the US elections were important for Russia, but 34 percent held the opposite view. By June 2008, these figures had changed to 51 percent and 31 percent, respectively, and 18 percent were noncommital. However, as indicated previously, by September some 55 percent of Russians believed the elections had significance for Russia. Polls conducted in November 2008 indicate that by the time the elections were held, nearly seven in ten Russians had expressed some interest in the campaign and the results. Those residents with higher education and from the major cities demonstrated the highest levels of interest during the election cycle.[73]

Throughout the campaign, where they showed preferences for candidates, Russians tended to support Democratic candidates, albeit without overwhelming enthusiasm. In March 2008, Russians viewed a prospective Democratic victory more favorably than a Republican one (19 percent to 4 percent). At this stage in the campaign Hillary Clinton was the favorite amongst Russians, with nearly one in five supporting her candidacy. Obama was the closest competitor garnering 4 percent of Russians' approval. No other candidate polled higher than 1 percent. Nevertheless, at that stage fewer than half found it difficult to identify a preferred candidate, and one in four would avoid going to the polls even if they were enfranchised for the vote. By June both camps' supporters were elevated. Just over one in four Russians felt that a Democratic president would be better for Russia than a Republican victor and 5 percent of Russians held the opposing view. At this stage only Obama remained in contention for the Democratic nomination. Accordingly, he led the candidates with 22 percent of Russians hoping he would be elected in November. Conversely, Republican McCain who held only 1 percent of Russian's support three months previously now had 6 percent of Russians considering him the better candidate. While the percentage of those who found it difficult to answer reduced significantly (from 46 percent to 31 percent), the share of those who felt that they would not vote in the elections if they had the opportunity to do so rose to 41 percent. By September, McCain's level of support remained the same and Obama's rose to 27 percent. The levels of those who could not make up their minds on the matter rose to one in three. However, those who would not participate declined to 34 percent. By November, however, support for Obama was elevated to 38 percent and 4 percent preferred McCain. Nevertheless 37 percent still would not have voted. It is significant to acknowledge that overall some 60 percent of Russians believed that it would be possible for an African-American politician to win the presidency. This included majorities in all age groups, with nearly two in three aged 35–44 having the strongest opinion on this matter.[74]

Russians expressed mixed views of the election result. On one hand, slightly fewer than one in four Russians viewed Obama's victory as a positive development. Nevertheless, nearly one in three did not think that there would be any change in Russo-American relations. Moreover, only 12 percent felt that there would be improvements between the two countries. However, this was more than double those who felt that there would be a decline in Russian-American relations. Across the political spectrum,[75] voters for the socially oriented pro-Kremlin party Just Russia (44 percent), United Russia (43 percent), Liberal Democratic Party of Russia (41 percent), and the Communist Party of the Russian Federation (38 percent) envisaged that matters would improve between the two countries following the election. This contrasted with 3 percent of Communist voters, 5 percent of United Russia and Just Russia voters, and 10 percent of Liberal Democrat voters believing that things would get worse. Only Liberal Democratic Party–oriented voters' opinions exceeded the national average that there would be no change (37 percent). Significant shares of Communist Party (31 percent), United Russia (28 percent), and Just Russia (26 percent) shared the same viewpoint. However, throughout the political spectrum, Liberal Democratic voters held the most clearly formulated opinions about the outcome of the election. Only 13 percent of them found it difficult to answer what the future held. The other parties' electorates were close to twice as likely to respond in this manner (Communists, 28 percent; Just Russia, 25 percent; Unified Russia, 24 percent).[76]

Following Obama's inauguration, Russians seemed to express positive opinions toward the new president and the potential for improved relations between Russia and America. While one in four Russians still found it hard to gauge the impact that the Obama Presidency would have on Russia, about a third felt that he would be good for Russia, including 3 percent who felt he would be among the best presidents. Slightly fewer than one in four felt he would be an average president. However, only 5 percent felt that he would be bad for Russia. One thing that rang through all sections of political opinion was that Obama should not follow in the footsteps of his predecessor, an opinion shared by nearly two-thirds of all Russian voters. This included 65 per cent of Just Russia voters, 68 percent of United Russia Voters, 70 percent of Liberal Democratic Party voters, and nearly 72 percent of Communist Party voters (). Most emphatic, however, were voters who supported the democratic movements and parties who were not represented in the State Duma. Among them an overwhelming 83 percent felt that Obama needed to pursue new measures, in contrast to those the Bush Administration pursued.[77]

CONCLUSION AND POSTSCRIPT

It is possible to identify several trends from an analysis of Russia's interest in the 2008 US presidential campaign. First, there was a very strong disaffection with Bush Administration policies, particularly in relation to foreign affairs. In particular, they were very concerned about creeping US and Western influence in former Soviet states, including the prospect of NATO membership, as well as overt support for Georgia and its President Saakashvili, which they considered a significant threat to Russian security. In these circumstances, the Russian electorate and opinion makers were very critical of the Republican candidate McCain, and very fearful that, being from the same party as Bush and having historically expressed negative feelings toward Russia, his victory would not be in Russia's best interest. There were some who felt that it might be easier to deal with McCain, however, because Russians were more familiar with him and felt that his policies and actions would be more predictable than those of Obama, whom they felt was a relatively unknown in international relations and who also lacked the seniority in these matters that his elder opponent had.

Second, Russians believed that, in general, Americans harbor significant anti-Russian sentiments. As such, notwithstanding who won, the victor would not produce results that would either improve Russia-US relations or provide benefits for Russia.

Third, and related to the second point, while Russians were more inclined to consider that an Obama victory would be more preferable than McCain occupying the White House, they were not convinced that his election victory would really change much in the relationship between the two countries. It is possible that he was viewed, at least until the election and his inauguration, as the lesser of the two evils. Opinion polls indicate that, across the political spectrum, about a third of Russians hold out some hope for the future of relations between their country and the United States. Moreover, a significant proportion also appears to be willing to give President Obama the benefit of the doubt that he is likely to make a difference. Most of all, however, they have some hope that things might improve if he does not pursue his predecessor's policies.

Shortly after the elections, Russian officialdom sent out messages that the new president may find it difficult to deal with his new counterparts. In his first address to the Federal Assembly, President Medvedev blamed the United States for the global economic disaster, railed against NATO expansion and the war in Georgia, and strongly criticized its proposed missile defense system in Poland and the Czech Republic. Additionally, he threatened to install Iskander missiles in Kalingrad to counter this proposed system. Nevertheless, he expressed some hope that there could be some improvement in relations between the two countries.[78] Thereafter, Russian diplomacy provided some potential complications for the new administration, as Russia offered to wipe out Kyrgyz debts and grant it US$ 2 billion in loans in exchange for not renewing the US lease on Manas airbase. Such a move may greatly hinder US operations in Afghanistan, as that facility played an important role in supplying US and other forces fighting against the Taliban and other terrorist and insurgent forces.[79]

Nevertheless, there have been some positive developments. For instance, the Obama Administration has expressed some interest in negotiating with Russians on the missile shield in Poland and the Czech Republic. Obama initially proposed a trade-off to Medvedev in which the United States would not deploy the missiles if Russia agreed to cease supplying Iran with nuclear technology. Medvedev rejected this tit-for-tat measure. He did, however, welcome the measure as an indication that the Obama Administration was more willing to negotiate than its predecessor.[80] In this respect, it may be possible to suggest that both sides' desires to engage in dialogue on key issues, such as the missile shield, may give Russians, Americans, and the world at least some glimmer of hope for general optimism, as opposed to the "Russian optimism" referred to earlier at the start of this chapter, in Russo-American relations.

NOTES

1. Department Informatsii i Pechati, Ministerstvo Inostrannykh Del Rossiiskoi Federatsii, (Hereafter MID RF), "Rossiisko-Amerikanskie otnosheniya (spravochnaya informatsiya)," May 6, 2008. From http://www.mid.ru, accessed December 28, 2008.

2. Information on Russian newspaper circulation is taken from "The Press in Russia," *BBC News*, May 16, 2008, http://news.bbc.co.uk/2/hi/europe/4315129.stm, accessed January 27, 2009.

3. Alaskan Department of Commerce and Economic Development, "Russian Heritage." From http://www.dced.state.ak-us/oed/student_info/learn/russianheritage.htm, accessed January 20, 2009.

4. Brookings Institution, "50 Facts About US Nuclear Weapons." From http://www.brookings.edu/projects/archive/nucweapons/50aspx, accessed January 20, 2009. MID RF 'Rossiisko-Amerikanskie otnosheniya....'"

5. MID RF, "Rossiisko-Amerikanskoe sotrudnichestvo v bor'be s terrorizmom (spravochnaya informatsiya)" (April 20, 2008). Located at http://www.mid.ru, accessed December 28, 2008.

6. MID RF, "Rossiisko-Amerikanskie otnosheniia...."; Federal'naya sluzhba Gosudarstvennoi statistiki, "Ob inostrannykh investitsiyakh v yanvare-sentyabre 2008 goda." From http://www.gks.ru/bgd/free/b04_03/IssWWW.Stg/d010/164inw18.htm, accessed February 2, 2009; Lúcio Vinhas de Souza, "Foreign Investment in Russia," *ECFIN Country Focus*, 5, 1 (January 11, 2008).

7. *Konstitutsiia Rossiiskoi Federatsii* (Moscow: Iuridicheskiya literatura, 1993).

8. Tsentral'naya Izbiratel'naia Komissiia Rossiiskoi Federatsii, "Postanovlenie O rezul'tatakh vyborov Presidenta Rossiiskoi Federatsii," no. 104/777–5

(March 7, 2008); Tsentral'naia Izbiratel'naia Komissiia Rossiiskoi Federatsii, "Vybory Prezidenty Rossiiskoi Federatsii: Rezultaty vyborov" (March 7, 2008).

9. Bill Clinton, *My Life* (New York: Alfred A. Knopf, 2004), 869–870, 882, and esp. 904, 908.

10. On these matters see the memoirs of former Russian Prime Minister Yevgeny Primakov, *Russian Crossroads: Towards the New Millennium*, Felix Rosenthal (trans.) (New Haven, CT: Yale University Press, 2004), esp. chapters 7 and 9.

11. Peter Lentini, "The Shanghai Cooperation Organization and Central Asia," in Marika Vicziany, David Wright-Neville, and Pete Lentini (eds), *Regional Security in the Asia Pacific: 9/11 and After* (Aldershot: Edward Elgar, 2004), 138.

12. Ibid., 132–141.

13. Peter Lentini, "Russia and the Iraq Crisis: The Triangulation of Foreign Policy?" Paper presented to Monash University European Studies Forum, "The Coalition of the Unwilling," March 25, 2003.

14. Vserossiiskii Tsentr Izucheniia Obshchestvennogo Mneniia (Hereafter VTsIOM), "Rossiyane o SShA: Konflikt na Kavkaze b'et po imidzhu Ameriki." Press release no. 1043 (September 19, 2008). From http://wciom.ru/arkhiv/tematicheskii-arkhiv/item/single/10673.html, accessed February 6, 2009.

15. See for example, "Tainyi raschet Saakashvili," *Argumenty i fakty*, August 12, 2008, http://aif.ru/politic/article/20202, accessed August 27, 2008; Evgenii Belikov, "S kem spat´, a kogo vystavit´ za dver´, Rossiia budet reshat´ bez Vashingtona," *Komsomol´skaia pravda*, July 30, 2008, http://kp.ru/daily/24138/356702/, accessed August 27, 2008; Vitalii Tsepliaev, "Obama: `nash´ kandidat?," *Argumenty i fakty*, June 11, 2008, http://www.aif.ru/politic/article/18847, accessed August 27, 2008.

16. See for example, Artur Blinov, "Obama protiv iskliucheniia Rossii iz G8," *Nezavisimaia gazeta*, July 14, 2008, http://www.ng.ru/week/2008-07-14/8_world.html, accessed August 27, 2008; Vladimir Skosyrev, "Mest´ Makkeina," *Nezavisimaia gazeta*, August 27, 2008, http://www.ng.ru/world/2008-07-29/1_maccane.html, accessed July 29, 2008.

17. Eduard Lozanskii, "Vybory SShA: kogda oba khuzhe," *Komsomol´skaia pravda*, July 2, 2008, http://www.kp.ru/daily/24123/344713/, accessed August 27, 2008.

18. Artur Blinov, "Problema-2009 dlia Putina i Medvedeva," *Nezavisimaia gazeta*, April 14, 2008, http://www.ng.ru/courier/2008-04-14/13_problem2009.html, accessed August 27, 2008.

19. See for example, "Prem´er Chekhii: Radar PRO pod Pragoi popravlen protiv Rossii," *Argumenty i fakty*, September 5, 2008, http://aif.ru/politic/article/20807, accessed September 8, 2008; Viacheslav Kostikov, "Nu, za Kondolizu!," *Argumenty i fakty*, September 3, 2008, http://aif.

ru/politic/article/20679, accessed September 8, 2008; Iuliia Kuprina, "Makkein somnevaetsia naschet sotrudnichestva s RF v kosmose," *Komsomol'skaia pravda*, August 27, 2008, http://www.kp.ru/online/news/132617/, accessed August 27, 2008; Artur Blinov and Tat'iana Dvoinova, "Vashington pytaetsia nakazat' Moskvu," *Nezavisimaia gazeta*, August 14, 2008, http://www.ng.ru/world/2008-08-14/1_washington.html, accessed January 20, 2009.

20. Aleksandr Dugin, "Rossiia pobedila v bitve, no eshche ne v voine," *Argumenty i fakty*, August 25, 2008, http://aif.ru/politic/article/20496, accessed August 27, 2008.

21. Aleksandr Gamov, "Amerika ne yspokoitsia. Nam nado byt' k etomu gotovymi," *Komsomol'skaia pravda*, September 9, 2008, http://kp.ru/daily/24160/374130/, accessed September 16, 2008; Larisa Kaftan, "Rossiia oboznachala na karte mira 2 novye strany. Chto dal'she?," *Komsomol'skaia pravda*, August 28, 2008, http://kp.ru/daily/24154.3/369260/, accessed September 1, 2008; Andrei Kolganov, "Kavkazskaia voina i narodnye interesy," *Nezavisimaia gazeta*, September 11, 2008, http://www.ng.ru/ideas/2008-09-11/10_alternative.html, accessed September 23, 2008; Viktoriia Kruchinina, "Novaia politicheskaia geografiia," *Nezavisimaia gazeta*, August 13, 2008, http://www.ng.ru/politics/2008-08-13/100_gepgraphy.html, accessed January 20, 2009.

22. Matthew Chance, "Transcript: CNN Interview With Vladimir Putin," *CNN*, August 29, 2008, http://edition.cnn.com/2008/WORLD/europe/08/29/putin.transcript/index.html, accessed January 14, 2009. See also "Vladimir Putin: My ne khotim ni s kem rugat'sia, ni s kem voevat'," *Argumenty i fakty*, August 29, 2008, http://aif.ru/politic/article/20626, accessed September 1, 2008.

23. Artur Blinov, "Obama i Makkein vykhodiat na finishnuiu priamuyu," *Nezavisimaia gazeta*, September 1, 2008, http://www.ng.ru/courier/2008-09-01/22_usa.html, accessed September 8, 2008.

24. Andrei Terekhov, "Makkein zamakhnulsia na Severnyi Kavkaz," *Nezavisimaia gazeta*, August 28, 2008, http://www.ng.ru/world/2008-08-28/6_caucasus.html, accessed September 1, 2008.

25. Evgenii Belikov, "Saakashvili podpisal vse," *Komsomol'skaia pravda*, September 16, 2008, http://kp.ru/daily/24160/374618/, accessed September 19, 2008; Andrei Parshev, "SShA planiruiut novuiu voinu s Rossiei," *Argumenty i fakty*, August 14, 2008, http://aif.ru/politic/article/20306, accessed September 1, 2008.

26. Artur Blinov, "Vitse-prezident dlia Obamy—senator Dzhozef Baiden," *Nezavisimaia gazeta*, 25, August 2008, http://www.ng.ru/week/2008-08-25/7_world.html, accessed August 27, 2008; Blinov, "Obama i Makkein," *NG* Web site; Andrei Baranov, "Obama vybral svoim vitse-prezidentom nedruga Rossii," *Komsomol'skaia pravda*, August 24, 2008, http://kp.ru/daily/24151/367476/, accessed August 27, 2008.

27. Vladimir Vorsobin, "Makkein reshil osvobodit′ Chechniu," *Komsomol′skaia pravda*, August 28, 2008, http://kp.ru/daily/24154.4/369481/, accessed September 1, 2008.

28. Sergei Vladimirov, "Bol′no i strashno, kogda stuchit v ushakh i vo vsei golove!," *Komsomol′skaia pravda*, October 2, 2008, http://kp.ru/daily/24174.4/384720/, accessed October 13, 2008. For other anti-McCain statements, see for example, "Rais nedarom zlitsia. Proshla ee pora…" *Komsomol′skaia pravda*, September 20, 2008, http://kp.ru/daily/24167/379532/, accessed September 30, 2008; "Ugroza SShA budet iskhodit′ ot stran, nazvanii kotorykh my ne znaem," *Nezavisimaia gazeta*, October 8, 2008, http://news.ng.ru/2008/10/08/1223445121.html, accessed October 13, 2008; Iurii Karash, "Kak my budem delit′ kosmos s Amerikoi," *Nezavisimaia gazeta*, September 16, 2008, http://www.ng.ru/politics/2008-09-16/3_kartbalnsh.html, accessed September 23, 2008.

29. See for example, Artur Blinov, "Obama stolknulsia s fenomenon Peilin," *Nezavisimaia gazeta*, September 16, 2008, http://www.ng.ru/world/2008-09-16/9_usa.html, accessed September 23, 2008; Evgenii Belikov, "Kandidat v vitse-prezidenty SShA ot respublikantsev Sara Pelin: `Nam nuzhno prismatrivat′ za Rossiei′," *Komsomol′skaia pravda*, September 13, 2008, http://kp.ru/daily/24163/376640/, accessed September 16, 2008.

30. "Prem′er Chekhii." See also Evgenii Belikov, "Dzhon Makkein obeshchaet ladit′ s Rossiei," *Komsomol′skaia pravda*, September 5, 2008, http://kp.ru/daily/24158/373444/, accessed September 8, 2008.

31. "Zalozhniki tret′ikh stran," *Nezavisimaia gazeta*, October 27, 2008, http://www.ng.ru/courier/2008-10-27/11_zalozhniki.html, accessed November 7, 2008.

32. Elena Chinkova, "V glazakh Putina Makkeinu mereshchat bukvy," *Komsomol′skaia pravda*, September 27, 2008, http://kp.ru/daily/24171/382707/, accessed September 30, 2008; Aleksandr Dugin, "Ves′ mir rano ili pozdno budet na storone Rossii," *Argumenty i fakty*, August 22, 2008, http://aif.ru/politic/article/20473, accessed August 27, 2008.

33. Dar′ia Aslamova, "Zbignev Bzhezinskii: Rossiia riskuet prevratit′sia v pustoe prostranstvo," *Komsomol′skaia pravda*, October 30, 2008, http://kp.ru/daily/24190.4/397290/, accessed November 7, 2008; Blinov, "Obama i Makkein," *NG* Web site; Gamov, "Amerika ne yspokoitsia."

34. Dar′ia Aslamova, "Afroamerikantsy boiatsia, chto Obamu ub′iut, kak Kennedi," *Komsomol′skaia pravda*, October 30, 2008, accessed November 7, 2008.

35. "Zalozhniki tret′ikh stran," *NG* Web site. See also Dmitrii Saims, "Vyigrat′ mir trudnee, chem pobedit′ v voine," *Nezavisimaia gazeta*, August 18, 2008, http://www.ng.ru/politics/2008-08-18/3_kartblansh.html, accessed January 20, 2009.

128   JEREMY DWYER AND PETER LENTINI

36. Sergei Rogov, "Krizis strategicheskogo partnerstva," *NG* Web site," *Nezavisimaia gazeta*, September 19, 2008, http://nvo.ng.ru/concepts/2008-09-19/1_crisis.html, accessed September 23, 2008; Aleksandr Gamov, "Seichas luchshe ne dergat´sia," *Komsomol´skaia pravda*, September 19, 2008, http://kp.ru/daily/24166/379133/, accessed September 30, 2008; Azmat Tynaev, "Shamil´ Enikeev: Pora zadumat´sia o sozdanii treugol´nika Tashkent—Astana—Bishkek," *Komsomol´skaia pravda*, September 18, 2008, http://kp.ru/daily/24166.4/378659/, accessed September 30, 2008.
37. Andrei Sedov, "Rossiia vstala s kolen. Kuda poidet dal´she?," *Komsomol´skaia pravda*, September 4, 2008, http://kp.ru/daily/24158.3/372433/, accessed September 8, 2008.
38. Nikolai Zlobin, "Khren red´ki ne..." *Argumenty i fakty*, October 28, 2008, http://aif.ru/politic/article/22219, accessed November 7, 2008.
39. Aleksei Malashenko, et al., "Rossii vygodno spasat´ Ameriku, no polnotsennuiu pomoshch´ nasha ekonomika ne potianet," *Argumenty i fakty*, October 21, 2008, http://spb.aif.ru/opinion/opinion/opinion_id/420, accessed November 7, 2008. Some of these themes are also explored in Tamara Miodushevskaia, "Vanga: Vybory `chernogo´ prezidenta unichtozhat SShA," *Argumenty i fakty*, November 2, 2008, http://aif.ru/politic/article/22389, accessed November 7, 2008.
40. Evgenii Grigor´ev, "Pol´sha priniala amerikanskuyu PRO," *Nezavisimaia gazeta*, August 21, 2008, http://www.ng.ru/world/2008-08-21/7_poland.html, accessed January 20, 2009; Rogov, "Krizis strategicheskogo partnerstva."
41. Evgenii Belikov, "Makkein prosit deneg u Rossii," *Komsomol´skaia pravda*, October 21, 2008, http://kp.ru/daily/24184/392891/, accessed November 7, 2008; Tamara Miodushevskaia, "Makkein poprosil vzaimy u Rossii," *Argumenty i fakty*, October 21, 2008, http://aif.ru/politic/article/21974, accessed November 7, 2008; Iuliia Petrovskaia, "Mesiats nezavisimosti i raznoglasii," *Nezavisimaia gazeta*, September 24, 2008, http://www.ng.ru/politics/2008-09-24/3_kartblansh.html, accessed September 30, 2008.
42. See for example, Artem Anis´kin, et al., "Bush ukhodit, chto dal´she?," *Komsomol´skaia pravda*, November 5, 2008, http://kp.ru/daily/24192/399185/, accessed November 7, 2008; Blinov, "Problema-2009"; Artur Blinov, "Moskva i Vashington pered shansom nachat´ vse snachala," *Nezavisimaia gazeta*, October 27, 2008, http://www.ng.ru/courier/2008-10-27/9_usa-rf.html, accessed November 7, 2008; Rogov, "Krizis strategicheskogo partnerstva."
43. "Bol´shinstvo Amerikantsev ne schitaiut Rossiiu vragom," *Argumenty i fakty*, August 25, 2008, http://aif.ru/politic/article/20482, accessed August 27, 2008; Baranov, "Obama vybral,"; Blinov, "Obama i Makkein."
44. See for example, Gamov, "Amerika ne yspokoitsia,"; Larisa Kaftan, "Prezident Iuzhnoi Ossetii Eduard Kokoity zapadnym analitikam: `O

muzhskikh kachestvakh Saakashvili ne govoriu, ikh net'," *Komsomol'skaia pravda*, September 11, 2008, http://kp.ru/daily/24162.4/375924/, accessed September 16, 2008; Aleksei Malashenko, "Privychnoe sostoianie nestabil'nosti," *Nezavisimaia gazeta*, October 8, 2008, http://www.ng.ru/ideas/2008-10-08/7_nestabilnost.html, accessed October 13, 2008; Terekhov, "Makkein zamakhnulsia"; Vorsobin, "Makkein reshil osvobodit' Chechniu."
45. Zlobin, "Khren red'ki ne…"
46. Blinov, "Problema-2009."
47. Iurii Gromyko, "My vse pomerznem? Chto ugrozhaet energeticheskoi bezopasnosti Rossii," *Argumenty i fakty*, September 29, 2008, http://spb.aif.ru/opinion/opinion/opinion_id/399, accessed October 13, 2008.
48. Artem Anis'kin, et al., "Bush ukhodit, chto dal'she?," *Komsomol'skaia pravda*, November 5, 2008, http://kp.ru/daily/24192/399185/, accessed November 7, 2008.
49. Ekaterina Kugalina, "Amerikantsy progolosovali za perestroiku," *Komsomol'skaia pravda*, November 6, 2008, http://kp.ru/daily/24193.4/399719/, accessed November 7, 2008.
50. Viktor Barenets, "Ia chut' ne prospal dolzhnost' ministra oborony," *Komsomol'skaia pravda*, November 8, 2008, http://kp.ru/daily/24194/400675/, accessed November 12, 2008.
51. Dmitrii Gornostaev, "Igra v kumira na volne radosti," *Nezavisimaia gazeta*, November 10, 2008, http://www.ng.ru/courier/2008-11-10/14_obama.html, accessed November 12, 2008.
52. Vladimir Kvint, "Obama prineset Amerike novyi finansovyi krizis?," *Argumenty i fakty*, November 5, 2008, http://spb.aif.ru/opinion/opinion/opinion_id/437, accessed November 7, 2008.
53. Iuliia Petrovskaia, "Obama vykhodi na mirovuiu arenu," *Nezavisimaia gazeta*, November 10, 2008, http://www.ng.ru/courier/2008-11-10/9_obama.html, accessed November 12, 2008.
54. See for example, Tamara Miodushevskaia, "Novym prezidentom SShA izbran Barak Obama," *Argumenty i fakty*, November 5, 2008, http://aif.ru/politic/article/22432, accessed November 7, 2008; Andrei Terekhov, "Opasnyi khod Moskvy," *Nezavisimaia gazeta*, November 10, 2008, http://www.ng.ru/courier/2008-11-10/15_dangerous.html, accessed November 12, 2008.
55. Elina Bilevskaia, et al., "Poslanie s sensatsiiami," *Nezavisimaia gazeta*, November 6, 2008, http://www.ng.ru/politics/2008-11-06/1_message.html, accessed November 7, 2008; Dmitrii Medvedev, "Vrag No. 1: korruptsiia," *Komsomol'skaia pravda*, November 6, 2008, http://kp.ru/daily/24193.4/399731/, accessed November 7, 2008; Miodushevskaia, "Novym prezidentom"; Sevost'ian Repov and Andron Fufyrin, "Blin vziatochnyi," *Argumenty i fakty*, November 12, 2008, http://aif.ru/politic/article/22536, accessed November 12, 2008; "MID Rossii rasschityvaet na vzaimodeistvie s administratsiei

Obamy," *Nezavisimaia gazeta*, November 5, 2008, http://news. ng.ru/2008/11/05/1225882192.html, accessed November 7, 2008.

56. Evgenii Belikov, "Obama pozval veteranov," *Komsomol'skaia pravda*, November 7, 2008, accessed November 7, 2008.

57. Andrei Terekhov, "Tsvetnaia amerikanskaia revoliutsiia," *Komsomol'skaia pravda*, November 5, 2008, http://www.ng.ru/world/2008-11-06/1_obama.html, accessed November 7, 2008.

58. Terekhov, "Tsvetnaia amerikanskaia revoliutsiia."

59. Vladimir Kozhemiakin, "100 dnei posle voiny," *Argumenty i fakty*, November 12, 2008, http://aif.ru/politic/article/22579, accessed November 12, 2008.

60. Iurii Simonian, "Petitsiia dlia Saakashvili," *Nezavisimaia gazeta*, November 6, 2008, http://www.ng.ru/cis/2008-11-06/6_saakashvili. html, accessed November 7, 2008.

61. See Belikov, "Obama pozval veteranov"; Tamara Miodushevskaia, "Voprosy PRO: Medvedev i Obama gotoviatsia k peregovoram," *Argumenty i fakty*, November 10, 2008, http://aif.ru/politic/article/22516, accessed November 12, 2008; Petrovskaia, "Obama vykhodi na mirovuiu arenu."

62. Iuliia Petrovskaia, "Plany Medvedeva vstrevozhili Zapad," *Nezavisimaia gazeta*, November 7, 2008, http://www.ng.ru/world/2008-11-07/7_medvedev.html, accessed November 7, 2008.

63. See Miodushevskaia, "Novym prezidentom," *AiF* Web site; Terekhov, "Tsvetnaia amerikanskaia revoliutsiia," *KP* Web site; Terekhov, "Opasnyi khod Moskvy," *NG* Web site.

64. Gornostaev, "Igra v kumira," *NG* Web site.

65. "Zalozhniki tret'ikh stran," *Nezavisimaia gazeta*, October 27, 2008, http://www.ng.ru/courier/2008-10-27/11_zalozhniki.html, accessed November 7, 2008.

66. Gornostaev, "Igra v kumira," *NG* Web site; Petrovskaia, "Obama vykhodi na mirovuiu arenu."

67. Ekaterina Kuznetsova, "Raznoglasiia s Evropoi ostanutsia," *Nezavisimaia gazeta*, November 10, 2008, http://www.ng.ru/courier/2008-11-10/13_europe.html, accessed November 12, 2008 On a similar point, Stanislav Belkovskii proposed that improving US-EU relations might be to Russia's disadvantage because it could not play the US and Europe off against one another as it had been doing. See Vladimir Kvint, et al., "Obama ne imeet opyta otnoshenii s nashei stranoi," *Argumenty i fakty*, November 6, 2008, http://aif.ru/opinion/opinion/opinion_id/718, accessed November 7, 2008.

68. Tat'iana Ivzhenko, "Kiev stavit na Obamu," *Nezavisimaia gazeta*, November 6, 2008, http://www.ng.ru/cis/2008-11-06/6_war.html, accessed November 7, 2008.

69. Anis'kin, et al., "Bush ukhodit."

70. Aleksei Bogaturov, "Konets kontrliberal'nogo tsikla?," *Nezavisimaia gazeta*, November 10, 2008, http://www.ng.ru/courier/2008-11-

10/15_contrliberal.html, accessed November 12, 2008. See also Anis′kin, et al., "Bush ukhodit," *KP* Web site.

71. Kvint, "Obama prineset Amerike," *AiF* Web site.

72. See "Eksperty: novomu prezidentu SShA mozhno tol′ko puchu-vstvovat′," *Komsomol′skaia pravda*, November 6, 2008, http://kp.ru/daily/24193.4/399686/, accessed November 7, 2008; Kugalina, "Amerikantsy progolosovali za perestroiku," *KP* Web site; Miodushevskaia, "Novym prezidentom," *AiF* Web site; Terekhov, "Opasnyi khod Moskvy," *NG* Web site.

73. VTsIOM, "Rossiyane—za Khillari Klinton," Press Release no. 899 (March 12, 2008). From http://wciom.ru/arkhiv/tematicheskii-arkhiv/item/single/9798.html, accessed February 6, 2009; VTsIOM, "Vybory v SShA: Rossiyanie progolosovali by za Baraka Obamu." Press Release no. 991. From http://wciom.ru/arkhiv/tematicheskii-arkhiv/item/single/10331.html, accessed February 6, 2009; VTsIOM, "Rossiyanie o SShA...."; VTsIOM, "Vybory v SShA: Temnokozhii Prezident—eto normal'no!." Press Release no. 1098 (November 20, 2008). From http://wciom.ru/arkhiv/tematicheskii-arkhiv/item/single/1109.html, accessed February 6, 2009.

74. VTsIOM, "Rossiyane—za Khillari Klinton"; VTsIOM, "Vybory v SShA: Rossiyanie progolosovali by za Baraka Obamu"; VTsIOM, "Barak Obama vo glave SShA i perspektivy Rossiisko-Amerikanskikh otnoshenii." Press Release no. 1077 (October 24, 2008). From http://wciom.ru/arkhiv/tematicheskii-arkhiv/item/single/10862.html. accessed February 6, 2009; VTsIOM, "Vybory v SShA: Temnokozhii Prezident...."

75. This survey represents the political opinions of voters who support those parties represented in the State Duma.

76. VTsIOM, "Rossiya i Amerika pri Medvedeve i Obame: perspektivy dvustroronnykh otnoshenii." Press Release no. 1114 (December 8, 2008). From http://wciom.ru/arkhiv/tematicheskii-arkhiv/item/single/11095.html, accessed February 6, 2009.

77. VTsIOM, "Rossiyane sovetuiut Baraku Obame: ne sledui kursom Dzhordzha Busha!." Press Release no. 1144 (January 29, 2009). From http://wciom.ru/novisti/press-vypusk/single/11312.html, accessed February 5, 2009.

78. Dmitrii Medvedev, "Poslanie Federal'nomu Sobraniiu Rossiiskoi Federatsii" (November 5, 2008). From http://www.kremlin.ru/appears/2008/11/05/1349_type63372type63381type86234_20874.shtml, accessed December 28, 2009; ABC (Australia), "Russian President Slams US in Election Aftermath"(November 6, 2008). From http://www.bigpond.com.au/news/breaking/content/20081106/2411488.asp, accessed November 6, 2008.

79. Elizabeth Bumiller and Ellen Barry, "U.S. Searches for Alternative to Central Asian Base," *The New York Times*, February 5, 2009.

80. Helene Cooper and Nicholas Kulish, "Biden Signals U.S. Is Open to Deal with Russia on Missiles," *New York Times*, February 8, 2009; Peter Baker, "Obama Offered Deal to Russia in Secret Letter," *New York Times*, March 3, 2009; Ellen Barry, "Russia Welcomes Letter From Obama," *New York Times*, March 4, 2009; Ellen Barry, "Russia Says No to US Iran Deal," *The Age*, March 5, 2009, 14.

7

Israeli Views on the US Presidential Election: Between Perception and Reality

Ronnie Olesker

Introduction

The Israeli perspectives on the US presidential elections are characterized by the dichotomy of perception and reality. That is to say, most of the Israeli perspective is based on perception rather than reality. Perception of the candidates and their positions on Iran, the Israeli-Palestinian peace process, Israeli settlements, arms control, and the relationship each of the candidates would have with Israel, all these affected Israeli preferences. The dichotomy between perception and reality has also infiltrated the 2009 Israeli election campaigns of the parties and their leading candidates insofar as they presented themselves as the candidates of "change" or as those most likely to work well with the incoming Obama administration, despite the political realities that may indicate otherwise. This has been referred to as the "Obama effect."[1]

According to Alon Pinkas, former consul general of Israel in New York and current head of the Rabin Center Institute for Israel-US relations, Israel was one of three countries to prefer the candidacy of John McCain over that of Barack Obama. The other two being Georgia and the Philippines.[2] In contrast to American Jews, who voted overwhelmingly for Obama, US absentee voters in Israel supported McCain over Obama by 3:1. This is to be expected, however, since most Americans living in Israel tend to be orthodox Jews who are conservative hawks, and they would not have necessarily represented the general Israeli opinion. Once Obama was elected, however, there was tremendous elation, particularly in the media, about that election and the historical change it symbolized.

The overall argument presented here is that despite the perceptions of most Israelis regarding Obama, and the expectations of many that the rise in power of the right in Israel following the elections there in February 2009 will lead to tensions between Israel and the United States, it is not expected, at least not in the first Obama term, that much will change in the relations between the two countries. In fact, early Obama appointments indicate a return to policies of the Clinton administration, which also did not manage to pressure Israel into concessions it felt it could not live with. Possible clashes may exist, I later argue, if the Obama administration achieves diplomatic concessions from Iran to halt its development of a nuclear program, in which case the American administration would be in the position to exert pressure on Israel regarding its own nuclear armament.

For the most part, this chapter focuses on the viewpoint of the political elites, which determine policies in Israel often independent of the public. The Israeli electoral system is based on a party system in which party politics, rather than individual representation, matters. While individual leaders such as Benjamin Netanyahu, Tzipi Livni and Ehud Barak represent the "face" of their party, Israelis do not elect their leaders directly. Nevertheless, where relevant, I invoke public polling data and news reports to support my analysis.

I begin by discussing the stakes Israelis feel they have in American politics in general and in the presidential elections in particular. I will then discuss which of the candidates was viewed more favorably and why, and what was seen as the distinguishing factors in them. In the fourth section of this chapter, I examine the political issues that are regarded as critical in this election and what effect, if any, the Obama election may have had on those issues. Before concluding, I analyze the effects the Obama victory has had on the Israeli election campaign in early 2009 and the implications of those elections for the bilateral relations between Israel and the United States. Following the 2009 Israeli elections, the right bloc in the Israeli political map increased its relative power, leading President Simon Peres to ask Benjamin Netanyahu of the Likud party, rather than Tzipi Livni of Kadima, to form the next government (even though Likud received one mandate less than Kadima did).

For scholars studying the bilateral relations between the United States and Israel, it is important to explore the results of the Israeli and American elections, as the nature of their relations may be affected by the results of the latest elections in both countries.

ISRAEL'S STAKE IN THE ELECTION

Israel has shared a close relationship with the United States from its inception. President Harry S. Truman, rejecting the advice of his Secretary of State

George C. Marshall, immediately gave Israel de facto diplomatic recognition after its proclamation of independence on May 14, 1948. Since then, the strong and close relationship Israel enjoys with the United States stands as Israel's most strategic, albeit unofficial, alliance. The military and political relationship grew stronger after 1967 when it was evident that the "Zionist experiment" had become a viable state and that Israel was here to stay. While the financial support for Israel has been steadily decreasing,[3] the United States is still overwhelmingly committed to Israel through military support. Indeed Israel is the top recipient of US foreign aid in the world. Recently the head of Military Intelligence argued that the relationship with the United States was one of the most vital proponents of Israeli security.[4]

Because of the diplomatic and military support Israeli received from the United States, any and every Israeli government is dependent on the American administration. Because of this dependency, the United States is practically the only country in whose domestic politics Israel is truly interested. Moreover, any Israeli government that does not have good working relations with the Americans finds it hard to survive politically. The Likud government headed by Yitzhak Shamir, who resisted the Bush-Baker administration's Middle East peace initiative in 1991, fell in 1992 when Yitzhak Rabin and a Labor government were elected. Similarly, the Netanyahu government, which did not get along with President Clinton and Secretary Albright, fell in 1999 when the Labor government led by Ehud Barak was elected. Because Israel sees the United States as the sole credible mediator in the Arab-Israeli conflict and the heavy US investment in resolving that conflict, it is very difficult to conduct Israeli foreign policy without US support. Thus, Israeli governments that did not enjoy the support of the US administration found it hard to survive when they were unable to move the peace process forward. As a result, the nature of the American administration and the identity and policies of its president are crucial for Israeli politics.

The relationship with the United States is not only a vital interest of Israeli policymakers, but also an important interest for the Israeli voter as well. Israeli voters take into consideration the relationship their leaders have with the American administration. This was evident during the recent election campaign in Israel when the candidates from the leading parties, Kadima, Likud, and Labor, all campaigned that they would be able to work effectively and build a positive relationship with the Obama administration. Benjamin Netanyahu emphasized that he met with Obama twice and both meetings were positive. Both Tzipi Livni and Ehud Barak presented their foreign policy as most compatible with the objectives of the Obama administration, since they support a diplomatic peace process with the PLO (but not Hamas), even before the American President made his objectives clear. In fact, following the elections in Israel in February 2009,

Livni explained her resistance to join a coalition led by Netanyahu by stating that she would be betraying her voters who viewed her as the "candidate of peace."

This is not lost on the Israeli voter. The military and diplomatic support Israel receives from the United States is particularly important today when Israel has few friends in the international community. Israelis therefore paid close attention to the election campaign in the United States, particularly once Obama and McCain had been chosen as the nominees of their respective parties.

Israeli interest in American politics is not new. Writing on past Israeli involvement in US election campaigns, political commentator Shmuel Rosner noted, "Israel has always promised to keep from intervening in America's internal political affairs—and then intervened. And when not intervening, it has demonstrated involvement." In fact, as Rosner describes, in 2004, the then prime minister, Ariel Sharon, refused to meet with John Kerry, the Democratic presidential nominee, demonstrating a clear preference for the incumbent president. More recently Prime Minister Ehud Olmert saluted President Bush's policies in Iraq on the eve of the 2006 midterm elections, angering many congressional Democrats.[5]

Given the tremendous stake Israelis feel they have in the relationship with the United States it is not surprising that they have demonstrated a strong interest in the American elections throughout the years. What happens in American politics has an impact on Israel and thus demands the attention of the public and, in some cases, even the active involvement of its leaders.

The following sections discuss the Israeli viewpoints on issues seen as crucial to Israel. To understand those viewpoints it is first imperative to examine the Israeli perspectives on the candidates and their stand on those issues.

THE AMERICAN CANDIDATES FROM THE ISRAELI PERSPECTIVE

Throughout the election campaign, beginning in the fall of 2006, Rosner of the *Haaretz* newspaper led a project titled "The Israeli Factor," which ranked the potential presidential candidates in the 2008 elections based on their attitude toward Israel. This project serves as yet another indication of the level of Israeli involvement and interest in those elections. Each month, a group of eight distinguished Israeli experts on American politics gathered to assess the candidates' positions on various Israel-related topics and to rank the best candidate for Israel. The panel included Dore Gold, the president of the Jerusalem Center for Public Affairs, advisor to former prime minister Benjamin Netanyahu, and former Israeli ambassador to the United Nations, as well as Alon Pinkas, the former Consul

General of Israel in New York, chief of staff for foreign ministers David Levy and Shlomo Ben-Ami, and member of the Israeli delegation at the Israel-Syria peace talks in 2000 *and current head of the Rabin Center Institute for Israel-US relations.* Also participating was Dan Halperin, who served as minister for economic affairs at the Embassy in Washington and negotiated the free trade agreement between the two states, as well as Zvi Rafiah, who served at the Israeli diplomatic missions in Iran and Turkey. The Panel included academic scholars on Israeli-US relations, Avi Ben Tzvi, Eytan Gilboa, Ron Rubin, and Yossi Shain.

Each of the candidates was marked on a scale from 1 to 10 (10 being the "best" for Israel and 1 being the "worst"). In the final "Israel Factor" issue, Republican nominee John McCain received a score of 7.75 while Democratic nominee Barack Obama received a score of 5.12. Before bowing out of the race, Hillary Clinton received a score of 7.5.[6]

While not intimately familiar with either candidate's positions, the general Israeli public clearly demonstrated a preference for McCain over Obama as well, with 46 percent of Israelis polled in October 2008 stating that they would vote for McCain if given the opportunity while only 34 percent said they would vote for Obama, and almost half of those polled said that they believed McCain would better impact Israel.[7] This stands in contrast to the international public opinion.

Israelis perceived McCain more favorably for several reasons. First, McCain was a known commodity and his hawkish image as well as his military background is one that most Israelis could relate to. Issues of national security dominate Israeli politics. In its sixty-year existence, Israel has fought numerous wars, some existential, and it has been engaged in a protracted conflict with the Palestinians for close to a century. Its founding narrative as a homeland for the Jewish people is based on a history of persecution, culminating in the Holocaust. It is not surprising, therefore, that security not only dominates politics but also supersedes all other issues.

Many leading figures in Israeli politics are former military officers. Indeed one could argue that the path to the office of Prime Minister is paved through the position of Military Chief of Staff. Ehud Barak was chief of staff of the military before embarking on a political career, as was his predecessor, Yitzhak Rabin. Tzipi Livni was an officer in the IDF and served in Israeli Mossad for many years. Although this trend has changed with Ehud Olmert, who was injured during his military service and completed it as a journalist, Olmert's rise to power was quite haphazard, marked by the early and unexpected incapacitation of Ariel Sharon after suffering a series of strokes in 2006.

Not surprisingly, then, much of John McCain's appeal to the Israelis may be found in his military experience. In Israeli perception, McCain understands the world as they do. Israelis believed that he would prefer a military course of action to a diplomatic one in cases where vital interests were involved and would support Israeli action to defend itself. McCain's hawkish position on Iran, which was more in line with the Israeli view, strengthened this perception. There is consensus among the Israeli political leadership on the issue of Iran. Both the political and military leadership view the nuclear armament of Iran as an existential threat to Israel and all favor a strong, military approach toward Iran. Even after the elections in Israel, and though refusing to join his coalition, Livni nevertheless indicated that she would support Netanyahu's government on issues relating to Iran from the opposition. Israel has been pressing the UN to bring more international pressure to bear on Iran, and recently it has been made public that the Israeli government sought and was denied approval from the Bush administration to strike Iran's known nuclear sites in 2007.[8] McCain and Obama disagreed on how to approach Iran, with the latter supporting no preconditions to high-level talks while McCain supported a view that was perceived by the Israelis as more militant and thus favorable to their interests.

A third reason for Israeli preference of McCain relates to the perception of Obama. Whereas Israelis related to the familiarity with McCain, Obama represented the unknown and therefore led Israelis to make several assumptions about him. Despite the Bush administration's refusal to support an Israeli strike in Iran and the successful association made by the Obama campaign between Bush and McCain (which could lead one to conclude that McCain too, would refuse to allow Israel to take similar action against Iran), Israelis still perceived Obama as "soft" on Iran. Many Israelis believed that Barack *Hussein* Obama would be more sympathetic to "Third World causes."[9] These causes include, inter alia, campaigns against Israeli occupation and support for Palestinian statehood. By virtue of his identity, as well as some of his earlier policy positions, Obama was perceived by Israelis as suspect.

Furthermore, Obama was perceived by most of Israel's political elites as more supportive of multilateral diplomatic action than reliance on military power. This was seen as a cause for concern. However, it should be noted that following the election of Obama there was tremendous excitement in the Israeli media about that historic election, and the political elites also seem to have quickly come to terms with the outcome. While the initial reaction of the political and military elites in Israel to the candidacy of Obama was one of deep concern, by the end of the campaign there was an increased sense of resolution and acceptance of his victory despite the preference for McCain. Responding to Obama's election, the then Prime Minister Olmert stated that "Obama has proven to the world his abilities and leadership skills...The Israel-US relations are special relations based on shared values and interests and characterized by tight cooperation."[10]

Speaking about Obama, Livni commented that she was impressed with Obama's commitment to Israel's safety. "Israel looks forward to a continued strategic cooperation with the new administration...and to a strengthening of the ties between the two nations," she added.[11] In fact, in a recent interview Rosner indicated that there seemed to have been a "bandwagon effect" in which the political elites were now "spinning" the results of the American elections as one that is "good for us."[12]

Despite the support for McCain, the "bandwagon effect" may explain the recent attitude of Israelis, which seem to now show support for the election of Obama. Contributing to this may be Obama's choice of his foreign policy and national security team, particularly Hillary Clinton as Secretary of State and General James Jones as National Security Advisor. Daniel Kurtzer, the former US Ambassador to Israel and his strategic advisor Dan Shapiro, both Jewish supporters of Israel, are also among Obama's senior advisors. The appointment of Dennis Ross, Bill Clinton's former envoy to the Mideast, who is regarded favorably by the Israelis for his involvement in the Israeli-Palestinian peace process, as special advisor to Secretary of State Hillary Clinton on the Gulf region, including Iran, and southwest Asia, speaks volumes in this regard. If Obama moves forward with US-Iranian talks, the appointment of Ross may serve as a signal to the Israelis that their interests will not be abandoned. These choices seem to have quelled lingering Israeli concerns about the incoming administration, as they indicate that the Obama administration will be a revival of the Bill Clinton Presidency, which was viewed as one of the most popular US administrations among Israelis.

Finally, Obama's refusal to comment or take action to intervene in the Israeli offensive into Gaza in September 2008 increased Israeli acquiesce to the new administration. Here is where Obama's test may truly emerge. Great leaders are often assessed by their ability to turn crises into opportunities. Richard Nixon and Henry Kissinger were able to leverage the Arab-Israeli War in 1973 into a political opportunity, which culminated with the signing of the Israeli-Egyptian Peace Treaty in 1979. President George H. W. Bush and James Baker were able to leverage the successes of the first Gulf War into a relaunching of the Arab-Israeli peace process in Madrid in 1991, which later produced the Oslo Accords and changed the status of Israel in the region. President Clinton leveraged Israel's offensive into Southern Lebanon in 1996 into a political process on the Palestinian front, which culminated with the signing of the Hebron and Wye Agreements by the Netanyahu government in 1997 and 1998, respectively. In this regard, one of George W. Bush's failures was that he did not intervene in the Israeli-Hezbollah war in Lebanon in 2006 and did not attempt to leverage that crisis into a political opportunity on the Lebanese/ Syrian front or create linkages to the Israeli-Palestinian peace process.[13]

"Obama's test will be whether he can leverage the war with Hamas into a political opportunity."[14]

It stands to reason that it may not be until Obama is well settled into the Oval Office that we start to see the true Israeli attitude toward his administration. What is clear is that despite Israeli early perceptions about the incoming administration, very little is likely to change, at least in the short term, with regard to the relationship Israel enjoys with the United States. This is largely because it can be expected that Obama will preoccupy himself in the first stage of his administration not with the Israeli-Palestinian conflict but rather the financial crisis. I discuss this in further detail in the following section when analyzing the issues seen as critical to Israelis and how the Obama elections may affect those issues.

THE ISRAELI VIEW ON THE POLITICAL ISSUES IN THE US ELECTION

There are several political issues that are crucial to Israelis and on which the US presidential candidate's position is important to them. Those issues include the Iranian nuclear threat and nuclear arms control, the "War on terror," the Syrian front, Lebanon and Hezbollah, the Palestinian peace process, which includes settlements, US-Israeli relations, the Iraq war, and US-United Nations (UN) relations, or more specifically, the diplomatic coverage the United States offers Israel at the UN Security Council. Referring back to the "Israel Factor" panel's ranking of McCain and Obama, the average scores indicated a preference for McCain, although the averages may be misleading as results were nuanced on each issue. With respect to the Iranian issue, however, there was consensus among the panelists with a clear preference for McCain (on a scale from 1 to 5, 5 being the highest score, McCain received a score of 4.25 while Obama received a score of 2.5), but on other issues, particularly the Syrian and Palestinian questions, among some panelist Obama often scored better than McCain although ultimately the average score indicated an overall preference for the latter.[15] Even though many Israelis viewed Obama as the candidate of "pressure," meaning that he would be more likely to pressure the Israeli government into political concessions, particularly on the Palestinian front, there were those who believed that some pressure was needed in order to move a diplomatic process forward. A poll conducted by the Rabin Center for Israel Studies found a preference for McCain on the issue of Iran, with over half surveyed believing he possessed the skills needed to deal with the security threat Iran poses to Israel.[16]

To assess the effects of the election of Obama as President of the United States, it is important to identify the possible areas of contention between America and Israel. This is because of the weight Israelis placed on good relations with the United States. Despite the Israeli fear of Obama's "soft" position on Iran, the question of Iran provides little opportunity for conflict between the United States and Israel. Israelis and Americans are in complete agreement that Iran's acquisition of a nuclear weapon would pose a threat to international security. As recent as December 2008, Obama told NBC's "Meet the Press" that Iran's threats against Israel are "contrary to everything the US believes in."[17] Moreover, Israel cannot strike at Iran unilaterally without US consent, as clearly indicated by the fact that it sought authorization and, when not received, took no action. Zbigniew Brzezinski, the former national security advisor to President Jimmy Carter, warned Israel not to lobby Washington for a strike on Iran as this may have detrimental effects on the bilateral relations between the two.[18] No Israeli leader, however, whether from the political left or right, may strike at Iran without US approval. It is both diplomatically and operationally impossible and thus Brzezinski's warning was misguided.

Where the Obama administration may exert more pressure on Israel, than perhaps a McCain administration would have, is in the areas of Israeli settlements in the Palestinian territory, nuclear disarmament, and the issue of self-defense versus excessive use of force. I will discuss these possible contentious issues later in this chapter. However, initially it is important to point out that Obama's refusal to intervene in the Israeli offensive into Gaza, which took place during the transition period, may indicate the temperance of his administration, refuting early Israeli perceptions and fears of significant US involvement.

Furthermore, state interests determine bilateral relations, particularly with regard to United States and Israeli foreign affairs. There are issues that are seen as vital to the United States and where it sees little to no legitimate Israeli interest. Here the United States may not compromise with the Israelis. In 2000, Israel canceled an arms sale to China just hours before Congress was to vote on blocking funds to Israel. On issues such as this, Israel has no influence on the United States and even a favorable Republican-led Congress would not sacrifice what it viewed as vital US concerns for Israeli interests. Similarly, as previously discussed, even President George W. Bush, arguably the most accommodating president for Israel, refused to allow it the use of Iraqi airspace in order to launch an attack on Iranian nuclear sites, as this would put US soldiers stationed in the Gulf at risk (in case of an Iranian and/or insurgent retaliation) and undermine US objectives by destabilizing the region.

On the other hand, there are issues that are of importance to the United States, but with respect to which Washington does not have a stake in a particular outcome. On these issues, such as the peace process with the Palestinians, the United States follows Israel's cue most of the time. When the Israelis defined the PLO as a terrorist organization and refused to directly negotiate with it, the Americans followed suit. Similarly, the United States defines Hamas as a terrorist organization and refuses to negotiate with its members directly, following Israeli policy. In between these two exists a grey area that includes policies toward Iran and Syria, and other Arab states that the United States has formed an alliance with, namely, Iraq, Egypt and Saudi Arabia. While taking into consideration the Israeli position and interest on these issues, the United States ultimately determines its policy independently. While the United States will consult with Israel on Iran's nuclear armament, it will not allow, as previously discussed, for an Israeli attack on Iran's nuclear sites even though that attack may enhance Israeli security.

However, on other issues, the reverse can be true as well. When President Bush refused to talk to the Syrians, connecting them to the "axis of evil" by virtue of their alliance with Iran and attempts at destabilizing Iraq through acquiescence to insurgents crossing their borders, the Israelis nevertheless attempted to renew the negotiations with the Syrians. While these are areas where possible disagreement may arise, the United States will not punish Israel for pursuing its own interests independent of US policy.

According to journalist Aluf Benn,[19] there are only three areas of possible contention between the US administration and Israel. The first is the balance between what Israel views as self-defense and what the international community often condemns as excessive use of force. Nowhere has this been more evident than in the recent Israeli military operation in Gaza (operation "Cast Lead"). The Israelis argued that the Gaza offensive was necessary for its security and in retaliation for years of Hamas' rocket firing onto Israeli towns. The massive casualties and infrastructure damage, however, including the striking of the United Nations Relief and Works Agency for Palestine Refugees (UNWRA) compound in Gaza city, destroying a warehouse full of food and medicine, led to calls of condemnation at the UN. It is on these issues that the Israelis and the incoming American administration may clash.

Second, the United States and Israel may find themselves at cross roads regarding the issue of arms control. The Iranian nuclear project has caused concern not only in Tel Aviv, but in Riyadh and Cairo as well. Both the Saudis and the Egyptians are fearful of Iran as a rising Shia regional hegemon. In response to the change in status quo, both are looking at the option of nuclear weapons programs of their own. In an attempt to prevent such proliferation in the Middle East, Washington may offer a deal of "Natanz for Dimona"[20] in which a cap will be placed on Israel's nuclear arsenal. Israeli nuclear capability, as the lone nuclear force in the region, is regarded not only as of vital interest to them but an existential one. For Washington a few Iranian bombs alone may not change the status quo in the region, but their effect will likely cause neighboring states—Egypt, Saudi Arabia, and Turkey in particular—to develop their own nuclear programs. From their viewpoint, they would only be responding to the threat of the rising Shia power. If Washington introduces a policy of regional nuclear arms control to deal with the Iranians, but by doing so "pay in Israeli security currency," it will find itself on a collision course with Tel Aviv. Obama's ability to exert pressure on Israel regarding its nuclear armament largely depends on whether he can prevent the Iranians from developing a bomb. If he is successful in this regard, and thus returns the status quo to the region, he will be able to exert more pressure on the Israelis regarding their nuclear arsenal. If he does not, however, and the dreaded scenario of a nuclear Iran materializes for the Israelis, Obama will find it difficult to pressure the Israelis into concessions on their own nuclear force.[21]

Finally, the issue of Jewish settlements in the occupied territories may situate the American and Israeli administrations at odds with each other, particularly regarding the issue of freedom of movement and roadblocks. It can be expected that an Obama administration may be more concerned with the humanitarian plight of the Palestinians than a McCain administration would have been, and as a result exert more pressure on the Israelis to evacuate illegal settlements and reduce the amount of roadblocks in the West Bank to allow for increased Palestinian movement. Even here, however, the Israeli concern about Obama may turn out to be unwarranted. No American administration would deny Israel the right to defend itself. It would merely take one suicide bomber who manages to slip into Israel for it to justify the reestablishment of those roadblocks with little objection from the United States. Moreover, given the state of the US and global economies, it is highly unlikely that Obama will dedicate much of his personal attention to the Palestinian-Israeli issue, at least initially. Previous experiences have shown that without direct presidential involvement, very little can be achieved. Because of this it is unlikely that the Israelis and the Americans will clash on these matters, at least not in the first half of Obama's term in office. Like many of his predecessors, it can be expected that if Obama wins a second term in office, he might dedicate that time to trying to move the Arab-Israeli peace process forward.

In conclusion, despite the Israeli preference for McCain, subsequent reactions to the election of Obama both among the general population, but more importantly among the political elite, indicate a resolve to establish close and good relations with the Obama administration. Moreover, on the core issues, there is very little opportunity for clashes between Obama's administration and the Israelis. Where Obama's election has figured into Israeli politics is surprisingly on the domestic level within the Israeli election campaigns, and this will be the subject of the following section.

Obama's Election and Israeli Domestic politics

In the following section I focus my analysis on the implications of the election of Obama as President of the United States for the Israeli elections in February 2009. Unlike the strategic bilateral relations that I argue are not crucially affected by the election of Obama, where the "Obama effect" could be felt immediately was the unlikely domain of election campaigning, with each of the leading candidates adopting the message of "change," which Obama has come to represent.

Following the elections in the United States, the Obama campaign slogans, messages, and use of the Internet as a vehicle for mobilizing support made its way into the Israeli election campaigns. Livni, the head of the centrist Kadima party, tried to convince voters that Netanyahu, the hawkish leader of the Right wing Likud party, would conflict with Washington because of his resistance to the peace process and his support for striking Iran militarily. In response, and to demonstrate his readiness to work closely with the Obama administration, Netanyahu was quick to state that in the two meetings he has held with Obama thus far, one in Washington in 2007 and the other during Obama's visit to Israel in the summer of 2008, the two had good chemistry and both meetings were productive. Of course, at the time of the first meeting Obama had not yet been selected as the Democratic presidential nominee and in the second meeting he had not yet been elected as president and was running close in the polls with McCain. Therefore, there was no reason for contention or conflict between the two.

Here again we find the dichotomy between perception and reality. While all three leading candidates, Livni, Netanyahu and Barak, were in agreement regarding Iran's nuclear armament, viewing this development as an existential threat to Israel, all three candidates, but particularly the candidates from the Center and Left (Livni and Barak), tried to "spin" the election of Obama in their favor.

The idea that any one of these candidates could represent a new way of conducting business in Jerusalem, in the same way that Obama has come to represent a new vision for Washington politics, is not only a parody of Obama's campaign message, it is antithetical to the structure of the Israeli electoral system, which is largely based on party politics.

Nevertheless, Obama's appointment of the old Clinton Middle East policy team has played into Livni's and Barak's campaigns, signaling a continuation of Clinton's Mideast policy, which would favor Livni's and Barak's approaches to the peace process over that of Netanyahu. Moreover, Netanyahu does not have a good rapport with the Clintons ever since he, as prime minister of Israel in the mid-1990s, sidetracked President Clinton and appealed to the Republican-controlled Congress to prevent having to negotiate with the PLO and Yassir Arafat.

The "Obama effect" was also evident in the campaign messages of the various candidates and parties. For example, all three candidates presented themselves as the "candidate of change," borrowing a page from the Obama campaign. This was particularly ironic given that two of the three—Barak and Netanyahu—were former prime ministers of Israel and Livni was the Foreign Minister in the Olmert government. Moreover, Netanyahu not only learned from Obama's campaign but also copied his use of the Internet as a means to spread his message to potential voters and mobilize support. According to Ethan Bronner and Noam Cohen of the New York Times:

> The colors, the fonts, the icons for donating and volunteering, the use of videos, and the social networking Facebook—type options— including Twitter, which hardly exists in Israel—all reflect a conscious effort by the Netanyahu campaign to learn from the Obama success.

The authors report that those who created the Obama Web site admitted that the Netanyahu one resembles Obama's more "than any others that they have seen."[22]
Netanyahu presented himself in the campaign as the candidate of new ideas for peace with the Palestinians, focusing on "economic peace," which would concentrate on building the Palestinian economy in the West Bank rather than negotiate with them while the Israelis wait for Palestinian attitudes to change, particularly their support of Hamas. This approach builds peace from the ground up and focuses on improving the lives of Palestinians on a daily basis. Netanyahu later abandoned this message when it did not resonate with the Israeli voters, and he argued that he would negotiate with the Palestinians over a final status agreement, aligning himself with the perceived preferences of the Obama administration. This message contradicts the statements made on the Netanyahu Web site, where under "The Issues" the Web site stated: "We do not believe that the Palestinians are ready for any historical compromise that would truly put an end to the conflict." The idea that Netanyahu, the conservative candidate of the hawkish Right in Israel, a former prime minister and a member of Israel's political elite for three decades, can present himself as the "Israeli Obama" is perplexing, particularly given that the idea of economic peace had been the brainchild of Shimon Peres.

Obama also featured in Livni's campaign as she presented her positions on the Israeli-Palestinian peace process as most compatible with those of the incoming American administration. Moreover, the Kadima campaign presented Livni as the candidate of change. The campaign messages implied that Netanyahu had already had a chance to guide Israel and failed and that Livni will be different—signaling yet again a change in Israeli politics. Ironically, Livni, despite being the newest candidate on the political scene, had in some respects the hardest time presenting herself as the candidate of change since she had been the number two in the previous Olmert cabinet. This linked her directly to the policies of a government that is widely perceived as having failed and may have served as a barrier to convincing the Israeli public of the change she claimed to represent.

The "Obama effect" also appeared in the campaign of the Shas Party. This was particularly surprising given that Shas is an ultraorthodox religious party, representing largely the Mizrahi (Jews of Middle Eastern or Northern African descent) religious Jews. The campaign adopted Obama's slogan "Yes We Can." Walking in the street of Israel, one could not escape the Shas slogan—on buses, on posters, and even bumper stickers. When Obama told Americans that they could, he was referring to the ability to come together as one. He first referred to the slogan after Hillary Clinton's victory in the New Hampshire primaries. He then spoke of the "destiny of a nation" proclaiming that "Yes we can heal this nation." He was not just referring to Democrats but to all Americans. Nothing could be farther from the truth in the Shas case. If Obama's subtext was *Yes We Can* come together to achieve a common goal, Shas' subtext was more in line with *Yes We Can* achieve eighteen mandates (in the Israeli Parliament, "The Knesset"). This is exactly the statement made by MK Eli Yishai (the Chairman of Shas) when he unveiled the slogan in early December. The use of the slogan is particularly baffling given Shas' stated policies, which are antithetical to the message Obama propagated in the presidential election campaign. Shas has consistently used its power in the Knesset to extract sectarian benefits for its supporters in exchange for political support for the governing coalition. If Obama sought to inspire young and old, black and white Americans to go to the polls for the first time regardless of their party affiliation, Shas seeks to inspire only its sectarian base to go to the polls.

The emphasis on the narrative of change in all of the campaigns seems to be in response to the perception of the Israeli public's yearning for change. Following the election results in the United States, many Israeli commentators wrote about Israel's need for change. For example, in an essay published a few days prior to the American elections in *Haaretz* titled "The Middle East also wants a change," Akiva Eldar writes:

> The new president will be sworn in not long before the citizens of Israel go to the polls. They deserve to know what Middle East policy the new prime minister they are about to elect will encounter when he (or she) comes to visit the White House. This will help them choose the direction of the change that they want at home.[23]

To summarize, perhaps the most interesting effect Obama has had on Israeli domestic politics is in the area of election campaigning. Despite the attempts of the candidates and their parties to portray themselves as candidates of change, or the use of Obama's messages to mobilize the voters, the reality is that not much has changed in Israeli politics. The same politicians, with the same policies, are trying to move Israel forward, often to no avail. While Livni managed to maintain Kadima's strength (garnering only one mandate less than Kadima had before), Netanyahu's campaign, which took Likud from nineteen to twenty-seven mandates, was clearly more successful. However, as I argue in my final concluding remarks, this had more to do with the developments in the Israeli-Palestinian conflict, namely, the Gaza offensive, than with the election of Obama in the United States.

Conclusion

The objective of this chapter has been to assess the Israeli perspective on the US presidential elections and the effects, if any, of those elections on the bilateral relations with Israel. Given the little that was known initially about Obama's impending Mideast policies, assessing these effects is no easy task. Despite several campaign speeches relating to Israel and a few statements indicating Obama's support for the two-state solution and Israel's security, there is very little we know about Obama's vision for the region. Moreover, as expected, Obama has initially at least been preoccupied with the economic crisis. Still, the appointment of many former "Clinton hands" indicated a continuation of the policies of that administration. The fears of the Israelis that a Netanyahu government would therefore be at odds with the US administration may be exaggerated. Ultimately, much of those implications depends on the circumstantial developments on the ground. By this I mean that the extent to which an Obama administration can pressure Israel and lead to tensions between Washington and Jerusalem largely depends on what Obama can achieve vis-à-vis the Iranians and the developments in the Israeli-Palestinian conflict. This in turn will depend on the state of the American economy and Obama's ability to dedicate much of his personal attention to the conflict in the Middle East.

Obama's election did figure in the Israeli election campaigns, particularly in the campaigns of Netanyahu and Livni. Both tried to present themselves and their policies as most compatible with the policies of the incoming US President. Obama's victory could have helped Livni's candidacy, but the Hamas rocket attacks and the subsequent offensive in Gaza in September 2008/09 increased support for Netanyahu. While the relations may be stressed by the results of the Israeli elections, ultimately, the strategic interests of both states have not changed, and those interests will determine the bilateral relations more than anything else. The relationship between the two countries is strong and, while threats can be made, it can be expected that with the looming Iranian threat the Obama administration would not cut US aid to Israel or hesitate in showing it diplomatic support, particularly in the UN.

Strategic interests notwithstanding, the relationship between Jerusalem and Washington somewhat depends on the composition of the Israeli government after the elections. With the far right party of "Israel is Our Home" winning fifteen mandates (more than Labor, which won only thirteen) and becoming Israel's third-largest party, MK Lieberman's radical views on the Palestinians will certainly be at odds with Obama's, and could create tensions. Nevertheless, Netanyahu, learning from his past mistakes, will seek to build good relations with Washington and— for that reason alone—may deny Lieberman the position he seeks as foreign minister. The pursuit of a coalition government with Livni's Kadima party also indicates that Netanyahu may not want to create a far Right government that would find it hard to cooperate with the Americans on the Palestinian front.

Israelis can expect an administration that is more involved in the region than the previous one. However, it is unlikely that such pressure would force Israel to make concessions it clearly cannot live with.

In conclusion, while many believe that the euphoria surrounding Obama's victory may translate into concrete policies that will yield results in the region, in the end, despite Obama's message of change, very little may change in the bilateral relations of the countries and, unfortunately, in the Arab-Israeli conflict. We may believe in change, as Obama asked Americans to do, but we will likely not see it.

NOTES

1. Aluf Benn, "Obama Will Star in Israel's Election Campaigns," *Haaretz.com,* November 11, 2008, http://www.haaretz.com/hasen/spages/1035177.html (accessed February 10, 2009).
2. Roni Sofer, "Poll: Israel Votes McCain in US elections," *Ynetnews. com*, October 27, 2008, http://www.ynetnews.com/articles/0,7340,L-3613689,00.html (accessed February 23, 2009).
3. United States Agency for International Development, "U.S. Overseas Loans and Grants [Greenbook]," *USAID.org*, http://qesdb.usaid.gov/gbk/ (accessed February 23, 2009).
4. Aluf Benn, personal communication with the author, November 19, 2008.
5. Shmuel Rosner, "Not meddling—involved," *Haaretz.com*, February 14, 2008, http://www.haaretz.com/hasen/pages/rosnerBlog.jhtml?itemN=954292&contrassID=25&subContrassID=0&sbSubContrassID=1&listSrc=Y&art=1 (accessed February 20, 2009).

6. Rosner's Domain: A Special Project, "*The Israel Factor: Ranking the presidential candidates*," http://www.haaretz.com/hasen/pages/rosnerPage.jhtml (accessed February 2).

7. Roni Sofer, "Poll: Israel Votes McCain in US elections," *Ynetnews. com*, October 27, 2008, http://www.ynetnews.com/articles/0,7340,L-3613689,00.html (accessed February 23, 2009).

8. Aluf Benn, "U.S. Puts Brakes on Israeli Plan for Attack on Iran Nuclear Facilities," *Haaretz.com*, August 13, 2008, http://www.haaretz.com/hasen/spages/1010938.html (accessed February 2, 2009).

9. Aluf Benn, "Israel's Dilemma: Obama vs. Qassams," *Haaretz.com*, November 5, 2008, http://www.haaretz.com/hasen/spages/1034570.html (accessed February 2, 2009).

10. Roni Sofer, "Olmert: Obama Proved His Leadership," *Ynetnews.com*, November, 5, 2008, http://www.ynet.co.il/english/articles/0,7340,L-3617987,00.html (accessed February 21, 2009).

11. Roni Sofer, "Olmert: Obama Proved His Leadership," *Ynetnews.com*, November, 5, 2008, http://www.ynet.co.il/english/articles/0,7340,L-3617987,00.html (accessed February 21, 2009).

12. Shmer Rosner, personal communication with the author, November 18, 2008.

13. Aluf Benn, "Leveraging as Leadership," *Haaretz.com*, October 23, 2008, http://www.haaretz.com/hasen/spages/1030263.html (accessed February 4, 2009).

14. Aluf Benn, personal communication, November 19, 2008.

15. Shmuel Rosner, "Israel Factor: Panel Doesn't Worry about Obama on Israel-Palestine," *Haaretz.com*, August 18, 2008, http://www.haaretz.com/hasen/spages/1012788.html (accessed February 22, 2009).

16. Roni Sofer, "Poll: Israel Votes McCain in US elections," *Ynetnews. com*, October 27, 2008, http://www.ynetnews.com/articles/0,7340,L-3613689,00.html (accessed February 23, 2009).

17. *Meet the Press*, MSNBC, December 7, 2008, http://www.msnbc.msn.com/id/28097635/page/3/ (accessed February 15, 2009).

18. Natasha Mozgovaya, "Zbigniew Brzezinski: Israel's Push for Iran Strike May Hurt U.S. Ties," *Haaretz.com*, December 12, 2008, http://www.haaretz.com/hasen/spages/1044635.html (accessed February 10, 2009).

19. Aluf Benn, personal communication, November 19, 2008.

20. Aluf Benn, "Will Obama Press Israel to Allow Nuclear Inspection of Dimona Reactor?" *Haaretz.com*, December 19, 2008, http://www.haaretz.com/hasen/spages/1048024.html (accessed February 15, 2009).

21. Aluf Benn, "Israel Must Adapt to Reality of U.S.-Iran Dialogue," *Haaretz.com*, October, 19, 2008, http://www.haaretz.com/hasen/spages/1029675.html (accessed February 3, 2009).

22. Ethan Bronner and Noam Cohen, "Israel Candidate Borrows a (Web) Page from Obama," *nytimes.com*, November 15, 2008, http://

www.nytimes.com/2008/11/15/world/middleeast/15bibi.html
(accessed February 18, 2009).

23. Akiva Eldar, "The Middle East Also Wants a Change," *Haaretz.com*,
    October 31, 2008, http://www.haaretz.com/hasen/spages/1033074.
    html (accessed February 15, 2009).

8

PALESTINE'S VIEW OF THE 2008 US PRESIDENTIAL ELECTION

Mohammad Masad

SKEPTICISM AND HOPEFULNESS AMONG MOST PALESTINIANS

Palestinian perception of the 2008 US presidential elections was characterized by a mixture of indifference and cautious optimism. The American obsession with the elections was only marginally echoed among Palestinians, and almost exclusively within the political elite, intellectuals, and circles within the youth and American-educated professionals. For these groups, there was a clear, though sometimes hesitant, support for the candidacy of Barack Obama. In the presidential race, John McCain was perceived to be more in line with the Bush policies and the pro-Israel lobby, while Obama, despite some of his controversial positions, was seen as a more decent and hopeful figure. His new approach, sensitive attitude toward Arabs and Muslims, and serious effort to deal with the question of Israel-Palestine as a top priority won him praise and admiration among many Palestinians. Moreover, his humble background, African origins, Muslim father, global upbringing, young age, Internet appeal, and charismatic persona, which endeared him to many global audiences, also contributed to his favorable image among Palestinians. And so for those who followed his campaign, Obama became the elections; and with other candidates out of the picture, he became the subject of criticism, debate, speculation, admiration, and adoration, whether in street conversations, newspaper articles, stories in the blogosphere, or messages and postings in the social networks.

Unlike McCain, who was seen as an extension of Bush and a blind supporter of Israel, Obama came to symbolize the hope for a real change in American foreign policy toward Palestine. The outcome of this change should ideally lead to a new and more active role for the United States in the peace process. This would translate into an active engagement that would curb Israeli aggressive policies, especially Jewish settlements, and goad them to deal with the elected Palestinian leadership to facilitate a two-state solution. In addition to this aspect of political change, the US elections was also seen by some as an example of the power of democracy and the civilized transition of power, a fact that prompted a degree of self-critique, given the despair, disunity, and internal fighting among the Palestinians. Obama's win was celebrated as a milestone for humanity and a new age of optimism, marked by multilateral diplomacy and change for the better. And while detractors took a dim view of Obama's choice of some advisors and cabinet members, others saw his appointment and dispatching of George Mitchell as special envoy to the Middle East as an early sign of Obama's quest for serious consideration of the Israel-Palestine conflict; his statements and actions seemingly signaling the arrival of the long-awaited diplomatic effort that has the potential for a change and which the people of Palestine can believe in.

Though the whole picture is rather complex, most evidence seems to suggest that for a majority of Palestinians, the elections were a nonevent. In addition to discontent with traditional American policies, the harsh social and economic situation in the Palestinian Occupied territories (POT) made daily survival a priority for most people. However, as far as it is possible to gauge people's perspective(s) on the elections, indications show that most Palestinians held a more positive view of the first ever African-American candidate when compared to his rivals. This is true mainly of the Palestinian communities in the POT, and excludes the majority of the Palestinians, who live in the refugee camps in several Middle Eastern countries and the diaspora.[1]

PALESTINE: SEEMINGLY NOT ON THE US PRESIDENTIAL CANDIDATES' AGENDAS

Palestinians are no strangers to democratic elections. During the past fifteen years, and as part of setting up the Palestinian Authority (PA) and its institutions, Palestinians participated several times in local elections, presidential and legislative. The last round in January 2006, when Hamas won a decisive majority in the Palestinian Legislative Council (PLC) at the expense of Mahmoud Abbas's ruling party, Fatah, was judged by international monitors to be one of the fairest and freest in the Middle East. Yet many Palestinians did not seem that interested in following the longest and most spectacular presidential elections in the world. This disinterest is a function of the deteriorating situation in Palestine as much as a result of the somewhat irrelevant nature of the issues that dominate American presidential politics and elections.

One possible reason is the sense of betrayal felt by Palestinians after the 2006 elections in the West Bank and Gaza. The negative reaction to Hamas's victory in the PLC elections by the United States and the EU, which decided to boycott the PA, was seen as a cruel irony. People wondered about the true value of democracy, high on the list of neoconservative objectives in the post-Cold War era, if their democratic choice was being rejected. To add insult to injury, the United States and its allies seemed unconcerned about Israel's arrest and detention of PLC Hamas members. The American and European approach to this issue smacked of hypocrisy. They demanded that Hamas first meet certain conditions specified by the Mideast Quartet to get it off the terrorist list before they can have official dealings with the PA.

Democracy, whether practiced at home or observed abroad, may seem to be a luxury, or a nuisance, when people have much more pressing needs on their minds; such is the situation for the bulk of ordinary Palestinians, whose lives are preoccupied with the requisites of daily survival under deteriorating conditions of socioeconomic adversity. One report in 2006 concluded that "the situation for 'poor' households in both the West Bank and the Gaza Strip had significantly worsened over the previous four years."[2] The following year, a UN survey found that 56 percent of Palestinians in the West Bank and 70 percent of those in the Gaza Strip live below the poverty level, with extreme poverty affecting 26 percent and 42 percent of them, respectively.[3] The situation became bleaker in 2008, especially for Gaza, as a survey by the Palestinian Central Bureau of Statistics (PCBS) found that 80 percent of Gaza families and 47 percent of those in the West Bank were living below the poverty line, and that the estimated per capita GDP was expected to fall by 7.4 percent.[4]

The relative indifference of the Palestinians to the US elections at the popular level can be illustrated in a number of examples. During Obama's visit to the West Bank city of Ramallah in June 2008, one reporter who accompanied the candidate ventured out in the streets, while Obama was meeting the PA President, to get a sense of people's reactions to the visit and what they thought of the Democratic candidate. The experience was quite revealing:

> We drove around in the heat searching for Obama supporters or fans, but even at venues with names in English, such as the Stars & Bucks cafe or Supermarket Baghdad, there were no Gobama banners to be seen. When a local radio newscast announced that the Senator had "confirmed to President Mahmoud Abbas that he will be a constructive partner in the peace process" and would "not waste a minute" if elected, there was little visible reaction in a patio cafe. Most customers just kept sucking their narghila water pipes. Talk is just talk, no matter how it's parsed.[5]

But even as a mere talking point, the question of Palestine, which is so central to the US foreign policy in the Middle East, hardly made it into the presidential debates; this was another let down for Palestinians eager to see a real discussion of the main issue that defines their existence. Commenting on the presidential candidates' debate in October, one blogger testifies to this fact, a regular feature of all such events; she laments that, "once again the word Palestine was erased from the discourse of a presidential debate. Neither John McCain nor Barack Obama, nor any of the American voters asking questions, uttered the word Palestine. Nor did the words Gaza or the West Bank cross anyone's lips."[6]

Whether it is sound bites or lengthy epistles, the fact is that, for most Palestinians, McCain and Obama would have sounded very much the same speaking on the Israel-Palestine conflict. The discourse in each case is basically identical, steeped in the language of support for Israel and the metaphor of praising the closeness and friendship between the United States and the Jewish state. Following the second presidential debate on October 7, 2008, a freelance journalist from Ramallah, Wafa Jamil, was asked, on the World Focus program, about Palestinian reaction to the debate the morning after. Her answer indicated that people on the streets were not giving much attention to the American elections, the reason being the similar perspectives both candidates have in line with the usual support for Israel, and thus the belief that nothing will change. Asked if this meant that regardless of who will be elected, it is not going to bring change to the life of the Palestinians, she answered, "not at all."[7]

Palestinians with interest in American politics tend to view the US presidential elections as a one-issue event, revolving around the candidates' positions on the question of Israel-Palestine conflict. As a result, Palestinian perception of these elections became more or less fixed, reflecting the inflexible US view of the conflict, rooted in a strategic partnership with Israel and a perceived indifference (or even hostility) to Palestinian rights and aspirations. Important shifts in the American thinking, namely, recognizing the PLO, endorsing a two-state solution, and occasionally engaging in specific peace initiatives, such as Clinton's Camp David II and Bush's Road Map, was recognized by the Palestinian political elite but hardly inspired popular imagination, and the failure of such efforts only confirmed this attitude. Consequently, most Palestinians in the POT and the diaspora see the US elections, including the last round, as a highly irrelevant process, with little practical implications to their lives and the future of their cause beyond what they already have come to know over the years.

The US diplomatic effort has been mostly seen as inadequate, its timing, motives, and level of engagement never adding up to the credible and honest role the United States has been trying to project in the Middle East Peace Process. Promises to broker a just and lasting solution have been eclipsed by the American administrations' steady support for Israel and aversion to criticize its controversial policies and actions. A public opinion poll conducted by the Zogby Institute across the Arab world in March 2008 found that 83 percent of respondents have an unfavorable view of the United States, while the remaining 15 percent said they viewed the United States favorably.[8] The US support for Israel is the most tangible and persistent outcome of American involvement in the conflict, and it is never as clearly unconditional and unanimous as during the American presidential elections. In contrast, there is typically an almost complete absence of Palestine from electoral debates, and therefore little or no stake for its people in the American election scene.

Palestinians are typically wary and cynical about US politics and the political process, stressing the systematic failure of successive American administrations in using their influence to end the conflict, and the stark difference with which American leaders treat Israel and Palestine: the first with unreserved adoration and identification, and the other with little genuine care and often boldness bordering on animosity. As far as Palestinians are concerned, the US elections are a seasonal grand stage to profess by the hopeful candidates their loyalty and love for Israel, to the exclusion of everything else, including any meaningful articulation of the plight of Palestine. This is the context in which American elections are usually viewed, with most Palestinians paying scant attention to the political drama played out across the United States.

Nimmer Hammad, a political advisor to the Palestinian President, confirms this line of thinking by noting that from the perspective of past experience, public opinion is more likely to see history repeating itself. This means that "the Palestinian public believes that each new American administration will be more committed than its predecessor to cooperation with Israel. It will assist Israel even more than before and act with even more bias."[9] But there are Palestinians with somewhat different opinions. Mahdi Abdul Hadi of the Palestinian Academic Society for the Study of International Affairs (PASSIA) does not exclude the possibility of change in US foreign policy toward Palestine, but he thinks that Obama is still "ambiguous on foreign policy in spite of the warm receptions he received in Europe and the Middle East."[10]

Yet some segments of the Palestinian people saw the elections as a contest between two agendas: a Republican neoconservative philosophy of aggressively exporting their notion of freedom and democracy, and a Democratic agenda that is less war-driven and more rational in its overall approach and objectives. Those in Palestine who watched Senator Obama's victory speech after he won the Democratic Party nomination on June 3, 2008 were likely encouraged at the different tone and language, including his stress on the need to break clean from the previous administration. His declaration that, "America, this is our moment. This is our time. Our time to turn the page on the policies of the past," must have won him quite a global audience, including a Palestinian one.

This sentiment was clearly amplified after Obama's final win and his inauguration as the 44th US President. In an open letter to Senator George Mitchell, who had been appointed as Obama's special envoy to the Middle East, a Palestinian leader from the left-wing People's Party congratulates President Obama for his victory and choice of Mitchell. He also conveys the sense of wider support for Obama among Palestinians in the POT:

> It is possible to say that the entire Palestinian people sympathized with the candidacy and election of President Obama, at least because of the desire to change the Bush administration and the neoconservatives; and it is possible to say that there are expectations that President Obama will make a difference in the way the American administration deals with the Palestine cause and the issues of the region and the world, and certainly actions will be the judge on the level of these expectations.[11]

As the letter shows, the lack of confidence in the Bush presidency and the need for change were palpable. By 2008, Palestinians simply lost any hope that Bush's stated goal of creating a Palestinian state before leaving office was possible. The occasional shuttle diplomacy of Secretary of State Condoleezza Rice produced virtually nothing. The Annapolis Conference of November 2007 turned out to be another vacuous initiative, reaffirming the well-known principles of a peace settlement but generating little momentum in the peace talks. The 2008 Pew Foundation's survey of global attitudes to the Bush foreign policy includes no polling of the Palestinians. However, the poll results from Jordan are indicative, given its geography and demography. Jordanians responded with the largest percentage of dissatisfaction with the Bush administration among all polled nations. In responding to the question whether they trusted Bush's foreign policy, 89 percent indicated they had little or none, while only 7 percent said they had much or some confidence in Bush's policy.[12]

The view of an Obama administration can also be gleaned from the same survey. Jordanians responded more positively as to whether they think the new American president will cultivate better US international relations. About 19 percent of respondents believe Obama would change American foreign policy for the better; 37 percent said there would not be much change, and 36 percent thought it would change for the worse.[13] This is not very surprising given the traditional disdain with which many Arabs regard the United States, and their anger over what they see as American hypocrisy and double standards. This image was further tarnished during the years of the American involvement in Iraq, starting with the embargo during the 1990s and ending with the US invasion of Iraq in 2003. Palestinian views should not be that different.

WHAT DID THE CANDIDATES STAND FOR?

Not unlike the rest of the world, for many Palestinians the 2008 American elections presented an occasion for a refreshing change in what otherwise had become an almost meaningless transition of power. The main reason for this expectation of change is Obama. As he was poised to win the primaries, Obama was becoming a Palestinian favorite. His opponent for the Democratic ticket, Hillary Clinton, was not a very sympathetic figure. Her perceived blanket support for Israel and her vote in favor of the invasion of Iraq have not won her much good will. Obama, virtually unknown till then, seemed to represent a real potential for change within American politics. Palestinians were also encouraged by Obama's remark early in the campaign in Muscatine, Iowa, that, "Nobody is suffering more than the Palestinian people," even though later, responding to much pro-Israel indignation, he clarified that the comment was meant as criticism of Palestinian leadership. One report on NBC suggests that, at least till his statement on Jerusalem before the most powerful American Jewish lobby, AIPAC, Obama was enjoying a rising popularity. During his run for the Democratic nomination, "the sentiment toward him has been extremely warm on the streets of Gaza, the West Bank, and east Jerusalem. Many Palestinians...believe that because he is African-American, he knows what it is like to be discriminated against," and therefore will be more empathetic to the Palestinians and more balanced in his approach to peace making.[14]

This favorable reception notwithstanding, there were still lingering doubts about Obama's ability to break away from conventional American politics, including the heavy influence of the pro-Israel lobby groups such as AIPAC. As one observer put it early on in the campaign, "It is not possible to be elected in the US if one is not pro-Israeli. But...Palestinians hope that Obama, who will clearly win the democratic primaries and go up against Republican John McCain in the final race, will change his tune once he is the first black man in the White House."[15] The fears that Obama was going to be a reincarnation of previous pro-Israel presidents were heightened on a number of occasions. The combined effect of a series of high-profile actions was damaging to Obama's image among Palestinians. On the extreme negative side of the spectrum, he inspired some angry reactions and was vilified. Some cartoons and popular jokes portrayed him as a mere Zionist puppet, occasionally using his skin color (which for many Palestinians was a welcome change) as a dramatic element for hard-hitting and sometimes cruel satire.[16] Upon winning the presidency, one writer explains, the White House will remain white, even if its occupant is black, but this fact will not stop people from dreaming and from feeling happy for Obama's win.[17]

The true extent of the pro-Israel influence on American politics has been the subject of a major debate among political activists, writers, and scholars. Recently, some of the most interesting views seem to confirm the enormous power at the disposal of the Jewish and pro-Israel lobbies.[18] Though there is a tendency to exaggerate the reach of this lobby, the argument remains that no candidate can hope to get far in the race for the White House without the endorsement of the pro-Israel pressure groups, an endorsement that can be given only in exchange for their unequivocal support for the state of Israel. Obama probably had no choice but to play the game, regardless of what his true positions were and what might they become after the elections.

Many of Obama's critics among the Palestinians seemed to appreciate this perspective, and so not all of them thought of him purely in terms of a Zionist candidate. There was some recognition that expressing whole-hearted support for Israel was simply a necessary ritual of American presidential politics, and that it did not necessarily mean absolutely binding positions, as a result, some people were willing to give him the benefit of the doubt. One local analyst, writing one day after Obama's visit to Ramallah in July 2008, registers a cautious, realistic view of the African-American Senator, noting that Obama tries to project a non-Republican image in his foreign policy orientation, but that he and McCain are similar in their support of Israel. The writer mentions Obama's visit to Sderot, his friendly meeting with the Likud leader Benjamin Netanyahu, and the expectation that he will be in line with the usual American policy toward Israel. The only potential difference in the Obama approach, according to the writer, could come as the result of a qualitatively different effort by the Palestinians to make their voice heard. However, the same commentator seems to be indirectly leaning toward Obama, as he is careful to indicate the more extreme positions of McCain, citing his declaration to Israel's Channel 2 T.V. that he will make the war on terror his top priority and that he will not allow another Holocaust to happen.[19]

McCain's open support for the annexation of Jerusalem as the capital of Israel during his visit there angered many Palestinians, including the usually more diplomatic PA officials. A top PLO leader, Yasser Abed Rabbo, "expressed his shock at the statement, which is an even more extreme position than that taken by current President Bush, and issued a condemnation."[20] As much as he tried to distance himself from Bush, McCain never managed to convince Palestinians that he was much different. As a matter of fact, McCain often came across as more supportive of Israel and dismissive of Palestinian rights than President Bush. His view, expressed in his AIPAC address, that, "America's unequivocal support

for Israel—not evenhandedness, no moral equivalence, not winking at
Palestinian violence—is the best guarantor of peace in the Middle East,"
gives nothing to Palestinians to feel hopeful or sympathetic about.

In contrast, Obama's critics sometimes tried to ameliorate his
overly pro-Israeli statements and actions. For example, one journalist, Muhammad Yaghi, praises the African-American candidate for his
pragmatism. He notes the fact that Obama spent most of the time
during his visit to the region in Israel, but doesn't criticize him for
that, stressing instead the significance of Obama's trip to Ramallah
(where McCain refused to visit), his travel from Jerusalem to Ramallah
by car, ostensibly to see Israeli checkpoints for himself, and his subsequent clarification of his AIPAC statement regarding the final status
of Jerusalem. He concludes by pointing out that Obama's visit to Israel
was directed at Jewish voters and pressure groups, and that what matters is that he, unlike McCain, maintained a sense of balance throughout.[21] A few months later, the same writer celebrated Obama's victory,
noting that he had never followed an American presidential election
this closely before, and praised Obama's appeal for a wide base of supporters in the United States and his rationalistic and humanistic views
on foreign and domestic issues. He also conceived of Obama's victory
as symbolic of the strength and moral power of American democracy
and values, as well as a proof of the real possibility for change within
the American system.[22]

One political analyst sounded very positive about Obama's agenda
of change, which, despite the limitations this change entails for the US
foreign policy toward Palestine, has the potential of actually spreading
farther. He begins his article by saying:

> It is within the right of Arabs and particularly Palestinians, plus all
> those who count on a global awakening and just solutions to the
> Palestine issue, to feel joyful for the election of Barack Obama, and
> to be armed with optimism, and to place more trust in the future, if
> not for the rise of Obama, with all the meanings, results, and oppor-
> tunities it carries with it, then at least because of the departure of the
> nightmare of President Bush, his Vice President Dick Cheney and the
> neoconservative team from the White House.[23]

More welcoming commentary for Obama's victory is evident in
what can be described as very extensive Palestinian press coverage. On
January 21, for example, *Al-Ayyam* newspaper leads with the inauguration
story, along with a color photograph of Obama taking the oath, with the
headline, "Took the oath amongst masses of millions and promised a new
beginning with the Muslim world. President Obama: the United States
is ready to lead again." The next day also sees more intense coverage,

with the leading story being Obama's phone call to the PA President, Mahmoud Abbas, the first foreign leader whom Obama called on his first day in office. The gesture was not lost on the newspaper, which saw that as a very encouraging step and a sign of change, praising Obama's appointed team, especially George Mitchell and Robert Gates.[24]

In the largest Palestinian daily, *Al-Quds*, editorials and commentaries expressed similar optimism at the election of Obama, though sometimes tinged with caution. Obama does not have a magic wand, the paper says, but his inauguration speech gives reason for limited optimism.[25] A similar line is adopted by one analyst, who says that the change is only in the style and not the substance and that the best Palestinians can expect from Obama is a policy similar to that of Bill Clinton; the writer then calls on Palestinians, especially Hamas, to be more realistic and not to gamble on regional powers such as Iran, concluding that there is no other way for Arabs to change the terms of a negotiated peace deal except by using their own power. One writer sees signs that Obama is not going to bend under Israeli pressure,[26] another one, a veteran journalist from *al-Hayat* newspaper, declares Obama's victory as a new chapter and an auspicious beginning, seeing him in a positive light and expressing his hope that the president will meet the expectations.[27]

Palestinian groups have different visions and strategies; however, there is a wide agreement over the two-state solution, a principle that is also a cornerstone of the American Mideast policy. This should offer an opportunity for Palestinians to engage American politics, including the election of a new president, from the perspective of this common goal. But this is easier said than done. From a Palestinian viewpoint, the Bush administration's policies had made a two-state solution more difficult to achieve. Israel's separation wall, the expansion of Jewish settlements in the West Bank and east Jerusalem, and continued siege and dismemberment of the POT have gone virtually unopposed by the United States. The complete identification with Israel seemed to be a defining feature of Bush's neoconservatism.[28]

In order for a meaningful peace process to go ahead, Israel would first have to cease its expansion of settlements, relax its control of Arab east Jerusalem, and lift the suffocating siege of the Gaza Strip. These three issues are among the top Palestinian priorities that any American administration that means business would need to tackle. For Palestinians who followed the US elections, McCain was clearly the less likely to do that. His public positions on these issues were actually more right-wing and extreme than that of the departing Bush administration. A continuation of the Bush policies in some other version was seen as a disaster. The most ominous of these issues, and one that has become symbolic of the whole conflict, is Jewish settlements. With Israel itself clearly unwilling to stop, it was becoming clear to Palestinians that Israel's facts-on-the-ground approach in the POT can only be stopped or reversed through serious American diplomacy. In his letter to Mitchell, Al-Salhi points out that the very first step the Obama administration should take as an honest peace broker is to halt the expansion of settlements and the building of the separation wall. He then adds that, "Mr. Mitchell knows perfectly well how critical and important this question is, since he dealt with it in his report in 2001 [investigating the violent 2000 uprising in the POT], and now it has become even more challenging and dangerous."[29]

Palestinian passion about issues such as the settlements and Jerusalem are often strangely matched by American vagueness or stale diplomatic formulae. It is rather interesting that a crucial issue such as settlements occupies no more than a shy footnote in the American approach to the conflict. No presidential candidate seemed interested in deviating from the cut-and-dried position, and therefore one problem for Palestinians following the elections has been the lack of clarity on such questions. The 2008 election campaigns were dominated by domestic issues, especially the unfolding financial crisis and the global economic downturn, as well as the most pressing and contentious of the foreign policy issues, namely the wars in Iraq and Afghanistan and the prospect of a nuclear Iran. Given the relative difference between the two candidates in their personalities, approaches, and some specific positions, Obama was the clear favorite. His message of change and hope won the day.

THE WAY FORWARD: THE NEW OBAMA PRESIDENCY THROUGH PALESTINIAN EYES

For the different political parties in the POT, the US elections were an opportunity to look forward to a closer and more effective relationship with a new American administration. In this context, Fatah and Hamas are well aware of the connection between US elections and internal Palestinian politics. However, Fatah is interested in the process from the position of a government seeking more legitimacy and authority. In the Bush years, the PA was reduced to a powerless and limited civic authority, recognized and praised by the US administration, but hand-tied by Israel and challenged by a resurgent ultranationalist, Islamic opposition. The sense of paralysis and hopelessness peaked during the Israeli offensive on Gaza, which showed the Bush administration's unwillingness to curb Israeli actions.

An administration that would change the Bush course would be instrumental to assist the PA to regain the initiative and improve its standing, both among its own people and at the negotiating table with Israel. A shift in the US administration's position was made all the more significant by the predictable and anticipated outcome of the Israeli elections in 2009, which brought a more right-wing or fundamentalist government into power. This is one area where Obama's position was clearly more attractive. At the very least, the candidate's declared determination to strongly intervene in the Israel-Palestine issue was seen as a hopeful sign.

The need for a strong American role is also attested by a joint opinion poll of the Truman Research Institute at the Hebrew University and the Palestinian Center for Policy and Survey Research (PCPSR), conducted after the elections in mid-December. The survey shows that 57 percent of Palestinians want to see a more active American role in the peace process under Obama's presidency. In contrast, 35 percent of Palestinians do not want any intervention by the United States, and only 4 percent approved of a continuation of the current (i.e., Bush's) American role. As for the prospects of a strong American role, 49 percent of Palestinians expected the US efforts to be successful, while 30 percent thought it would fail, and 16 percent said the US role would be useless.[30]

For the PA, this would mean the kind of material, political, and moral support that strengthens its tenuous hold on power in the West Bank, and eventually help it regain its control of the Gaza Strip. For the Fatah activists, who dominate the PA, a friendly administration would be instrumental in extracting symbolic concessions from Israel, such as granting more free movement of people and goods across the POT, and an end to the expansion of settlements and closure of Jerusalem, which would be no small achievements, given the intransigence of Israel on these issues and the extent to which such steps could enhance the PA's position among Palestinians as it prepares to negotiate with Israel the issues concerning the final status of Palestine.

The fate of Hamas and by implication the unity of Palestinian leadership and its representational status is one cluster of issues that are linked to the American elections. The Western boycott of Hamas and its government in Gaza has not weakened the movement, neither did the 2009 Israeli winter offensive against it. Similarly, the Abbas government in Ramallah has been marginal and ineffective. A unity government between the two groups will risk another boycott, unless the ban on Hamas is lifted. There are indications that an Obama administration might be willing to consider a more flexible policy in dealing with Hamas, especially if the movement also shows some flexibility toward the Mideast Quartet's conditions. Hamas has made an effort to be positive toward Obama, something that caused Obama some problems during the campaign, with some Republicans describing him as the Hamas candidate. So far the Obama administration has not publicly shifted its position, but the signs for a possible change cannot be ignored.

In fact, Hamas also congratulated Obama on his victory and asked him to deal with Palestinians with fairness. According to some reports, "the incoming Obama administration is ready to abandon George Bush's doctrine of isolating Hamas…The move to open contacts with Hamas, which could be initiated through the US intelligence services, would represent a definitive break with the Bush presidency's ostracizing of the group."[31] Such rapprochement would accelerate Palestinian efforts for national unity and reconciliation and remove an important obstacle from the path of peace. In addition to solving a political crisis, the rehabilitation of Hamas would also help solve the humanitarian problem in Gaza, since any such political process would entail the end of the siege. It is the civilian population of the impoverished and crowded Gaza Strip that bears the brunt of the punishing Israeli restrictions and international isolation. Only basic humanitarian needs and a minimum of human movement have been permitted for them, subject to the approval of Egyptian authorities and Israeli forces. A political solution should bring with it an end to this humanitarian suffering.

Another issue likely to be impacted by the US elections is the future of democracy in Palestine, given the impasse between Fatah and Hamas. The crisis, which started soon after the formation of a national unity government in March 2007, culminated in a Hamas military coup in Gaza in summer 2007, ending the unity government and splitting the POT into two territories governed by opposing factions, and paralyzing the normal functions of the Palestinian nascent democratic institutions. Neither side recognized the other and a bitter rivalry deepened every day. President Abbas's term expired in January 2009, when Gaza was under attack by Israel, and the two parties seemed equally unsure of what to do next. The representational legitimacy of Palestinian institutions hinges on agreement on a new unity government, as well as on American, European, and international support of new Palestinian elections and robust democratic institutions. Along with the donations to rebuild Gaza in the aftermath of the latest war, Palestinian democracy, in order to thrive, will require consistent and significant material and moral support from the United States. It is quite telling that the two groups, Fatah and Hamas (though with important differences in their approaches and agendas), seem to be counting on the new Obama administration to help them overcome the current crisis and consolidate Palestinian democracy.

While this is expected to be relatively easy for Fatah, it is not that clear how Hamas can do that without changing key aspects of its strategy and ideology. Some Obama enthusiasts have recognized this dilemma and asked Hamas to forge a new image based on a reality check of its tactics and objectives. One writer predicts that a new US administration will not change the traditional American positions toward Israel and the region, including a ban on dealings with Hamas till the movement transforms itself. Consequently, the writer calls on Hamas to be more pragmatic and to reevaluate its regional relations with countries such as Egypt and Iran, and revise its strategy and tactics, concluding that he sees no other way for Arabs to change their negotiating terms except by working through an enlightened leadership that acts from a position of realism.[32]

There was also much awareness of the American elections as a peaceful and credible way of political and leadership change. Contrasted with the intra-Palestinian fighting, and the continued animosity between Fatah and Hamas, the US elections offered a more civilized model of democratic politics that is currently sorely missing from Palestine. In the case of the 2008 elections, there was also the extra lesson of the triumph of the underdog, with Obama capturing the presidency against all odds, overcoming stereotypes and a long history of racism and discrimination. As one commentator put it reflectively, "I personally was happy for the man's win, not out of any love for him or the Democratic party...but because America managed to triumph over racism. I wonder if the Israelis learn the lesson? Will we learn the lesson?"[33]

Another journalist, commenting on the Palestinians' outcry over Obama's statements during his visit to Sderot, indirectly blames Hamas for the negative press, pointing out that if it was not for the missiles fired on the town from Gaza, the town would not be what it is, and therefore Obama would have had more time to visit Palestinian communities and be in a better position to understand the situation.[34] Self-critique, whether pointing the finger at the mistakes of Palestinian groups, demystifying some of the myths and stereotypes connected to American elections, or drawing important lessons from the American democratic system, was one important way for Palestinians to relate to the 2008 US presidential elections.

IN THE END: INDIFFERENCE, SKEPTICISM, AND SOME HOPE

Palestinian views of the US presidential elections are based on a crude cost-benefit analysis, driven mostly by the desire for change and the expectations suggested by a different style and approach. The two candidates' core positions toward the crucial issues that concern the Palestinians are too close for many people to make it a meaningful base for viewing the candidates differently. The positions repeated throughout the campaign by McCain and Obama are typical, pledging absolute support for Israel, its existence and security, and avoiding any criticism of Israel's actions. As alienating and disappointing as this might be for many people, the fact is that the 2008 presidential elections were also as such a contest of styles and agendas. This contrast, plus important symbolic differences in the candidates' positions on Palestine, did register with different sectors within the political elite, intellectuals, and the Western-educated professionals and young people. The extent to which the campaign was a genuinely popular or street issue is debatable. There is, however, no reason to doubt the impression that ordinary people in general took no notice of the US elections, or only followed it in the most superficial way. For almost all of those who actually had a real interest in the elections, Obama was the favorite candidate.

The logic of most of the US election discourses disproportionately favors Israel and prioritizes its security and existence, casting the US-Israel relation in terms of shared values and strategic interests. Compared to this powerful and often emotional image, reinforced by the pro-Israel lobbies, Palestine is conspicuously absent from the presidential debates and electoral politics. This is a pattern that has not changed much over the years, and to the extent American presidential elections have ignored Palestine, Palestinians also have ignored American elections. However, the Obama-McCain contest represented more of an exception to this rule. The Obama candidacy, with its vibrancy and global appeal, on the heels of the disastrous Bush legacy, also made some waves in different quarters within the POT. To Palestinian observers, Obama's approach reflected more respect, sophistication, conviction, and determination to change past policies.

In the history of American presidential elections, no other campaign has evoked the kind of mixed response, energy, enthusiasm, and activism like the 2008 campaign. The interest in the elections was a genuine reaction to the contrast between the candidates and possibly their different approaches in foreign policy, and it was also a way of looking beyond the current situation to new political horizons of the post-Bush era. It is also a natural outcome of the power of the globalized media, of which Palestine is an integral part. Although mostly united in their support for Obama, Palestinian perspectives of the Democratic candidate included a spectrum of views, from the cynical to the cautious to the welcoming, but all hoping that his promise of treating the question of Palestine as a top priority will be honored and that he will oversee the birth of a Palestinian state and bring peace to the Middle East.

Obama's soaring and eloquent proclamation that "change has come to America!" has captured a unique moment in American history and presidential politics. It is hard to know if this change is credible enough to encompass American foreign policy in the Middle East and the Israeli-Palestinian conflict. During his first major interview after inauguration, given to the Dubai-based Al-Arabiya channel, Obama appealed to his Arab audience to judge him not on his words but on his actions. One would hope that his actions would truly vindicate those Palestinians who believed in him and also give a reason to those who were very skeptical of him to see him in a different light. Only time will tell if this is going to be the case.

NOTES

1. To be sure this is not truly a view from Palestine, since Palestine, as a nation, is so dispersed globally and form many different communities whose opinions of the US elections can only be understood and analyzed through a different and more comprehensive study. The reference to Palestine here is therefore restricted to the POT.

2. ICRC, *West Bank and Gaza: ICRC Household Economy Assessment*, November 21, 2006, http://www.icrc.org/web/eng/siteeng0.nsf/htmlall/palestine-report-211106?opendocument (accessed December 15, 2008).

3. UNDP, "Poverty in the Occupied Palestinian Territory 2007," *Development Times* 1, July 2007, http://www.undp.ps/en/newsroom/publications/pdf/other/dtpov.pdf (accessed December 11, 2008).

4. Palestine Monitor, "Poverty in Palestine: The Facts," Exposing Life Under Occupation, 18 December 18, 2008, http://www.palestinemonitor.org/spip/spip.php?article13 (accessed January 19, 2009).

5. Jan McGirk, "Obama in Ramallah," *Huffpost's Off the Bus*, July 23, 2008, http://www.huffingtonpost.com/tag/obama%20ramallah (accessed November 7, 2008).

6. Marcy Newman, "How About Just Three Commandments?," October 8, 2008, http://bodyontheline.wordpress.com (accessed December 29, 2008).

7. Wafa Jamil, interviewed by Peter Ford, "World Watches McCain, Obama Debate," World Focus, Blogwatch, October 8, 2008, http://worldfocus.org/blog/2008/10/08/world-watches-mccain-obama-debate/1703/ (accessed January 14, 2009).

8. Shibley Telhami, *2008 Annual Arab Public Opinion Poll: Survey of the Anwar Sadat Chair for Peace and Development at the University of Maryland (with Zogby International)*, March 2008, University of Maryland and Zogby international, 2008, http://www.brookings.edu/topics/~/media/Files/events/2008/0414_middle_east/0414_middle_east_telhami.pdf (accessed October 20, 2008).

9. Palestine News Network, March 19, 2008 http://english.pnn.ps/index.php?option=com_content&task=view&id=2546&Itemid=5 (accessed September 12, 2008).

10. Ibid.

11. Bassam Al-Salhi, "An Open Letter to Mr. Mitchell: For the Sake of Real Peace and not a 'Pax Romana,'" January 28, 2009, http://www.alquds.com. All citations from Arabic sources are direct translations by the author.

12. "Global Public Opinion in the Bush Years (2001–2008)," Pew Global Attitude Project, December 18, 2008, http://pewglobal.org/reports/display.php?ReportID=263 (accessed February 13, 2009).

13. Ibid.

14. Lawahez Jabari, "Obama's AIPAC Speech Riles Palestinians," *NBC*, June 5, 2008, http://www.worldblog.msnbc.com/archive/2008/06/05/1117964.aspx (accessed November 7, 2008).

15. Kristen Ess, Palestine News Network (PNN). May 7, 2008, http://english.pnn.ps/index.php?option=com_content&task=view&id=2743&Itemid=5 (accessed September 9, 2008).

16. "Obama: Jerusalem is Israel's unified capital," cartoon in *Filastin*, June 8, 2008, http://www.filastin.com (accessed October 9, 2008).

17. Hani Habib, "Obama's Win: The Cynics are Frustrated!," *Al-Ayyam*, November 9, 2008, http://www.al-ayyam.com (accessed December 29, 2008).

18. See for example, John J. Mearsheimer and Stephen M. Walt, *The Israel Lobby and US Foreign Policy*, 2007 (London: Allen Lane, Penguin books Ltd., 2007); and William A. Cook, *Hope Destroyed, Justice Denied: The Rape of Palestine* (Groningen, Netherlands: EXPATHOS, 2008), Reviewed in *Palestine Chronicle* by Jim Miles, October 21, 2008.

19. Rajab Abu Syrieh. "Barack Obama: The Journey in Search of Jewish Vote," *Al-Ayyam*, July 25, 2008, http://www.al-ayyam.com (accessed November 14, 2008).

20. PNN, March 19, 2008, http://english.pnn.ps/index.php?option=com_content&task=view&id=2546&Itemid=5 (accessed November 15, 2008).

21. Muhammad Yaghi, "Obama Learns Navigating the Middle East," *Al-Ayyam*, July 25, 2008, http://www.al-ayyam.com (accessed December 14, 2008).

22. Muhammad Yaghi, "The Moral Power of Obama's Victory," *Al-Ayyam*, November 7, 2008, http://www.al-ayyam.com (accessed December 14, 2008).

23. Hani Hourani, "A New American President: Him or Us?," *Al-Ayyam*, November 5, 2008, http://www.al-ayyam.com (accessed January 9, 2009).

24. Al-Ayyam, January 22, 2008, http://www.al-ayyam.com (accessed November 5, 2008).

25. Al-Quds, January 21, 2008, http://www.alquds.com (accessed November 5, 2008).

26. Atallah Mansour, "The First Challenge to the New President," *Al-Quds*, January 21, 2009, http://www.alquds.com (accessed January 21, 2009).

27. Jihad Al-Khazen, "And the Reign of Barack Hussein Obama Begins," *Al-Quds*, January 21, 2009, http://www.alquds.com (accessed January 21, 2009).

28. Andrew Sullivan, "A False Premise," Sullivan's Daily Dish. *The Atlantic*. February 5, 2009, http://andrewsullivan.theatlantic.com/the_daily_dish/2009/02/a-false-premise.html.

29. Al-Salhi, "An Open Letter," 2009.

30. "Following Obama's Election, Palestinians and Israelis Seek a More Active Role of the US in Moderating the Conflict," *Palestinian Center for Policy and Survey research* (*PCPSR*), 2008, http://www. pcpsr.org/index.html (January 18, 2009). Incidentally, the poll measured both Palestinian and Israeli public opinion and the results among the Israelis had a similar ranking, though the numbers were mostly slightly different.

31. Suzanne Goldenberg, "Obama Came Prepared to Talk to Hamas," *The Guardian*, January 9, 2009, http://www.guardian.co.uk (accessed January 23, 2009).

32. Alaa Abu Amer, "Obama President: Is There Something New for Us?," Al-Quds, January 26, 2009, http://www.alquds.com (accessed January 30, 2009).

33. Adel Al-Ustah, "Footnotes to Obama's Victory," Al-Ayyam, November 9, 2008, http://www.al-ayyam.com (accessed January 30, 2009).

34. Waleed Batrawi, "The Road to the Presidency," *Al-Ayyam*, July 25, 2008, http://www.al-ayyam.com (accessed January 30, 2009).

9

THE UAE AND THE GULF VIEWS OF THE US PRESIDENTIAL ELECTION

Kenneth Christie

INTRODUCTION

This chapter assesses how the United Arab Emirates (UAE), a small, oil rich Gulf State in the Middle East, in particular, and how the neighboring Gulf States in general, viewed the US presidential election of 2008, and to some extent the aftermath of that election.

Certain caveats have to be addressed when dealing with this kind of analysis in this particular regional context. First and foremost, to a large extent we are engaged in generalizing from specifics. The views and opinions described and investigated here are not necessarily representative of all members of society or even a majority of the population. In the Middle East, little political research is done when it comes to opinions, precisely because these societies in general lack transparency, do not conduct democratic practices, and fail to allow for a broad freedom of expression. Government statistics are sorely lacking and dissenting views from the elites often remain unheard.

This is especially true for the sorts of issues under investigation here. So it is difficult to know the general "flavor" of politics. Indeed, politics itself seems to have been depoliticized in the UAE, for obvious fears that political behavior might encourage dissent. There is little real discussion in newspapers, nor are there any meaningful debates or in-depth internal analysis about the politics of the United Arab Emirates. In fact, many political decisions are taken in secret, and the general public is left to learn about it after the decision has been taken. This is especially true of the information relating to the ruling families. Information initially filters down in the form of gossip, and hard facts are difficult to establish. Pro-Government newspapers are full of congratulatory pieces about how positive public policy is, but they are severely lacking in debate regarding the actual direction of that policy.

Moreover, in terms of the coverage of the US elections, many online pieces were relegated to secondary, hard-to-find pages, making information on Web sites more difficult to access. In addition, many articles were also simply lifted from the sites of Reuters and the Associated Press.[1]

However, it is important to understand the domestic context of this situation. Despite the fact that the recent global credit crunch has had such a big impact on the world economy, little has been written in UAE newspapers that would place the UAE in a critical light and point toward their increasing economic problems. The new $1.5 billion Atlantis Hotel, based on the famous Palm Jumeirah Island, for instance, opened in October 2008. While thousands of workers had to be laid off, $14.5 million were spent on fireworks alone—without this becoming a point of contention in the media. A recent gag order on the local media not to report negatively on the UAE economy has done little to allay fears. State-sanctioned projects or those with a significant amount of local money invested in it are rarely, if ever, portrayed in a critical vein.

Furthermore, one must be aware of the near schizophrenia of pro-Palestinian and anti-Israeli views expressed constantly in official media while at the same time the UAE state maintains an overwhelming reliance on an American security blanket. Here, too, the media is not a reliable tool to gauge what the decision-making elites are really thinking.

Largely to respond to these challenges, this chapter has been organized into several sections. First, I provide an overview of the UAE and its politics. Second, I ask the question of context and why people who live here might be interested in US politics. I will then look at opinions of people here on a range of issues related to the economy and foreign policy, the two major issues that cause interest and controversy. Lastly I will make an assessment on how they viewed the US presidential candidates.

Several primary sources were used here, including local media, such as, most prominently, the "*Gulf News*" (which is pro-government), and the "*Khaleej Times*" (less so), a new daily broadsheet called "The National," which is based in Abu Dhabi and tends to offer more critical views of politics, as well as "7 Days," a free paper, but one that has interesting outlooks on the pulse of Dubai. In addition, the attitude surveys conducted by James Zogby, the Arab-American pollster, are another excellent and extensive source of people's preferences.

Clearly, there has been some interest in the US presidential elections in the UAE. However, one has to understand that the UAE does not have an open and free press, which engages in critical dissent of the ruling elites. More often than not it toes the ruling elite's line, and while it is more likely to publish criticisms of the United States in different forms, there are still certain restraints on the media. Mass politics in any Western sense of the term does not exist. Despite this, however, in recent years there has been a growth in blogs and other forms of Internet activity in the UAE. These will also be assessed.

Background and Context

The UAE is a Middle Eastern federation of states situated in the southeast of the Arabian Peninsula on the Persian Gulf, bordering Oman and Saudi Arabia. Its growth is predicated on oil and the resources produced by oil, and in particular Dubai has been seen as a model of development for much of the Arab world. Seen as a relatively marginal state, the discovery of oil ensured that Dubai and Abu Dhabi (the capital) would be able to sustain growth and development, initially based on trading. The UAE has gone from a peripheral backwater of the world's economy under the British Empire to a relative economic powerhouse in the region and one that many states are seeking to emulate.

The oil boom of the 1970s transformed the power and social structure. Furthermore, to decrease the risk of being oil dependent, the country has increasingly sought to diversify its economy through massive construction projects including shopping malls, hotels, and a burgeoning touristy industry. However, in the light of the recent economic meltdown, many of these projects have been placed on hold, scaled back, or in some cases even abandoned altogether. Nevertheless, the long and, until very recently, largely uninterrupted economic growth has allowed the rulers of the country an opportunity to undertake comprehensive social and economic development. Political development, however, has not occurred at the same rate and the UAE is known for its lack of democracy and civil society.

Only a minority of the population living in the UAE is accorded citizenship, and the state relies on a massive imported labor force that work in construction, often under very poor conditions. On the other hand, among professional expatriates, the Gulf is seen as a tax-free paradise rewarding them in lucrative style. Under such conditions political awareness is slow to develop and in fact discouraged. People seem disinterested in local politics. This is further reinforced because the media, which is government controlled, has tight censorship on newspapers and other news sources. Expatriates come to places like Dubai to make money and return home after a short period of time. There is little sense in them staying for extended periods of time.

The UAE still primarily relies on expatriates not only in menial labor roles but also at the highest levels of planning and management. This is a fact that causes resentment among the local population who see their culture as increasingly marginalized in their own country and under threat by globalization. And yet globalization and Dubai seem to be synonymous. If ever there was a state that was the result of global commerce, then Dubai is that state. A real estate boom after 2003 created speculation that quickly reached completely unrealistic proportions and saw house prices rise by 43 percent in the first quarter of 2008 alone.[2] And "as of June (2008), Dubai had 42 million square feet of office space under construction, more than any other city in the world, even Shanghai. What was a flat desert 20 years ago is today an urban canyon."[3] The globalization of property acquisition fuelled a property boom in Dubai as buyers and investors sought to make quick profits. However, this appears to be in a state of freefall now with the increasing shortage of capital available.

However, this economic globalization and massive growth has not translated into greater political awareness. One problem in examining Emiratis' attitudes toward the American elections and presidential candidates is their degree of apathy toward politics in general. The UAE is not a democracy but a monarchy, and there is no voting or similar system of clear representation. Personality and individuals with strong family connections tend to run politics in the UAE, and there is a great deal of control by these individuals who exercise it in a paternalistic fashion. Little, if any, dissent is brooked. The government allows limited protests over the Palestinian issue, but, in general, the civil society of the kind seen in the West or indeed in other parts of the Middle East is nonexistent. Yet, because there are great material benefits for the local citizens who are highly privileged over the overseas workforce, there appears little incentive to change the system, and the people generally go along with it.

Relationship Between the USA and the UAE

The United States and the UAE have a long-standing relationship. First, these ties are related to oil production and the oil industry. Second, the United States supplies a security blanket to the Gulf including the UAE. Third, the UAE and the United States share strategic and geopolitical interests, which include fighting terrorism and providing docking facilities for US war ships. Fourth, both countries have a common problem in Iran and Iraq. Iran remains a contentious security issue for the UAE because of an ongoing dispute over Iran's occupation of the islands of Abu Musa and Greater and Lesser Tunb since 1971, which both claim sovereignty over. It is doubtful whether, in the pantheon of conflict-related issues, this could ever become more than a minor spat involving name-calling. However, recently the UAE purchased significant quantities of missiles from the US weapons manufacturer Raytheon at enormous sums, despite the fact that there appears very little likelihood of an attack on UAE soil. The United States seems content to provide the UAE with a firewall between it and Iran despite low threat levels.[4]

In the Gulf, the UAE is considered one of the largest markets for US products, and more than 750 American firms are based here. In 2007, the United States exported $11.6 billion worth of goods and services to the UAE, making it the largest export market in the Arab world.[5] Moreover, the United States is involved heavily in the development of higher education institutions in the UAE with the establishment of a number of new universities and the creation of university partnerships. Similarly, American institutions are setting up new health care facilities in the region; these are partly franchises of established institutions and private clinics. Finally, In 2007, Halliburton, the controversial US oil services company, decided to move its global seat of operations to Dubai, a sign of how US companies were becoming more integrated into the political economy of the region.

It might be fair to say that the UAE has clearly mixed feelings about the former president, George W. Bush, and his policies. There was clear delight in the media and, on an anecdotal basis, in Dubai when an Iraqi journalist threw a shoe at Bush on his final visit to Baghdad in December 2008.[6] And yet at the same time there is an understanding that the UAE is dependent on the United States for military security and that the United States affords them a level of protection that other countries cannot offer.

Despite the strong relationship and ties between the UAE and the United States, there have been problems. These have come about most notably in recent years as Dubai has entered the global arena and expect to play a larger role. In 2007, for instance, a commercial deal was concluded for the sale of port management operations in six major US ports to a company based in the UAE. This was done by the UAE in an effort to secure an attractive investment opportunity and also to gain a degree of influence in the United States. This created a major security debate in the United States. The issue was whether such a sale would compromise their port security and therefore their national security. Although the executive branch of the Federal Government approved the sale, various senior US elites argued that the takeover would compromise US port security. In the end, a legislation was introduced in the US congress, whose members ultimately prevented the sale.

Citizens of the UAE viewed this in large measure as an attack on their integrity. More generally, the controversy surrounding the attempted bid to take over US port operations by a company from the UAE reinforced fears in the Middle East that investments in the United States have become politically risky for Arabs and Muslims. Some commentators have expressed concern that the controversy was being driven by racist hysteria and xenophobia on the part of the US Congress, notably James Zogby of the Arab-American Institute.

PUBLIC OPINION IN THE ARAB WORLD AND THE UAE

Perhaps the most extensive surveys of Arab public opinion on these types of issues have come from an Arab-American based in the United States who consistently organizes polls across the region in order to tap attitudes. Zogby, the president of the Arab-American Institute, conducted a survey in mid-March across the Arab world with more than 4000 respondents. He argues that "[in] 2008, Arab attitudes towards the United States remain at alarmingly low levels. Concern with US policy is the reason. And because the US role in the region is so critical, interest in the American elections is high across the Arab world."[7] Detecting a general sense of dissatisfaction is not necessarily surprising. However, with such survey data, Zogby has been able to provide hard evidence to back up what many have intuitively claimed.

In fact, much of the reasons for the anti-American attitudes in the region could be traced to American foreign policy rather than to any inherent disagreement with US values or attributes. This is an important finding and a critical distinction to make. Figures obtained on Arabs in general and Emiratis in particular show that both groups broadly conceive US foreign policy as designed to secure energy supplies (oil), protect Israel, and dominate the Muslim world. Anti-Americanism in this broad light, however, appears to have little to do with attacking the American "creed" or the "American dream" as posited by the former president, George W. Bush, but, rather, with the outcomes of policy in several areas. In comparison to the other Arab states surveyed, the UAE respondents were fairly positive toward the United States and saw many positive aspects in it. But then again, this might be a reflection of the low levels of political awareness. In Muslim societies with a more active civil society, like Morocco, Lebanon, and Egypt, for example, levels of approval toward the United States were far lower. Again, this may have to do with the levels of depoliticization in the UAE and lack of awareness at a general level. Many UAE citizens obtain their images of the United States from Hollywood and the media, which tend to give them an illusory picture.

Concretely, Zogby found that 71 percent of people in the UAE displayed an unfavorable attitude in general toward the United States, with 22 percent in favor of it. The problematic factors cited were the war in Iraq, the pro-Israeli stance of the US government, and, very critically, the US treatment of Muslims at home..

In fact, the Arab-American Institute poll showed that in the UAE, Saudi Arabia, and Lebanon, treatment of Muslims in the United States was the most important policy concern. This is because they have had direct or at least some indirect personal experience of treatment of their citizens when travelling, studying, or working in America. Responses are also conditioned by the strict entry measures applied against Saudis and Gulf states citizens instituted by the US Government following the September 11 attacks. In other words, it is a direct personal concern for the treatment of themselves, family members, and relatives who have been affected by the post-9/11 legislation. This appears more relevant than external issues or the politics of the region. Positive attributes ascribed to the United States (not surprisingly, given the Middle East's democratic deficit) include "personal freedom," "opportunity," and American "entertainment" and "products."

The number of UAE citizens who personally knew Americans was higher in the region (four in ten claimed to know Americans) and exposure to US media and entertainment is quite high in the country. Nearly 50 percent claimed they received their ideas about the United States from a mixture of books, movies, and watching US television. Given the low levels of reading behavior amongst Emiratis, however, it is more likely they received most of their information from the latter two forms.[8] Most Emiratis would probably deny, for instance, that there were two Emirati citizens directly involved with the 9/11 terrorist attacks in the United States. This is because, in general, Emiratis have little critical resources with which to make objective or critical evaluations of their country and society. There is little open media, little transparency, and it is nearly impossible to obtain correct statistics.

Finally, Zogby's study of 2008 also found that the outcome of the US presidential election had fairly little significance for people in the area and that fewer than 40 percent had actually shown an interest in the election.[9] As Zogby noted before the presidential elections, "public opinion remains sour on the U.S., with unfavorable ratings ranging from a high in the 80% range in Egypt and Jordan, to a low (though still high) 71% in the UAE and Morocco."

Much more specifically, in terms of the US presidential elections, the survey found that about a third of the respondents in the UAE were indeed following the United States election closely. Nevertheless, the fact that a substantial proportion of the population paid close attention to the event still did not translate into overwhelming support for any particular candidate.

A Global Experiment

The Economist magazine attempted an experiment to measure peoples' support for US presidential candidates around the world, with the idea to create a "global electoral college." The unanimous decision (85 percent to 15 percent) favored Obama over McCain as the next President of the United States. With only one exception, the majority of the Gulf States showed an even larger preference for Obama than the international average. The respective countries' votes were (Obama-McCain):

1. Bahrain 95 percent-5 percent
2. Kuwait 79 percent-21 percent
3. Oman 97 percent-3 percent
4. Qatar 95 percent-5 percent
5. Saudi Arabia 89 percent-11 percent
6. UAE 94 percent-6 percent

Even Iran (85-15), Pakistan (81-19), and Lebanon (87-13) contained majorities supporting the Democratic hopeful.[10] There was clear and overwhelming support for the Democratic candidate for president at the time, and it could mean several things. In terms of the Republicans and the lack of support for McCain, it is clearly because he was linked to the Bush policies and administration, one that was viewed extremely negatively in the Middle East as a whole. In terms of the Democratic candidate it seems that Obama represented change, that is, change from what was widely seen as disastrous policies. It would be a fresh beginning and there was little stomach in the region for a continuation of US policy.

The UAE and Foreign Policy in the US Election

One of the main driving forces in US politics is the approach to foreign policy by candidates in elections, especially at the presidential level. The economy and foreign policy are crucial to the electoral success or failure of candidates for the highest office. There were major differences of opinion between the Democratic candidate Obama and the Republican candidate McCain. Obama has been far more expressive of developing relationships and working through diplomacy to achieve goals. His promise to visit a major Islamic state within 100 days of his inauguration sparked a great deal of interest in the Middle East and promoted Obama as the candidate of choice for most Arabs in the region. McCain, on the other hand, was still associated with failed policies; he appeared to offer nothing new except a reiteration of the "war on terror" strategy, and people in the region perceived this with great negativity.

In the Gulf and the UAE, the foreign affair issues that typically dominate the headlines in local newspapers are the Israeli-Palestinian conflict, the war in Iraq, and the issue of Iranian nuclear capabilities.[11] The latter is especially pressing to the UAE who are involved in a dispute with Iran over islands that both sides claim as their territory, as mentioned before.

If asked about these issues directly, a typical response, and one that reflects the general viewpoint among Emiratis, might be like this: "In terms of the Arab-Israeli conflict, many Arabs feel that US foreign policy completely favors Israel and does not support Palestine at all." In the recent Israeli air strikes conducted against Gaza in late December 2008/January 2009, there was massive outrage in the local newspapers, with stories dominated by bloody pictures of Palestinians lying dead in the streets of Gaza. Students at a major university, for example, organized events around the issue, mostly of a nonpolitical nature, to raise money for victims of the air strikes. Nevertheless, they were trying to make an important statement, which by its very nature has a political connotation.

Furthermore, special days were set aside for the Palestinian issue by student groups, and the ruler of Dubai, Sheikh Mohammed, cancelled the New Years Eve celebrations in hotels across Dubai as an expression of sympathy with the Palestinian plight in the face of the Israeli onslaught. Moreover, there is enormous latent resentment among the local population in the UAE and the Gulf states at the treatment of the Palestinians. This resentment is furthered by what in the eyes of many is perceived as unconditional support of the United States for Israel. A case in point, in the eyes of the people in the Gulf, was how the United States in typically combative fashion simply blamed Hamas for provoking the attacks on Gaza in 2008/2009.

Among the population of the Gulf states, a broad consensus existed that saw a clear imbalance between roughly 350 Palestinians dead in comparison to only four Israelis by the fourth day. Not much later, more than 1000 residents of Gaza had been killed, many of them children and women. These facts dominated the discussion and shaped the majority opinion about the conflict in Gaza among broad sections of the societies in the Gulf.

One theory that assesses US policy in the Middle East argues that some who influence US foreign policy in the Middle East (specifically the neoconservatives) see Arab countries as needing to be reshaped and remodeled by the power of the United States in order to suit Israeli strategic needs. Second, many Arabs feel that the United States must leave Iraq immediately and it was unjustified to invade Iraq in the first place. According to Arab views, Iraq under Saddam Hussein did not pose a threat to the United States but it did to Israel, which is the main reason Washington attacked Iraq. Similarly, saber rattling against Iran and its proposed nuclear capability by the US government does not promote peace in the region and is seen in a negative light in the region and the UAE. Obama appeared to adopt a much more conciliatory stance to these problems and appeared much more willing to engage with perceived enemies than the Republican leadership.

For Republicans, the Middle East has always seemed a more prominent issue than for Democrats, who appear more comfortable with US domestic issues. Today, the former still perceive foreign policy as directed through the prism of the "War on Terror." For Democrats, there are larger issues at stake, including global warming and the different threats and opportunities presented by globalization.

The Bush administration has been widely seen as pro-Israel, something that gives it a negative aspect in the eyes of most Arab and Gulf States. This view of Bush is shared in the UAE. Here, the negative view of Bush and his Middle Eastern policies meshes easily with the daily media coverage of hardship and deprivation of the Palestinians.

McCain was associated with the Bush administration and it was feared that, if elected, he would simply continue these policies. His future policies were also extrapolated from the fact that he had provided support for a "surge" in troop numbers in Iraq and had been arguing that these policies would be successful. His was an aggressive strategy willing the United States onto victory.

Similarly, he was very supportive of Israel. He argued that the Palestinian Hamas is a terrorist group, as the Israeli government argues. This not only put him in line with Israel's view, but also implied that Hamas, being a terrorist group, was not a group to be negotiated with. He treated Iran with similar bullishness, showing the standard concern over the development of nuclear weapons and arguing that military options for the problem might be appropriate.[12]

The Democrats, on the other hand, and most importantly Obama, have a much more nuanced position on these conflicts and less of a hardline position. This has appealed to UAE citizens and residents. During the election campaign, US Democrats talked openly about withdrawing troops from Iraq and pursuing negotiations with Iran. Obama pledged friendlier relations with Islamic states.

During the campaign, Obama also denounced the war in Iraq as a war that "should never have been authorized and should never have been waged."[13] He further rejected torture as a technique and argued early for the closure of Guantanamo and adhering to the Geneva conventions on the treatment of prisoners there. In short, Obama's position was a for more inclusive foreign policy that rejected the flouting of international law and an effort to gain more legitimacy for the United States and its policies after the perceived global illegitimacy of the Bush administration. There is no doubt that Hillary Clinton received much less coverage than Obama in the UAE press. This might be due to several factors. For one thing she was strongly opposed, as senator of New York, to the Dubai World Ports deal, causing controversy. And this is also partly because of her apparent strong links with the Jewish lobby in the United States. The other factor, of course, is that Obama was just seen as so popular and a real candidate for change that her coverage and media presence could never reach the same levels as Obama's.

Both American parties would clearly like to see more democracy in the region. However, this may not be easy to achieve given the difficult position they currently find themselves in, despite having spend massive amounts of money to fund many projects in the region. The global economic downturn and the state of the US economy have meant that much more effort has to be focused on the internal domestic problems of the United States.

The other major issue in US foreign policy in the Middle East is the handling of the economy. Clearly, an unstable Middle East is not good for business with the UAE. Fears of another war breaking out between the United States and Iran thus raised concerns. According to Watson, "Many Emiratis have watched with alarm as tensions between Washington and Tehran have escalated over the past year. They fear that if a war breaks out between Washington and Tehran, it would bring an end to the incredible economic growth their country has enjoyed, as oil prices have hit record highs of more than $100 a barrel."[14] In other words, the people of the Emirates hope that the next occupant of the White House will pursue a very restrained policy toward the Middle East. They hope for an assurance that the United States will stay out of Iran and avoid the possibility of war with Iran, which consequently will also involve Israel and could easily spillover into their territory.

The mess, which was created under the Bush administration regarding the DPW controversy, is also something that negatively influenced Emiratis toward the US Republican party.

OBAMA'S APPEAL IN THE MUSLIM WORLD

One of the special features of the 2008 presidential election campaign was the unprecedented appeal of presidential candidate Obama on the Islamic world. Large sections of Muslim populations on a global basis were fascinated by the campaign and hoped that Obama would achieve his goals. And the fact that this level of support came at a time when the Muslim world likewise displayed an unprecedented degree of anger and indignation over US foreign policy toward the Middle East is just as striking. This "Obama phenomenon" really seems to be encapsulated by the new president's willingness to be open and to talk to "America's enemies," a marked contrast from the Bush administration.[15]

Within the UAE, Obama came across as a very popular candidate. The fact that he lived for some time in a Muslim country (Indonesia) when he grew up, that as an African-American he came from a minority background in the United States, and that he appeared to have a radically different set of policies and ideas to that of the Bush administration certainly helped.[16] In this context, one must remember that Obama's predecessor in the White House was very unpopular in the UAE in particular and the Middle East in general. This support for Obama evinced itself in a generalized degree of support, even though it would be fair to say that many Emiratis are generally apathetic about politics.

It would also be fair to say that eight years of the Bush administration has tarnished America's reputation around the world and has been a cause of anti-Americanism at a very serious level. The radical change in leadership, which would have been unthinkable fifty years ago, has given people a kind of fresh impetus to become involved and be interested in politics.[17] This has had a kind of knock on effect (effect by association) where the UAE has paid a keener than usual interest in the US election. Moreover, the hype in the media and the interest generated by the primaries and the candidates in terms of this being seen as a landmark election has made people more interested.

Supporters of Obama in the Middle East viewed this candidate as a person with a diverse, international and interracial background and in this light was seen to be someone who would develop good relations with the Muslim world. In contrast, Bush was always seen in the region as the candidate more likely to provoke a "clash of civilizations."

Obama's declarations and policy positions also make him popular in the UAE. On the campaign trail he spoke out against the war in Iraq and called for a phased withdrawal of troops from there, as well as on the need to offer incentives and negotiate with Iran over its nuclear program.

THE PERCEPTION OF MCCAIN IN THE GULF REGION

McCain, the Republican candidate in the US presidential election, is problematic to assess in terms of how people in the Gulf region felt about him. One thing is certain, however, if Obama was the candidate of change, then McCain represented, at least to the UAE and Middle East, the candidate of the status quo. He represented the opposite of change. For most people in the UAE, he was simply seen as an extension of the Bush presidency and all the negative implications associated with that, including, in their eyes, support for Israel over the Palestinians, the continuation of the war in Iraq, further exploitation of Gulf oil resources, and an aggressive policy toward Iran, among others. These were all hallmarks of the Bush Administration's policies. Many Emiratis simply viewed McCain as the candidate who would extend the Bush Administration's policies in the region.

Furthermore, McCain was not supported by general public opinion in the Middle East, tending to be seen as an extension of Bush and the negative associations with that. McCain's policy on the Iraq War, for instance, is very different from Obama's. The Republican was strongly against withdrawing troops from Iraq, whereas the Democratic candidate publicly stated that troops would be withdrawn at some point.[18] In addition, McCain, as the representative of the Republican Party, was tainted with his party's traditional policy in the Middle East, which put him on a losing side from the beginning in the eyes of many Emiratis.

Immediate Reaction to the Election Outcome

The immediate reaction to the election of Barack Obama as the 44th President of the United States was overwhelmingly positive in the UAE. One newspaper based in Dubai ran a headline "A new dawn of American leadership."[19] The leaders of the UAE sent their congratulations to the new American President in fulsome verse.

The real constraints on the new president were all too apparent, however, particularly in the Middle East. Obama criticized Bush's policies in the Middle East and the handling of wars in both Iraq and Afghanistan as well as his policy toward Iran. But a full eight years of policy mistakes in the Middle East by the outgoing administration may well plague Obama's chances of success at attaining the peace sought so desperately in Iraq and Palestine.

Positive elements that commentators in the Middle East saw in favor of Obama included his oratorical skills and sense of diplomacy, his value of multilateral institutions and his sense of a global interdependence, all in sharp juxtaposition to the Bush administration's policies, which was viewed as notorious for its lack of subtlety and diplomacy in world affairs. On the other hand, some in the Arab press did not think the identity of the US president-elect would make much difference in his country's policy in the Middle East, given the fact that the presidential candidates publicly declared their support of Israel.[20]

Conclusion

Sometimes the results of research that political scientists produce on public attitudes toward public figures appear obvious and straightforward. In the case of the UAE's relationship with the United States it appears more difficult because the ties are complex and not always apparent. The UAE is a bastion of globalization and commerce in the Middle East; capitalism appears unfettered here and the role model for that is the United States. Also, the US military provides a security blanket in the region and in the UAE in particular, with American ships docking at its ports and the UAE purchasing massive amounts of US weaponry. Most importantly, with the overall presence of US firepower in the region, the UAE must tread lightly in its criticism of American policy.

And yet, at the same time, ordinary citizens felt dismayed by the policies of the Bush administration, which appear to be one-sided toward Israel and against the Palestinians and motivated by realist interests. Daily criticism of these policies in the newspapers is taken for granted even among UAE government channels.

Into this mix comes President Obama, a new and dynamic leader with some apparent Islamic background, presenting a reconciliatory tone toward Islam as opposed to an open clash with it. Obama positions himself as a proponent of diplomatic and multilateral approaches, as opposed to unilateral and often offensive tactics practiced by an imperial superpower under President Bush. The reaction in the Middle East to the US presidential candidate changed on this point, and the UAE in particular sees President Obama as a force for change. Public opinion toward Obama and his policies was highly positive, and opinion survey showed that Emiratis favored Obama more than any other candidate. There is little doubt that if Obama can maintain the impetus of change and apply this to the US foreign policy, then the United States and its president will achieve greater levels of positive public acclaim in years to come.

NOTES

1. Ashe Reardon, "Election coverage in the UAE," in http://international-newsroom.wordpress.com/about/links-to-student-blogs/super-Tuesday-coverage/uae/ (accessed February 2, 2009).
2. Christopher Dickey, "Is Dubai's Party Over," *Newsweek*, December 15, 2008, 22.
3. Ibid.
4. "Deal to Buy US Missiles for $3.3 billion," *The National* (UAE), December 20, 2008, 1.
5. "UAE-US Relations: Shared Strategic Interests." United Arab Emirates/UAE-US Relations. Http://www.uae-us.org/page.cfm?id=4 (accessed February 12, 2009).
6. Several of my students in Dubai, in what must mark the high point of their repertoire of political action, e-mailed me the video clip on You Tube.
7. James Zogby (May 13, 2008), "Arab Public Opinion towards the US in 2008. Cross-Cultural understandings." http://www.ccun.org/Opinion%20Editorials/2008/May/13%20o/Arab%20Public%20Opinion%20Toward%20the%20US,%20in%202008%20By%20James%20Zogby.htm (accessed February 12, 2009).
8. Khaled Dawoud, "Arab Opinion," *Al-Ahram Weekly*, http://yaleglobal.yale.edu/display.article?id=4305 (accessed February 1, 2009).
9. James Zogby (May 13, 2008), "Arab Public Opinion towards the US in 2008. Cross-Cultural understandings." http://www.ccun.org/

Opinion%20Editorials/2008/May/13%20o/Arab%20Public%20 Opinion%20Toward%20the%20US,%20in%202008%20By%20 James%20Zogby.htm (accessed February 12, 2009).

10. Joseph Kechnician, "President Obama and the Mideast." *Gulf News Online.* Http://archive.gulfnews.com/articles/0810/30/10255574. html (accessed February 15, 2009).

11. In one of the rare demonstrations of politics by students at my university in Dubai, the American flag was burnt in response to more Israeli attacks on Palestine.

12. Marwan Kabalan, "The US elections and the Middle East." *Gulf News Online.* http://archive.gulfnews.com/articles/08/04/18/10206490. html (accessed February 10, 2009).

13. Patrick Seale, "Obama is Good for Israel," *Gulf News Online*, February 2, 2008, http://archive.gulfnews.com/articles /08/02/29/10193473. html (accessed February 13, 2009).

14. Ivan Watson, "United Arab Emirates Both Resents, Relies on the US," *National Public Radio*, http://www.npr.org/templates/story/story. php?storyId=18056114 (accessed January 13, 2009)

15. Yasser Khalil, "Obama's Appeal in the Muslim World," *Gulf News Online*, June 17, 2008, http//:archive.gulfnews.com/ articles/08/06/17/10221577.html (accessed February 22, 2009).

16. Obama's middle name is Hussein, which is significant in the Islamic world as it is the name of the Prophet Mohammed's grandson. See Maryam Ismail, "US Elections: Hope is the Colour of the Future." *Khaleej Times Online.* http://www.khaleejtimes.ae/ DisplayArticleNew.asp?xfile=data/opinion/2008/May/opinion_ May70.xml&section=opinion&col= (accessed February 26, 2009).

17. Debbie Menon, "Why Barack Obama Holds Out Hope For All Of Us." *Khaleej Times Online.* http://www.khaleejtimes.com/ DisplayArticleNew.asp?col=&section=opinion&xfile=data/ opinion/2008/May/opinion_May74.xml (accessed February 26, 2009).

18. Pierre Tristam, "John McCain's Middle East Policy," http://middleeast.about.com/od/usmideastpolicy/a/me071122_2.htm (accessed February 25, 2009).

19. *The National*, November 6, 2008, 1.

20. Rasha Hassan, "Arab Perspective: Message to Winner of the US Presidential Election," http://archive.gulfnews.com/articles/00/11/10/2283.html (accessed February 27, 2009).

10

THE IRANIAN PERSPECTIVE ON THE US PRESIDENTIAL ELECTION OF 2008

Grace Cheng

Along with the Bush administration, all of the major prospective candidates for the American presidential race in November 2008 characterized Iran as the major threat to US interests in the Middle East. US presidents since Jimmy Carter, during whose presidency relations with Iran were severed, have viewed Iran as the main obstacle to peaceful order in the region. US policy toward Iran has been one of containment in the region and isolation internationally. Since the death of the first Supreme Leader Ayatollah Ruhollah Khomeini in 1989, there have been various opportunities to reestablish diplomatic relations. However, these have been thwarted by hardliners on both sides. Both Bill Clinton and George W. Bush refused to take steps toward any diplomatic engagement without prior basic changes in Iranian policy. Any breakthrough in US-Iran relations may benefit both countries, as Iran's economy continues to suffer from years of economic sanctions, while the United States could rely on Iran to play a constructive role in Iraq and Afghanistan. Therefore, the 2008 US presidential election was of interest to Iranians, to the extent that the presidential candidates of the two major parties approached US-Iran relations differently.

THE UNITED STATES AND IRAN SINCE 1979

The close diplomatic ties between the United States and Iran came to an abrupt end when in late 1979 revolutionary students took fifty-two American hostages in the former US Embassy in Tehran. Khomeini supported the students' action, which revolutionary ideologues still portray as "payback" for prior US interventions in Iranian affairs: from its role in the 1953 coup against popular Prime Minister Mohammad Mossadeqh to its support of Muhammad Reza Shah's repressive regime.

The United States' response to the hostage crisis, which lasted 444 days, was an imposition of an embargo on Iranian oil and all trade, except food and medicine, and a freezing of Iranian assets. Iran's Islamic Revolution aimed explicitly at establishing an alternative to the existing international order, which its leaders perceived as one of hegemonic design by the United States. Accordingly, the Iranian Constitution (Article 152) states that:

> The foreign policy of the Islamic Republic of Iran is based upon the rejection of all forms of domination, both the exertion of it and submission to it, the preservation of the independence of the country in all respects and its territorial integrity, the defense of the rights of all Muslims, nonalignment with respect to the hegemonic superpowers, and the maintenance of mutually peaceful relations with all non-belligerent States.[1]

The Islamic Republic's policy orientation thus threatened the existing order in the Middle East, most critically via the ambition to "export" the Islamic revolution through the creation and support of opposition groups throughout the region. Against the Islamic Republic's threat to the regional order, the United States sought to undermine the new Islamic regime in Tehran by supplying arms and intelligence information to Saddam Hussein's government during the devastating Iran-Iraq War of 1980–1989.

Although Tehran's commitment to exporting the revolution petered following the death of Khomeini, it still has close relations with and supports anti-Israeli opposition groups in Lebanon and the Palestinian territories, as well as Shi`a groups in Afghanistan, Pakistan, and now Iraq. This is one of the main causes of the United States' concerns today, along with Iran's nuclear program, which many US officials fear is making rapid progress in enriching enough uranium to build an atomic bomb. Despite US characterizations of Tehran as a "state sponsor of terrorism" and, since 2005, as defiant of the International Atomic Energy Agency's (IAEA) authority, the Iranian political leadership has refused to retreat on any of these policies, which the United States has held as preconditions to any talks that might lead to a restoration of diplomatic relations.

Citing Tehran's links to terrorist groups and its nuclear program, the George W. Bush administration not only continued the US government's post-1979 policy toward Iran but further threatened the existence of the Iranian regime in explicit terms. The US administration accused Iran of harboring members of al-Qaeda, while President Bush named Iran as part of an "Axis of Evil" in the 2002 State of the Union address. Along with other efforts to isolate Tehran, such rhetoric and threats from Washington, despite Tehran's constructive participation in the Bonn talks on the post-Taliban Afghan government and its contributions to Afghanistan's reconstruction (including a donation of $560 million, the largest amount from a developing country, made in 2002), discredited Iran's proponents of warmer relations with the United States and it led eventually to the hardening of the Iranian government's position, including their resumption of uranium enrichment activities in 2005 (suspended previously in 2003 under orders of the IAEA). President Mahmoud Ahmadinejad, who was elected later that year, proceeded to make uranium enrichment an issue of national sovereignty and a critical aspect of his administration over the next several years.

The Iranian population may not all be convinced of their government's claim that it has no ambitions to develop nuclear weapons, but many seem to be of the opinion that their country should not be denied a right to such technology or weapons when countries not party to the Nuclear Nonproliferation Treaty (NPT) are allowed to possess them, including countries hostile to Iran, such as Israel and Pakistan. However, reportedly the mood in Iran in 2008 was that of ambivalence about the issue of the nuclear program, as it brought more economic hardship with new United Nations (UN) Security Council sanctions. Weakened economically by years of sanctions as well as state mismanagement, normalization of relations with the United States would make available urgently needed economic aid and investment, but the Iranian leadership has not been willing to comply with US demands following such threats to the regime. With the Bush administration's harsh US rhetoric and policies of containment, the Iranian leadership has come to view the nuclear issue as part of the United States' effort to undermine the Iranian regime through US manipulation of the NPT and IAEA framework. Supreme Leader Ali Khamenei and other Iranian leaders and analysts perceive that the United States aims to undermine the Islamic Republic and that nothing less than an Iranian state subservient to US interests would be satisfactory. This has made constructive negotiations about Iran's nuclear program impossible.

What the Iranians want is to preserve their national interests, but their national interest is not uniformly defined. For those on the right, including Khamenei and Ahmadinejad, Iran's national standing would only be served if the United States treats Iran not only as a state like any other in the region but also as an equal in international relations and a critical player in the Middle East. These ideological conservatives reject the current US policy of containing Iran and often employ strong language insisting that the United States acknowledges its "wrong policies" in the region. The pragmatist and reformist members of the Iranian leadership want the United States to recognize Iran's legitimate interests and strategic concerns, such as the projected difficulties in meeting domestic demand for energy and the presence of nuclear-armed neighbors.

However, they do not see Iran's national interests served by Iran asserting its role in regional matters that do not have direct consequence for the
country. For the Iranian population, about two-third of which is under
the age of thirty, moving toward a normalization of relations would offer
great opportunities, economic and otherwise. The views of the government and the people of Iran about the US presidential elections were
filtered through their perceptions of which candidate was the more likely
to fulfill these interests.

EXPLAINING IRAN

Mainstream US representations of post-1979 Iran have consistently been
that of a viciously anti-American nation guided by a militant religious
ideology, characteristics that are embodied by key personalities such as
Khomeini and Ahmadinejad. While Ahmadinejad receives tremendous
press coverage for his outrageously bold statements on international
issues, there was a relative lack of interest in former reformist president
Muhammad Khatami's (1997–2005) efforts at promoting reconciliation
with the United States, including his launching of a Dialogue Among
Civilizations (a challenge to Samuel Huntington's "clash of civilizations" thesis) and his statements during an interview on CNN in 1998
of regret for the embassy takeover and categorical rejection of terrorism. This suggests the utility of negative imagery for legitimating the
United States' rigidly hostile position toward Tehran since the establishment of the Islamic Republic on April 1, 1979. Although throughout
this period the United States has maintained a policy of sanctions and
containment, this strategy has not encouraged the Islamic Republic to
change its orientation domestically or internationally. Despite its criticism of Tehran's human rights record, the United States has been most
concerned about the international role of the Islamic Republic, including
its efforts to export its counter-hegemonic revolutionary ideology and
rejection of the Arab-Israeli peace process. Since 1979 the United States
has assumed that the hard-line conservatives in Tehran who support this
foreign policy hold the key to Iranian foreign policy. This has effectively
been the case. However, Iranian politics is more complicated than the
typical American portrayal of an authoritarian regime dominated by religious conservatives who seek to crush the aspirations of a people desiring
freedom and liberation.

    For example, while Khomeini did indeed dominate Iranian poli-
tics while he was alive, Ahmadinejad (elected to the 2005–2009 term)
does not represent the views of all of the conservative Iranian political leadership despite the attention he receives in the American media.
Indeed, conservative leaders have often criticized Ahmadinejad, finding

his unrelenting outspokenness on the nuclear and other international issues to be disruptive of their goals. Also, his pronouncements on such matters are not insignificant politically, as the president of Iran in fact does not have any authority in matters of national security. Supported by the Revolutionary Guard Corps and the Guardian Council, the Supreme Leader Ali Khamenei is empowered by Iran's constitution to have the final word on such matters. Therefore, Ahmadinejad's public pronouncements on the issue have complicated the Iranian government's position, and he does not have the authority to make such decisions about the nuclear program and Iran's relations with the United States. In addition, Ahmadinejad's personal religious inclination has a millenarian quality that does not characterize the qualities of the conservative religious ruling elite.

The authority of the Supreme Leader and Council of Guardians, which was strengthened constitutionally following Khomeini's death, is a matter of huge contention among the different political factions in Iran. Khatami in particular sought to challenge this political imbalance while he was president. Iran's leadership factions may be divided into several major groups: on the liberal end are the reformists, such as former president Khatami; in the center are pragmatists, such as former president Hashemi Rafsanjani (1989–1997); Islamic leftists, such as former prime minister Mir Hosein Musavi and the majority in the *majles* (parliament) in the 1980s, who have since been sidelined; the ideological religious conservatives, such as Supreme Leader Ali Khamenei and members of the Guardian Council; and populist revolutionary revivalists, such as Ahmadinejad and his supporters. There are also a great number of dissidents and a radical opposition (such as the Third Force movement), who, although outside of the formal political institutions, play a critical role in Iranian political discourse. Iranian students and intellectuals typically support the reformist and opposition groups, which are oriented toward social and political liberties and realist perspectives of international relations, as well as sometimes more progressive, cosmopolitan views.

Aside from those calling for the restoration of the Pahlavi monarchy (who are currently in exile outside of the country), most Iranians are generally skeptical of the United States. While the inheritors of Khomeini's revolutionary Islamic ideology are in principle opposed to the United States, many pro-reform Iranians are also wary of the United States. Pro-democracy groups in Iran have steered clear of US State Department funds intended to support Iranian democracy, because US involvement in Iran historically has been tainted by the CIA's role in the overthrow of Mossadeqh in 1953 and the United States' subsequent support for Reza Pahlavi, even during the most repressive years of his rule. Therefore, historically US intervention in Iranian affairs has effectively undermined democratic forces in Iran. Owing to these factors, the United States lacks credibility in this area among even pro-reform Iranians.

Though these pro-reform Iranians receive the most press in the United States, Iran remains a highly polarized society, with a wide cultural and ideological gap between the middle-class consumers, who find reformist and liberal positions most appealing, and the conservative poor, many of whom comprise the growing urban migrant populations. These poor Iranians suffer from chronic housing problems, lack of adequate healthcare, poor sanitation, and unemployment. Furthermore, as Christophe de Bellaigue puts it, for the first generation of migrants to Iranian cities "urban life is a brutal assault on their traditions and their dignity."[2] The less privileged in Iran tend to be more conservative, devout, and less supportive of reinstating social freedoms, which they believe are the cause for "moral corruption." Ahmadinejad came to power with the support of this lower class. With his frugal lifestyle, unglamorous professional background (as transportation engineer), and populist appeals to their concerns about personal survival and sense of social justice, Ahmadinejad compared favorably with other politicians, such as former president Hashem Rafsanjani, who possesses great personal wealth and is associated with the lopsided results of the market reforms of his terms as president (1989–1997). As Iranians are generally very nationalistic, the Iranian president readily exploited the nuclear issue to appeal to the nationalist pride as well as anxieties of many Iranians. The Bush administration's threats and rhetoric against Iran helped to support the hardliners' claim that Iran needs a nuclear deterrent, but popular opinion may be turning against this because of the international and economic consequences of defiance against the UN Security Council on this matter. In addition, among the Iranians who did support Ahmadinejad in part because of his promises of redistribution of wealth, his popularity has declined alongside their economic situation.

Iran is a semi-democratic system, but its elections have been marred by interference by the Council of Guardians, who disqualified thousands of candidates in the past several *majles* (parliamentary) elections. Nevertheless, Iranian politics is far more open and subject to contestation, and Iranians enjoy more political liberties than the populations of other states in the Middle East. Given their past relations with the United States, those challenging the political order within Iran do not lend themselves to simple alignment with American perspectives. Rather, in their political calculations, Iranian understandings of how to best preserve their national interests typically are balanced by some degree of skepticism regarding US intentions for their country and the Middle East.

MCCAIN OR OBAMA?

Although the Iranian people were among the first in the world to hold spontaneous candlelight vigils for the victims of the 9/11 terrorist attacks on the United States, the Bush administration soon became extremely unpopular among Iranians by naming the country as the "Axis of Evil," despite the Iranian government's cooperation in Afghanistan and the pursuit of al-Qaeda. In addition, though they hated the Saddam Hussein regime in Iraq, Iranians perceived the Bush administration's war as an attempt to establish US hegemony in the Middle East, and having little consideration for Iraqi lives and security. With the instability of post-Saddam Iraq, Iranians were concerned with the Bush administration's willingness to resort to military means and its lax approach to post-conflict security and reconstruction. Bush's efforts to support democracy in Iran also drew strong criticism from opponents of the Iranian regime, because the funds supported US government-sponsored media and US-based opposition groups. Iranian dissidents felt that this and the Bush policy of threatening the Iranian regime shifted the country's domestic politics in favor of conservatives. This is reflected in a September 24, 2007 open letter to United Nations Secretary-General Ban Ki-moon by Akbar Ganji:

> Far from helping the development of democracy, US policy over the past 50 years has consistently been to the detriment of the proponents of freedom and democracy in Iran ... The Bush administration, for its part, by approving a fund for democracy assistance in Iran, which is in fact being largely spent on official institutions and media affiliated with the US government, has made it easy for the Iranian regime to describe its opponents as mercenaries of the US and to crush them with impunity.[3]

With video footage of one US presidential candidate, John McCain, in 2007 singing "Bomb, bomb, bomb, bomb, bomb Iran" to the tune of the Beach Boys' *Barbara Ann*, the preference of most Iranians for the next president of the United States was clear from the beginning of the 2008 campaign. Beyond his unwavering support for President Bush's unpopular policies in the "war on terror" and his rejection of Barack Obama's call for diplomacy with Iran, McCain's singing further suggested a disregard for the human toll of US military action against those it has conflict with, including, potentially, Iran. By reinforcing American associations of Iran with religious extremism, terrorism, and the "Axis of Evil," McCain and the amused audience he sang to revealed the extent to which the Iranian nation had been dehumanized in the minds of those rejecting diplomacy before military action with Iran. Further fueling Iranians' negative perceptions of McCain were video clips of supporters of McCain and his running-mate Sarah Palin explaining that they opposed Obama because they believed he is a Muslim and thus a terrorist. Their quick equation of Islam with terrorism was worrisome to Iranians, whose religion had become associated simplistically in the US media with the worst of the Islamic Republics. Images of such rallies suggested that McCain would perpetuate the "Islamophobic" attitude of the Bush administration, whose policies of detaining Muslims at Guantanamo Bay, Cuba, angered Iranians and other Muslims around the world. Given their expressed attitudes, McCain-Palin supporters suggested to Iranians the impossibility of advancing US-Iranian relations if the Republican Party candidates were elected to office.

As in most other countries around the world, Iranians widely supported Obama as the next US president. Obama's self-presentation as a would-be "antiwar" president who stood for a fundamental "change," along with his calls for talks with Iran "without self-defeating preconditions," set him apart from the Bush administration that McCain associated himself with. Many Iranian analysts believed that the Bush administration's inclusion of Iran in the "Axis of Evil" undermined former president Khatami's (1997–2005) reform efforts. Domestic political developments in Iran while Bush was in office reflected how the Bush administration's hard-line approach toward Tehran helped to solidify the political position of Iranian hardliners, who enforced stricter adherence to religious laws and restrictions on democratic rights. Although the political vacuum in Iraq has enabled religious figures and organizations to establish cross-border ties among fellow Shi`a and the Iranian government to assert its influence in the country, more conservative Iranians also considered the Bush administration's policies in Iraq, as well as in Afghanistan and in regard to the Israeli-Palestinian conflict, as aggressive efforts to establish the United States as a hegemonic power in the region. They perceive developments such as the US manipulation of the IAEA as elements of an American strategy designed to undermine the Iranian regime. The Bush administration's continued threats to destabilize Tehran, together with Iran's existing anxieties regarding its "nuclear neighborhood," helped secure the conservative claim of the necessity of a nuclear deterrent, and Ahmadinejad successfully exploited the issue of the country's nuclear program, presenting it as a matter of national right and interest during the early years of his presidency.

Prior to his nomination as the Democratic Party's candidate in 2008, Obama stressed that he would do "[e]verything in [his] power to prevent Iran from obtaining a nuclear weapon." However, he has also called for a diplomatic approach toward achieving this objective. The plan of Obama and vice presidential candidate Joe Biden called for "direct presidential diplomacy," although Obama also stated that "as president of the United States, I would be willing to lead tough and principled diplomacy *with the appropriate Iranian leader* at a time and place of my choosing" (italics by the author). Following his electoral victory, Obama's refusal to respond to Ahmadinejad's congratulatory letter has led to speculation that any diplomacy will not occur while Ahmadinejad is president. By apparently setting his own precondition for talks with Tehran, Obama may have been attempting to persuade Iranians to vote in the country's June 2009 election for a president who is less outspoken and more pragmatic. Relations with the United States were not an issue in the 2005 Iranian presidential election that brought Ahmadinejad into office, as the domestic situation took center-stage. Obama's statement and his stated willingness to negotiate may have been aimed at making US relations a critical matter in Iran's 2009 election. In any case, Ahmadinejad has since been reelected, as a result of international events that have evolved since the November elections in the United States (see below), and as he also has the support of Khamenei, who has stated publicly that he should continue as president.[4] On the other hand, when Obama mentioned holding diplomacy with the "appropriate Iranian leader," he may have been referring to the Supreme Leader, who effectively has the authority in national security matters, not the Iranian president. What Obama meant with this statement will be revealed only after some time during his presidency, and it will reflect how well and how differently he and his national security team understand Iranian politics.

SIZING UP PRESIDENT-ELECT OBAMA

Following Obama's electoral victory, the Iranian Ambassador to the IAEA, Ali Ashgar Soltanieh, said "that if Obama makes good on his campaign pledge to drop preconditions on talks with Tehran, it could pave the way for a significant cooling of tensions between the U.S. and Iran."[5] Soltanieh added, "We are fully prepared to sit at the negotiating table with all the countries, provided that there are no conditions and all are on equal footing." Iranian Foreign Minister Manouchehr Mottaki was cautious about any change that Obama would bring to US policy as president, but he took the opportunity to state a more optimist view following the announcement of Obama's electoral victory, that his election reflected a " 'clear sign' that Americans wanted changes in government policies."[6] However, the conservative position in Iran is that the government "should not wait for a change in US policy" but rather should take the initiative in setting the tone for US-Iran diplomatic relations.[7]

Ahmadinejad's November 6 letter of congratulation to Obama contained a list of criticisms of existing US policies and an explication of what "nations of the world expects" from President Obama.[8] Nevertheless, it was an unprecedented gesture by an Iranian leader in the history of severed relations between the United States and the Islamic Republic.

The conservative analyst Amir Mohebbian "urged that Obama write a letter to Ahmadinejad as a first step to contacting" the Supreme Leader, with whom he should negotiate substantive matters.[9] Obama's rebuff may signal a rejection of the Iranian president's legitimacy based on his remarks about the Holocaust and Israel, which French President Nicolas Sarkozy condemned openly (leading to Tehran's boycotting of Paris talks on Afghanistan in late 2008). It remains to be seen whether the Obama administration's position will be like that of Sarkozy's, which is to refuse to treat Ahmadinejad as a legitimate representative of the Iranian nation.

However, various Iranian analysts from different ends of the political spectrum have commented that Obama should not wait until after the Iranian presidential election to make contact with the Supreme Leader and his national security advisors.[10] They offer that the Iranian conservatives in charge would not wait for Obama to make a move. Such advice may be predicated on past experience of missed opportunities, which were followed by a hardening of the leadership's position. Before 2002, reformists in the Khatami government, as well as the clerics of the Guardian Council, debated the merits of the policy of rejecting Israel's legitimacy. Even after Bush's dubbing of Iran as part of the "Axis of Evil," Iranian leaders pursued this new stance toward the Middle East conflict with efforts to reestablish diplomatic relations with Egypt (and there was even a call by a reformist member of parliament for a "strategic realignment" with Egypt and Jordan). In May 2003, Iran's clerical leadership sent a proposal for talks to their American counterparts via the Swiss ambassador in Tehran. The proposal included an offer to freeze its nuclear program, cooperate fully with the IAEA, support for a non-religious democratic government in Iraq, and to end material support to Palestinian groups. It asked in return for the removal of Iran from the United States' terrorism list, the end of all sanctions, US support for Iran's claims for reparations for the Iran-Iraq war as part of the overall settlement of the Iraqi debt, the repatriation of Muhahideen-e-Khalq (MEK, a discredited opposition group, which has been in exile in Iraq since the early 1980s) members to Iran, and access to nuclear technology for peaceful purposes. The Bush administration flatly rejected the proposal, with Vice President Dick Cheney stating that "We don't speak to evil."[11]

Under US-led international pressure, Iran did halt its efforts at uranium enrichment and also cooperated with the IAEA on inspections in 2003 and 2004. By 2005, however, Bush's hard-line approach had led to the sidelining of the liberals and moderates within the Iranian leadership, as Khatami's term ended and Tehran refused the IAEA's request for another round of inspections. The subsequent IAEA Resolution against Tehran opened the door for referral of Iran to the UN Security Council and more sanctions. The Iranian perception now is that the United States was using the NPT and the IAEA for political means to set up the basis for a military strike against Iran, just as earlier Security Council resolutions were used to justify the United States' war against Iraq in 2003. Given their high level of skepticism, Iranian officials rejected the proposals offered in 2006 and 2008 by the permanent members of the Security Council and Germany, in part because they found the United States' concessions having little incentive.

It is clear that past US presidents' reliance on threats of force have not been effective in bringing the two countries toward improved relations or resolving issues of concern, such as Iran's nuclear program and regional matters. Therefore, a US president who has promised to choose diplomacy before coercion offers a new opportunity for reestablishing bilateral exchange. In stating his willingness to talk to Iranian leaders "without preconditions," Obama seems to be aware of the background of how the Bush administration's preconditions had evolved. However, assessing what to expect from Obama's administration has been difficult for Iranian policymakers and analysts. Obama's statements have been contradictory, calling for change and diplomacy while still characterizing Iran as a serious threat to the United States and the Middle East, and threatening to impose further sanctions in order to force Iran to stop its uranium enrichment program. Iranian leaders and analysts have been largely divided on the question. Gareth Porter reported that following the US elections, Iranian national security officials and political leaders were cautious regarding passing judgment on an Obama presidency. He found two views of Obama within the Iranian political establishment, which was echoed in the Iranian press. One was that his presidency would bring about a fundamental shift in US politics and thus an opportunity to change the nature of US-Iranian relations. The other was that President Obama, like any other US president, would be subject to pro-Israel and other political forces that would limit his approach to relations with Iran, including on the nuclear issue. It was important for Iranian leaders to determine whether Obama would really represent change in US policy, so as to enable them to consider "whether Iran should make any concessions in order to begin negotiations" with the next US president.

Several Iranian analysts based overseas have argued that the United States should delink the issues that concern them about Tehran—including its nuclear program, support of anti-Israel groups—in order to begin talks.[12] They suggest that in the end it may be mutual interests and concerns that bring the US and Iranian governments to the table, including their common interest in a stable Iraq and in preventing the reestablishment of a fundamentalist Sunni state under the Taliban in Afghanistan. They note the willingness of Tehran to cooperate on limited matters, as reflected in the Bush administration's efforts to take this approach, which included talks between US officials and senior Iranian diplomats in Europe in the aftermath of the US-led intervention in Afghanistan, as well as two meetings between the US Ambassador to Iraq, Ryan Crocker, and his Iranian counterpart in Baghdad during the latter part of the Bush administration. As such, these analysts suggest that the United States should set aside the nuclear issue and Iran's support for anti-Israel groups, and it should gain Tehran's cooperation on the two critical fronts for stability in Iraq and preventing the Taliban reestablishing themselves in Afghanistan in exchange for the lifting of sanctions and other economic incentives (although the US congress is likely to be against such actions which they may perceive as appeasement to Tehran). However, others have disagreed. President of the American Iranian Council Hooshang Amirahmadi argues that the issues that divide the United States and Iran "are part and parcel of other regional problems," including Iran's extreme isolation.[13] The makers of Iran's foreign policy hold the view that, instead of recognizing its own failure to solve the problems in Lebanon, the occupied territories, and Iraq, the United States has blamed Tehran for being behind all of the destabilizing forces in the region.

Obama's snub of Ahmadinejad's letter of congratulation was taken by some Iranians as a sign of hostility to the Iranian state and a suggestion that he would continue to treat Iran in much the same way as previous American presidents had.[14] Less than a week after the US election, an Iranian Foreign Ministry spokesman stated that Iran "should not expect much change or development in the strategic fundamentals of US foreign policy,"[15] which they perceive as establishing an "Israel-centered security arrangement in the Middle East."[16] Even before he took office, reports of president-elect Obama's plan to appoint Hillary Clinton—who in her bid for the Democratic Party nomination threatened to "obliterate" Iran—as his Secretary of State and his refusal to make a statement on the Israeli attacks on Gaza created skepticism about his promise of change, and Iranians perceived the Democrats as being more pro-Israel in their policies. Some Iranian commentators also suspected Obama's representation of himself as an antiwar president-elect, and one of them (Morad Velsi) pointed out Obama's support for boosting the war effort in Afghanistan and in Pashtunistan to weed out the Taliban and al-Qaeda.

Iranians will be watching carefully the Obama administration's response to the aftermath of the Israeli siege of Gaza, as many believe that any change that Obama might bring to US relations with Iran and to its "position in the world" is predicated on whether President Obama will act independently of "Zionist lobbies." Israel's relentless bombardment of Gaza has caused an outcry in Iran and around the world over the humanitarian disaster and the disproportionality of the Israeli attack.

However, some Iranians were ambivalent regarding Hamas' role in the conflict, and this suggests some differences among the people over the country's policy toward Israel. While some, like the reformists during Khatami's second term, feel that the rejection of Israel's existence is counterproductive to Iran's national interest, there are others who are committed to the constitution's stated support for Muslims, which is expressed through the centrality of the Israeli-Palestinian issue in Iranian foreign policy. Hard-line Iranian students even staged daily demonstrations and a six-day sit-in at the Tehran airport to demand that the government support volunteers in their efforts to go and fight in Gaza (although, according to Trita Parsi, Tehran did not provide hard support for Hamas, as Bush administration officials claimed).[17] Regardless of their positions on whether the Israel-Palestinian conflict should remain a central feature of their foreign policy, Iranians perceive the timing of the Israeli attacks in the last weeks of Bush's term in office, as well as its unilateral declaration of a ceasefire just prior to Obama's inauguration, as an opportunistic move to attack Hamas without facing consequences for its continued wreckage of Gaza's infrastructure. Iranians will judge whether Obama truly represents change by the extent to which he will be fair to Palestinian concerns in any post-conflict agreement and future efforts toward a two-state system.

For the most part, however, Tehran's approach to the Israeli-Palestinian conflict is driven by strategic concerns, and its support for Hamas and Islamic Jihad is largely symbolic, not as substantive as or comparable with its close relationship with Hezbollah, which is an organization of fellow Shiites in Lebanon, influenced by the ideology of the Iranian revolution. Parsi notes that Hamas, in contrast, has its ideological roots in the Sunni fundamentalism of Egypt's Muslim Brotherhood and that during the Iraq-Iran war (along with the PLO) expressed support for Saddam Hussein based on Arab nationalist sentiment. He also cites that Tehran has not committed any material support for the Palestinian groups when it did not coincide with Iran's immediate security concerns.[18] Various analysts have noted that Iran's hostility to the Arab-Israeli peace process is due to its exclusion from the talks. The strong Iranian sense of national identity and pride, rooted in a consciousness of the long history of its civilization, lends itself to the view that Iran should play a leadership role in the region. The Khomeinist approach of promoting the ideology of Iranian-style Islamic revolution internationally reflected the sense of the nation as a leader in world affairs. This has historically clashed with secular Arab nationalism. As a result, relations between Iran and Arab states have remained persistently strained due to their conflicting identity and ideological orientations. The fighting between Israel and Hamas during the last weeks of the Bush administration has further troubled Iran's relations with Arab states, whose slowness to condemn the impact of Israeli strikes was construed by some in Tehran as confirmation of a rumored understanding between Israel and secular Arab states who are leery of the democratically elected Hamas government. In particular, the Egyptian government's closing of the Rafah border crossing to Palestinians have created great tensions between Cairo and Tehran, despite earlier talk among Iranian leaders regarding normalization of relations with Egypt.

APPROACHING TEHRAN

Thus far, what is new in the dealings with Iran's nuclear program since Obama took office is a switch in the roles of the United States and the EU, with the former suggesting opportunities for talk and the latter increasing pressure on Iran. For example, in January 2009, European countries removed the MEK from their terrorism list, which unfreezes the group's assets and enables them to raise funds and resume activities, while the United States refused such a move and remains supportive of Iraqi government efforts to shut down the group's base in Iraq, as well as to prevent its acquisition of weapons.

However, having reignited tensions in the Middle East, the Israel-Hamas war and persisting exchange of fire after the ceasefire may undercut any new strategy that Obama may have for the region. The war has failed to resolve the conflict between the two sides, which promises to erupt again, as Israeli officials continue to assert, just as former Bush administration officials had, that Iran has been the instigating factor behind Hamas' strikes against Israel. Iranians perceive this effort to portray Hamas as an illegitimate, Iranian-backed group as a means to justify Israel's continued blockade of Gaza, as well as its ongoing attacks on the area to ostensibly force Hamas to disarm. With Likud candidate Benjamin Netanyahu elected as Israeli President in February 2009, it has become more difficult for the United States to delink issues, as he seeks to intensify efforts to sow division among Palestinian factions and mount pressure on Tehran. The characterization of Iran as the sponsor of the Hamas government in Gaza serves both to effectively postpone any meaningful resolution of political grievances among Israelis and Palestinians, which for many Iranians would reflect a lack of meaningful change in US policy, as well as to preserve an existing US policy to dismantle Iran's nuclear program under threat of further sanctions.

Given the indications of the past few years, Tehran would be willing to suspend its uranium enrichment program in exchange for technology for nuclear energy, removal of its case from the UN Security Council, and assurances about its security concerns, which include Israel's threats of striking Iranian facilities, as well as neighboring nuclear-armed

Pakistan and a destabilized Afghanistan, where, respectively, Pakistani Sunni extremists and the Taliban threaten to reemerge (both of which have strong anti-Shiite sentiments). Although some Iranians, including Khatami, a presidential candidate for the June 2009 election, have come to perceive the nuclear program as an obstacle to reestablishing Iran's relations with the Western world, most perceive a double standard in UN Security Council resolutions requiring Iran to submit to IAEA spot inspections. They are aware that Western claims of Iran's rapid progress toward producing weapons-grade uranium is based on overseas Iranian sources (including the National Council of Resistance of Iran, or NCRI, the political wing of the MEK), despite the 2007 US National Intelligence Estimate Report's conclusion that Iran was not moving toward such capability. Therefore, Iranians interpret the policy as evidence of an Israel-driven agenda in the United States, which, according to many news sources throughout and after the 2008 US election, is the basis for widespread pessimism among the Iranian population about any change in US-Iran relations.

Although at the time of writing this essay Obama had not yet made contact with Tehran, his cabinet appointments have suggested to Iranians that there was not likely to be any significant change in US policy toward Iran, at least in a manner that would satisfy the clerics in charge and also the critical Iranian analysts of US policy. Obama's retention of Robert Gates as US secretary of defense and his State Department appointments have been cause for pessimism. Gates has recently openly opposed a softened approach with Iran and has historically worked against anything less than a hard-line position. Iranian analysts have reacted negatively in particular to rumors that Obama would name Dennis Ross as special envoy to Iran. Ross was the chief negotiator in the Middle East talks for both Presidents George H. W. Bush and Bill Clinton and is affiliated with the Washington Institute for Near East Policy, which is viewed as a "pro-Israel" think tank, as well as with the Jerusalem-based Jewish People's Policy Planning Institute. Ross was also a key contributor to the Bipartisan Policy Center's September 2008 report, *Meeting the Challenge: US Policy Toward Iranian Nuclear Development*, which called for a strong stance against any perceived impertinent behavior on Iran's part, including deadlines for compliance with UN Security Council Resolutions to submit to IAEA inspections that, if not met, would lead to US attacks on Iran's nuclear and conventional military infrastructure. The report also calls for the expansion of US military forces in the Middle East and warns that European states make war more likely if they don't strengthen sanctions against Iran and end all commercial relations.[19]

Although Khatami offered a significant shift in Iranian policy in the Middle East and with the United States during his first two terms

as president, it is unlikely that his previous positions of rapprochement with Arab states and the United States as well as recognition
of Israel will have any chance to be repeated, given the developments
since the latter years of his presidency. At any rate, Khatami's chances
are not strong, as he poses a grave threat to the conservative domestic
agenda that even conservative critics of Ahmadinejad are likely to support Ahmadinejad in order to prevent a Khatami victory and a renewal
of liberalized domestic policies. For Iranians, domestic issues are still
key agendas, although their economic condition is tied to the isolation
resulting from the nuclear issue. However, given that foreign policy is
in the control of the Guardian Council, the Iranian vote for president
is normally based on domestic concerns. Regardless of their ideological inclination, many Iranians fear that domestic liberalizations will
encourage a new era of public protest that would divide and destabilize
the country. Therefore, according to many reports, many Iranians do
not bother to vote.

Since it is likely that the clerics in the Guardian Council will remain
in charge of Iranian foreign policy, I will conclude with a summary of
the policy shifts that they are likely to respond to. This group is guided
by a suspicion of a US grand design for the region, which includes support for Israel as well as undemocratic Arab states that do not welcome
a role for Iran. Therefore, successful talks between the United States
and Iran would have to address the following: the present exclusion of
Iran from matters concerning the region; the removal of the Iranian case
from the UN Security Council; a retraction of the designation of Iran
as a member of the "Axis of Evil"; and the severing of US contacts with
anti-regime elements based overseas, such as the NCRI. For the clerics in
charge of Iran's foreign policy, such shifts in US policy would represent
true "fundamental change." However, the Obama administration has
not indicated any moves toward changes approaching those on this list,
and rather persists in characterizing Iran's nuclear activities as "unaccept-
able." Obama's "bigger carrots, bigger sticks" approach to dealing with
Tehran—a donkey-cart analogy that is insulting to many Iranians—does
not promise any fundamental change in policy, and is likely to be only
a change in tactics. Without the lifting of sanctions that could alleviate
Iran's domestic economic crisis, a new president in Washington means
little to the average Iranian.

NOTES

1. The constitution is available online, for example, "Iran Online," at http://
   www.iranonline.com/iran/iran-info/Government/constitution-
   10.html (accessed February 12, 2009).

2. Christopher de Bellaigue, "New Man in Iran," *New York Review of Books,* Aug 11, 2005, 19–22.

3. From a summary by Akbar Ganji of the letter he sent to United Nations Secretary-General Ban Ki-moon in September 2007: Akbar Ganji, "The US and the Plight of the Iranians," *New York Review of Books* 54, 18 (November 22, 2007).

4. M. K. Bhadrakumar, "Biden May Hold Unclenched Iranian Hand," *Asia Times Online*, January 31, 2009, at http://www.atimes.com/atime/Middle_East/KA31Ak03.html.

5. "Iran Open to Wider Talks with Obama: Diplomat," *Tehran Times,* December 2, 2008, at http://www.tehrantimes.com/NCms/2007.asp?code=183814.

6. "Iran FM: Obama Win Shows Americans Want Change," *Iran Visual News Corps* (IranVNC), November 5, 2008 at http://www.iranvnc.com/en/home/.

7. Mina Ali Eslam, "Iran and the US Election Result," *Iran Diplomacy* (online), November 2, 2008, at http://www.irdiplomacy.ir/.

8. In his letter to the president-elect, Ahmadinejad also write that "nations of the world expect policies based on war, occupation, coercion, deception, humiliation of nations and imposition of discriminatory and unjust relations...would be changed into behavior based on justice and respect for rights of all human beings and nations, friendship and non-interference into internal affairs of others"; in *Ettala'at*, November 10, 2008.

9. Eslam, November 2, 2008.

10. Gareth Evans, "Iran Urges Obama to Start Talks—Now," *Asia Times Online*, December 16, 2008 at http://www.atimes.com/atimes/Middle_East/JL16Ak03.html.

11. Max Rodenbeck, "The Iran Mystery Case," *New York Review of Books*, January 15, 2009, 36.

12. Ali Ansari, *Confronting Iran: The Failure of American Foreign Policy and the Next Great Crisis in the Middle East* (Basic Books, 2006).

13. Hooshang Amirahmadi, "Iran and America: Can Obama Find a Political Solution?" Presented at the Le Cercle Conference, Washington, DC, November 14, 2008.

14. See Evan's series "The Tangled US-Iran Knot" in *Asia Times Online,* in which he cites numerous Iranian analysts on the importance of a respectful attitude in US dealings with Tehran, at http://www.atimes.com/atimes/Middle_East/JL13Ak02.html.

15. "Iran Not Expecting 'Much Change' under Obama," *Middle East Online*, November 10, 2008 at http://www.middle-east-online.com/english/?id=28710.

16. Hosein Alaie, "Sanctions Supporting Negotiations: The Future of Iran-U.S. Relations," *Iran Diplomacy* (online), January 15, 2009, at http://www.irdiplomacy.ir/index.php?Lang=en&Page=21TypeId=1&ArticleId-3704&BranchId=28&Action=ArticleBodyView.

17. Trita Parsi, "Israel, Gaza and Iran: Trapping Obama in Imagined Fault Lines," January 13, 2009, at http://www.huffingtonpost.com/trita-parsi/israel-gaza-and-iran-trap_b_157483.html.

18. Ibid.

19. *Meeting the Challenge: US Policy Toward Iranian Nuclear Development*, September 2008, at http://www.bipartisanpolicy.org/ht/a/GetDocumentAction/i/8448.

11

How Pakistan Viewed the US Election Campaign

Moonis Ahmar

Introduction

Perhaps no presidential election campaign in the United States in the recent past was a source of as immense interest to the people of Pakistan as the one that was carried out in the year 2008. The whole world took a great interest in the critical election campaign of Democratic Party candidate Barack Obama and the candidate of Republican Party John McCain. However, in Pakistan the situation was different because of the periodic US drone attacks on the tribal areas and the collateral damage caused as a result of these attacks, the Bush administration's rhetoric that Pakistan should do more to eliminate what Washington alleged were "safe heavens" for Taliban/al-Qaeda in the tribal areas of Pakistan, and the serious concerns in the Western circles about the deepening of chaos, disorder, and insecurity in some parts of Pakistan because of violence, terrorism, and unabated political unrest.

If one tries to analyze dominant perception in Pakistan about the difference in the approach and policy of Democratic and Republican Parties vis-à-vis Islamabad, hardly any qualitative difference could be figured out except that the latter is perceived o have some soft corner for Pakistan. But, the traditional "tilt" of the Republican Party in favor of Pakistan was not to be taken for granted even during the post-9/11 period, particularly when the images of Guantanamo Bay prison in Cuba, Abu-Ghraib jail in Iraq, and the Bengram detention center in Afghanistan shaped a highly negative perception against the United States not only among the majority of the people in Pakistan but also in other parts of the world. Obama's Afro-American heritage and his pledge to provide a better American leadership for a "just" world order generated some hope and optimism for Pakistani people who considered him a "lesser evil" than his counterpart, whose party was in power for eight years and had left a highly negative imprint on the minds of the people of Pakistan, particularly for their role in the violence ridden Muslim countries.

"Caught between the devil and the deep blue sea," for the Pakistani people, Obama's candidacy sounded better than McCain's, despite the former's election rhetoric in which he had used strong words in terms of targeting Pakistani tribal areas in order to eliminate the "safe heavens" of al-Qaeda. A section of Pakistani society during the US election campaign believed that it generally did not matter who won the American presidential elections because candidates from both parties were influenced by the pro-Indian and Jewish lobbies and were not considerate about Pakistan. According to this school of thought, despite Pakistan's critical role in the "War on Terror" and the enormous losses that it has incurred since 9/11, Washington is suspicious of Pakistan's seriousness in its efforts to curb terrorism and is threatening to continue drone attacks on its tribal areas. Anti-Americanism in Pakistan, which has permeated far and wide, gets its strength from the US policy of providing unlimited support to Israel, the occupation of Iraq and Afghanistan by the US-led coalition forces, and Washington's failure to redress Muslim grievances in different parts of the world. The 2008 election campaign in the United States was perceived by proponents of this school of thought as mere sustenance of the status quo in American foreign policy. However, this view still maintained room for anticipating a shift, even if only minor, of approaches and policies on some critical issues.

This article examines Pakistani perceptions on the US presidential elections by responding to the following questions:

1. How far were the 2008 elections in the United States *perceived* differently by the Pakistani people as compared to previous election campaigns?
2. What were the *expectations* and *fears* in Pakistan regarding the Democratic Party winning at the polls?
3. What is the level of *understanding* in Pakistan about American elections?
4. To what extent did the US presidential election campaign become a *source* of debate and discussion in Pakistani circles?

US ELECTIONS AND PAKISTAN

Issues having far-reaching impact on the state and society of Pakistan, like religious extremism, ethno-nationalism, violence, terrorism, judicial crisis, economic stagnation, political polarization, and weak democratic institutions also influenced Pakistan-US relations. Although, most of the aforementioned issues were not as such on the agenda of the Democratic or Republican Party election campaigns, both presidential candidates, Obama and McCain, considered Pakistan and some of its critical issues, such as terrorism, religious extremism, nuclear proliferation, and democracy, fundamental to American interests. While the 2008 US election campaign was dominated by domestic issues, foreign policy matters influencing America also figured high.

Four factors should be taken into account with regard to Pakistan and the 2008 American elections. First is the image that was depicted in the American media about the growing religious fanaticism in Pakistan, particularly the burning of girls' schools and targeting women in public places by religious fanatics. The failure of the Pakistani state to establish its writ on the Federally Administered Tribal Areas (FATA) and in the settled district of Swat of North Western Frontier Province (NWFP) also became a source of reference in the US election campaign. News reports of countless suicide attacks killing and injuring hundreds of innocent people and of sectarian violence in different areas of Pakistan portrayed the world's second biggest Muslim country as the "most dangerous place" on earth. Periodic drone attacks on the tribal areas of Pakistan and other military measures taken by the United States to neutralize what America perceived as terrorist hideouts got instant approval from the US presidential candidates. When Pakistan came to be seen as the most dangerous place on earth, the message was clear that the safety and security of the American people was at stake because of the remnants of al-Qaeda groups holed up in the tribal belt and other parts of Pakistan bordering Afghanistan. But, such an approach had a serious backlash in Pakistan because the majority of the casualties from these drone attacks were innocent people rather than terrorists.

Moreover, the deterioration of law and order in Pakistan and a serious leadership crisis in the post-Musharraf era raised questions about political stability and the rationale of Islamabad participating in the US-led "War on Terror." The flaring up of the squabble for power between the ruling Pakistan People's Party Parliamentarians (PPPP) and the opposition Pakistan Muslim League (N) following the refusal of the former to reinstate the deposed Chief Justice of the Supreme Court and other deposed senior judges[1] may have compelled the US presidential candidates to pursue a cautious approach on Pakistan.

Second, the perception in Pakistan and in other parts of the world that the US election campaign was in a way being "fought" in the tribal areas of Pakistan made some sense. Both Obama and McCain in their election campaigns were quite forceful in their resolve to track down the al-Qaeda leadership, particularly Osama Bin Laden who in their opinion was hiding in the "safe heavens" of Pakistan. The Republican Party and its candidate McCain were particularly vocal on the issue of Bin Laden and showed resolve to eliminate the al-Qaeda leadership in order to ensure the security of the American people. The intensity of US drone attacks prior to the November 4 presidential elections also proved the desperation of the sitting Republican Party administration to catch the most-wanted terrorist, hoping that such a success would translate into electoral gains and turn around the Republican Party's plunging poll results.

Were the people living in the tribal areas of Pakistan then victims of US election campaign politics or did the contesting parties genuinely believe that the al-Qaeda leadership had their sanctuaries in these areas? In fact, the US drone attacks on FATA areas despite strong criticism of Pakistan proved the link between American elections and the assumed presence of al-Qaeda leadership in the tribal belt bordering Afghanistan. The perception that the US election campaign was being fought under the name of assumed al-Qaeda sanctuaries in the tribal areas of Pakistan thus seemed to make sense.

Third, the perception that growing chaos and instability in Pakistan following the loss of the state's writ in FATA, the district of Swat in NWFP and parts of Baluchistan, raised serious doubts about the safety of its nuclear arsenal. While the state of Pakistan denied any threat of Pakistan's nuclear weapons falling into the control of religious extremist groups, some raised serious concerns about a scenario in which the Pakistani state was taken over by the group of Islamic extremists having their links with al-Qaeda. The gory drama at the "Red Mosque" in Islamabad in the summer of 2007 and the gradual taking over of territory in Swat by the Taliban groups, covered in the US media and in the think tanks, caused increased concern about the capability of the Pakistani state to withstand the pressures of religious fanatics. Though they were miles away from Islamabad, the activities of the Taliban in the settled areas of Pakistan were considered a nightmare not only by the Western elite of Pakistan but by all those who had never underestimated the intentions of Pakistani Taliban and their al-Qaeda supporters to take over the structures and institutions of the state and the nuclear arsenal. Finally, fragile democracy in Pakistan and particularly weak political institutions also caused concern in the US election campaign. Both Republican and Democratic Party candidates took the position of strengthening democracy in Pakistan, but Obama was critical of the Bush administration's rendering of support to what he termed Musharraf's dictatorial rule. Viewed in the context of militancy, extremism, terrorism, and the gradual loss of the government's writ in volatile areas of Pakistan, the issue of democratic stability and the capability of the Pakistani state and society to deal with the menace of religious extremism has been a source of enormous concern in the United States.

It was in the initial stages of the launching of the US election campaign that moves to remove General Pervez Musharraf from the presidency gained ground. It was believed in Pakistan that without seeking endorsement from Washington, the ruling PPPP-led coalition would not be able to remove Musharraf from power. It was only when PPPP and PML (N) decided to impeach Musharraf that the Bush administration expressed its neutrality in the whole episode of getting rid of the Pakistani President. However, unlike the soft tone of the Republican Party on President Musharraf, Obama expressed his criticism over the manner in which Musharraf failed to curb militancy and al-Qaeda/Taliban influence in the tribal areas and called for strengthening Pakistan's democratic institutions instead of supporting one individual officeholder.

On August 1, 2007, Senator Obama delivered an important speech in which he made critical remarks about the manner in which President Musharraf was handling the al-Qaeda threat in the perceived "safe heavens" in the tribal areas of Pakistan. He stated:

> Let me make this clear. There are terrorists holed in those mountains who murdered 3,000 Americans. They are plotting to strike again. It was a terrible mistake to fail to act when we had a chance to take out an al-Qaeda leadership meeting in 2005.[2]

He warned that he would send troops into Pakistan to hunt terrorists even without local permission if warranted: "If we have actionable intelligence about high-value terrorist targets and President Musharraf won't act, we will."[3] Likewise, in the presidential debate held in October 2008, Obama talked about Pakistan and the "War on Terror" by asserting that, "[i]f we have Osama bin Laden in our sights and the Pakistan government is unable or unwilling to take them [*sic*] out, then I think we have to act and we will take them out. We will kill bin Laden; we will crush al-Qaeda. That has to be our biggest national security priority." There was a sharp reaction in Pakistan to the statements of Obama as Pakistan's Foreign Office warned that "[a] military invasion could be risky, given Pakistan's hostile terrain and the suspicion of its warrior-minded tribesmen against uninvited outsiders." It was argued that Obama's harsh tone vis-à-vis Pakistan was because of the remarks made by his rival Hillary Clinton in which she questioned his abilities to be Commander in Chief of the US armed forces. The August 1 speech of Senator Obama, in which he had threatened to send the US military in order to track down al-Qaeda leadership hiding in the Pakistani tribal belt, was viewed adversely in Pakistan.

An editorial in a Pakistani daily talked about Obama's threatening posture toward Pakistan with respect to launching strikes to weed out what he called terrorist hideouts. Taking a positive note of Obama's tone on Pakistan, the editorial argued:

> The Democrat hopeful has spoken of being willing to conduct attacks within Pak territory, and on focusing on Afghanistan rather than Iraq. In contrast, Mc Cain's approach has been more conciliatory, focusing on the need to engage with Pakistan. This has been interpreted to mean that Obama will be bad for Pakistan, Mc Cain potentially better. But there is much more to the issue than this. While Obama has taken a tougher line on Pakistan, it is quite possible this approach may stand us in a good stead.[4]

It was not only the print and electronic media of Pakistan that took an offensive position on Obama's threatening posture on their country, various political parties and groups expressed serious concerns and reservations on what they saw as the Democratic Party's traditional hostile posture on Pakistan. One can agree or disagree with the domestic voices in Pakistan over Obama's election rhetoric, but concerns were also expressed against the Republican Party. After all, not only the people of Pakistan but also those in the Muslim world had developed a strong dislike against the Bush administration, and they considered the Republican Party no different than the Democratic Party in terms of issues sensitive to them, such as strong, unwavering support to Israel, far too often equating Islam with terrorism, and generally pursuing an offensive policy against Muslims, particularly since the terrorist events of September 11, 2001. For the Pakistani people, primarily those living in the tribal areas bordering Afghanistan, their lives had become miserable because of constant US drone attacks and the collateral damage inflicted by them on innocent people. For them, there was no difference between candidates from the Democratic or Republican Parties as both were seen as pursuing an aggressive, imprudent approach in dealing with the issue of terrorism.

For the majority of the people of Pakistan, the United States is not considered as a country that is either irrelevant or indifferent to their critical issues because of three main reasons. First, there is a history of Pakistan-US strategic, political, and economic ties since the early 1950s to date. This relation had several ups and downs on account of various reasons, ranging from Pakistan's role as a frontline state during the Cold War and the Soviet military intervention in Afghanistan, to the suspension of Pakistan military assistance during the 1965 and 1971 Indo-Pakistan wars, and to the imposition of democracy and nuclear related sanctions during the 1990s; one can argue that there is a love-hate relationship between the two countries. As a major non-NATO ally and a close strategic partner of the United States since September 11, 2001,

Pakistan is, however, not at ease with periodic drone attacks on its tribal areas and the tone used by some American officials about what they allege Islamabad's failure to "do more" in their efforts to get rid of the "safe heavens" of al-Qaeda and Taliban in the tribal areas of Pakistan.

Second, the perception in Pakistan about deep-rooted American involvement in the affairs of their country is also an important cause of friction in Pakistan-American relations. With the deepening of American involvement in Iraq and Afghanistan and its major support to Israel, the surge in anti-Americanism not only in Pakistan but also in other Muslim countries has been quite noticeable. During the long eight years of the Bush administration, in the post-9/11 era a large groundswell of anti-American sentiment has gathered in Pakistan, particularly in the conservative sections of society. If the elite of Pakistan were a beneficiary of the enormous US economic and military aid, the common people living in abject poverty considered America a major reason for their plight. Under the heavy influence of a clergy that turned anti-American since the termination of US engagement in Afghanistan following the departure of Soviet forces from that country, many ordinary people were corrupted by anti-American sentiments and were indoctrinated to launch a Jihad against the West. Madrassas were used to deepen anti-Americanism by a radical section of the clergy and religious students were lured by them to join the Jihad against the infidels. In light of this, and with more and more American military engagements in Iraq and Afghanistan and the US drone attacks on the tribal areas of Pakistan, hatred against America surged in some sections of Pakistani society.

Third, with the permeation of militancy and radicalism, particularly in the Pashtun belt of NWFP and Baluchistan, the stage was set for a direct clash between Pakistan's military and the religious militant groups. The growing American pressure on the then quasi-military regime of Musharraf to do more against the alleged terrorist groups hiding in the tribal areas and other hideouts of Pakistan made things difficult for the Pakistan Army. A military operation by the Pakistani military in FATA on what was seen as the direction of Washington was counterproductive and caused sharp reaction not only from the opposition parties but also among other groups, both religious and political. It was under these conditions that Pakistan observed the launching of the campaign for the 2008 US presidential election.

Pakistan as a Factor in US Polls

It is unrealistic to expect American voters and candidates contesting for the offices of president, vice-president, senator, and representative to focus merely on Pakistan. As a major global power, there are numerous domestic and foreign policy issues that impact on election campaigns

and presidential debates in America. However, in the 2008 US elec
tions, Pakistan was discussed more prominently, both in the contex
of the "War on Terror" and the dangerous situation in some territorie
of Pakistan where state authority and control was gradually being chal
lenged by the forces of religious and ethnic extremism. The Pakistan
population, already affected by the US-led military campaigns agains
terrorism, viewed the US elections with a semblance of hope and fear
hope in the sense that a new face in the White House may do some
thing to pursue a rational approach on targeting al-Qaeda groups insid
Pakistan; fear because of the possibility that no change will take plac
whether the presidency is claimed by the Republican or Democrati
party candidate. People living along the Pakistan-Afghan border wer
afraid that they would continue to face US drone attacks and other form
of military incursions. A feeling of despair loomed large in some section
of Pakistani society when Obama threatened to strike against what he
termed "terrorist hideouts" in the tribal areas of Pakistan. As pointe
out by a Pakistani writer:

> It really does not matter to us which party is in power in the U.S.
> American interests, or at least the perception of American interests, is
> what drives American policy towards Pakistan or any one else in the
> world. We would do well to remember that it was under Bill Clinton
> that American cruise missiles hit Afghanistan for the first time. The
> differences between the Republican and Democrats are limited to their
> domestic arena, and at best to the style of international diplomacy. Yes,
> Obama being quite possibly the first black president does send a good
> message to the world about America.[5]

A similar tone was struck by another Pakistani writer, although hi
focus was less on party affiliation:

> On the one hand, we have the charismatic and eloquent Obama, who
> most Pakistanis have taken a strong liking to because he promises a
> break with what are generally conceived by the common people here
> as pro-military dictatorship policies of the grand old party. But Obama
> has also engaged in rhetoric that scares most Pakistanis. The idea of
> a US attack on the NWFP isn't so much an issue of sovereignty as
> repercussions.[6]

Therefore, the divided perception among the majority of Pakistanis
on Obama and McCain was actually reflected in the dichotomy of hope
and fear, on one hand, and, along with that, in the indifference regarding who would actually occupy the White House. The future of US
involvement in Afghanistan and the clear stance of both Republican and

Democratic Parties' presidential candidates that they would not reduce or even end American military presence in that war torn country in the near future was seen as already implying more suffering and ordeals for the people of Pakistan. Particularly, Obama's pledge to increase the US military presence in Afghanistan in order to combat the Taliban and al-Qaeda threat also seemed to indicate that more pressure would be applied on Pakistan to "do more" to dismantle "safe heavens" of terrorists in the tribal areas of Pakistan.

However, Obama's commitment to democracy and democratic institutions in Pakistan raised expectations in some circles about possible US assistance for a people-focused, instead of state-oriented, US policy vis-à-vis Pakistan. Consequently, it was argued that "Obama is pledging to promote democracy in Pakistan, increase non-military aid to Islamabad, institute greater scrutiny of military aid, strike inside Pakistani territory if and when Islamabad is unwilling or unable to move on actionable intelligence about the presence of high value targets on its soil, send at least two more brigades of US troops to Afghanistan, build pressure on President Hamid Karzai to curb corruption in the Afghanistan government, control the drug trade, and establish the state's writ in much of the countryside."[7]

A Pakistani newspaper report shows how much US policy toward Pakistan had become politicized in the United States in the context of the presidential race:

> Pakistan, a key US allay in the war against terror, has also become a major election issue and is discussed even in congressional races otherwise dominated by local issues. At a debate in Kentucky, Republican Senator Mitch McConnell accused the Democrats of wanting to bomb Islamabad while Al-Qaeda leaders were hiding in the tribal region bordering Afghanistan. Congressman Gary Ackerman, Chairman of a House panel on South Asia, called Pakistan the most dangerous country on earth and accused it of using American dollars for buying weapons to fight India. His stance, obviously, won him the support of the powerful Indian-American community, which donated generously to his re-election campaign.[8]

Perceiving Pakistan as an "arc of crisis" and a "dangerous" country where terrorist groups can maintain sanctuaries, which in turn strengthens the US view of Pakistan as a major threat to the United States, was not the only factor that left its imprint on the US election campaign. The US perception was also affected by hostility between India and Pakistan. Islamabad's and New Delhi's drive to win over candidates contesting in the American elections depicted the polarized nature of the Indo-Pakistan relationship. Given both countries'

interest in carrying favor with the United States, it is not surprising
that this dynamic also impacted on American elections. Lobbying for
support from members of the US Congress seems to be the most crucial task of both Indian and Pakistani groups in the United States.
In addition to depicting Pakistan as a hub of terrorism and religious
militancy, the Indian lobby also embarked on a media campaign. This
campaign peaked when Indo-Pakistan tensions almost boiled over during the Kargil crisis, after the attack on the Indian parliament, and in
the post-Mumbai terrorist attacks. Yet, it was argued that Obama "is
also the first presidential candidate to stress the importance of trying
to facilitate a better understanding between Pakistan and India and to
try to resolve the Kashmir crisis so that they can focus not on India, but
on the situation with those militants. This has upset some Indians, who
stress that Kashmir can only be resolved bilaterally, but a helpful nudge
from Washington, if it can promote peace and understanding in the
region, should be welcome."[9] However, the reservations of India vis-à-
vis third-party mediation puts a limitation on the role Washington may
play in the New Delhi-Islamabad peace process and the resolution of
the Kashmir conflict.

One may term as pure fantasy the opinion held in Pakistan about the
nexus of an Indo-Jewish lobby in the United States to defame Pakistan.
However, there is a considerable convergence of interests and perceptions
between India and Israel on some of the issues that also involve Pakistan,
such as nuclear proliferation, support bases for al-Qaeda in the tribal
areas of Pakistan, and the role of various *Jihadi* organizations having
transnational linkages. To be sure, some political and religious groups in
Pakistan exploit any Indo-US-Jewish "axis" and use it to their advantage,
but most of their contentions are merely rhetorical in nature, are strictly
for political consumption, and are far from reality.

Like the media in many other countries, the Pakistani media, both
print and electronic, took much interest in covering the US presidential
elections, and contributed to forming opinions among their readers, lis-
teners, and viewers. Thus, it was pointed out how much coverage the US
election was in fact actually receiving in Pakistan:

> The recent US presidential elections seem to have caught the attention
> of Pakistan's media in a big way. This is obvious from the fact that 33 out
> of the 50-odd television channels were directly relaying American elec-
> tion results with full bloom commentaries from academics, retired civil
> and military bureaucrats, and all those who could read, write and speak
> English or were involved with the media in some shape or form.[10]

Moreover, Pakistani media clearly and directly made the connection
between the US presidential race and what the outcome may hold in

store for Pakistan. In other words, the relevance for Pakistan was center-stage, as the following report indicates:

> The debate about the merits of various American presidential candidates has focused almost completely in the Pakistani media on one of the two factors—their personal history or chemistry with Pakistan on the one hand, and the relative stance of their political parties regarding our country or the other. Both of these issues are trivial and of no consequence. In the current match up, much has been made of the Democrat Party's nominee Senator Barack Obama's statements that he would support unilateral American action inside Pakistani territory to attack Al-Qaeda leaders. Such has been the chorus of disapproval from Pakistanis both within Pakistan and in the US, that it has drowned out of the certain (muted) euphoria over the discovery that the Obama had close friends from Sindh whose homes he had visited during his college days. But if any Pakistani had any illusions about Obama's rival, the Republican Party candidate John McCain having greater concern for Pakistani's territorial sovereignty, they were certainly disabused of such notions during the presidential debates. McCain attacked Obama for his pronouncements about Pakistan, but mainly over style. "You do what you have to do" he told the American public, "but you don't say it publicly." So the choice for us is between some one who supports disregarding Pakistan sovereignty on the one hand, and on the other, some one who supports the same line but just doesn't want us to know.[11]

One negative and threatening statement by Obama about Pakistan raised several questions about his intentions. People in Pakistan jumped to conclusions when they heard Obama using tough language indicating his willingness to act tough if elected. They saw him talking tough about Pakistan and threatening to take direct action against what the US called a strategic ally in the "War on terror." Reflecting a critical sentiment of such talk, a Pakistani writer lamented that, "Obama's references to Pakistan have however been disconcerting, especially his comment that, we must make it clear that if Pakistan cannot or will not act, we will take out high-level terrorist targets like Osama bin Laden, if we have them in our sights."[12]

However, in actual fact, Obama was not that critical or negative about Pakistan during his election campaign as was perceived in some Pakistani circles. In an interview given to CNN, he said, "now you have got a fledging democratic government. We have to help their efforts to democratize. That means, by the way, not just providing military aid. It means also helping them to provide concrete solutions to the poverty and lack of education that exists in Pakistan. So I want to increase nonmilitary aid to Pakistan. We will have to make the case that the biggest threat to

Pakistan now is not India which has been the historic enemy. It is actually militants within their borders. And if we can get them to refocus on that's going to be critical for our success, not just in establishing Pakistan but also in finishing the job in Afghanistan."[13] Nevertheless, actually reducing or neutralizing the feeling of anti-Americanism that seems to have permeated far and wide, particularly in the areas along the Pakistan-Afghan border, even after a review of US policy on Afghanistan under a new Obama administration, would remain a difficult task.

Two important perceptions that prevailed in Pakistan about Obama's election rhetoric on targeting al-Qaeda safe heavens relate to the notion of the Democratic Party's traditional bias against Pakistan. The first view is that Obama also will not be able to undermine the traditional Zionist and Indian influence in the US power structures and that the United States will thus continue to follow the policy of his predecessors. That would mean sustaining political and military pressure on Pakistan and continuing drone attacks on its tribal areas. The second perception relates to the frustration that one can see permeating in American official circles over the looming failure in Afghanistan and the escalation of Taliban activities. As a result of such frustration, the Obama administration may act out of desperation and intensify its cross border attacks on what it perceives as "safe heavens" of terrorists in the tribal area of Pakistan. Such a scenario will have a serious backlash and may lead to a further surge of anti-Americanism, which would constitute a major setback for the present regime in Islamabad.

It seems Obama is in fact proceeding with a policy in line with the threats made by him to Pakistan during the election campaign. Since he moved into the White House, several drone attacks have indeed taken place in Pakistan's tribal areas and have claimed hundreds of lives. The more the Taliban intensify their attacks on US and NATO forces in Afghanistan, the more one can expect retaliation from the American side, and not only against the Taliban fighters in Afghanistan but also their counterparts in Pakistan. In addition, it is not anymore the Pakistani Taliban alone that poses a threat to the regime in Islamabad, as they seem to have begun coordinating with other like-minded groups to go after pro-American targets in Pakistan.

It would not be solely America's nightmare but a nightmare for the West as a whole if the Pakistani Taliban are given a free hand, which would then allow them to consolidate their political and administrative hold over some of the areas that are under their control. In such a scenario, the Afghan Taliban, who are already pitted against the US-led coalition forces, will not only get a boost but will intensify their pressure on foreign forces who, to a large extent, are not only from Western countries but also happen to be Christians. It was in this context that the United States expressed its reservations over reaching separate "peace deals" with the Taliban groups in FATA and in Swat. With respect to issues faced by the broader Muslim world, the US election campaign was about a fight against terrorism, particularly al-Qaeda and the Taliban. Some years earlier, it had been argued that the real threat for the United States came from *al-Qaeda* and its leadership and not from the Taliban. The latter had a local and narrow base, it was argued, whereas the former operated internationally. Now it seems that such a perception has changed because of the massive attacks launched by the Taliban fighters particularly against the US forces and their refusal to lay down arms and join the Afghan political scene.

Is it then not paranoia on the part of the United States and its policymakers to view the Taliban as a major threat to their interests in Afghanistan and Pakistan because of their growing support base and their capacity to withstand heavy US aerial and ground attacks? Fear, frustration, and fatigue seem to have added an extra dimension and contributed to an aggressive American policy in Afghanistan. This political environment in fact seems to have influenced the Obama administration's approach in dealing with such a critical issue. It was the al-Qaeda and Taliban factor in Afghanistan and also in Pakistan that prompted Obama to take a hard-line stand during his election campaign. His resolve to end the war in Iraq and to increase the number of American forces in Afghanistan also demonstrated how the Democrats viewed the nature of the threat, a threat that is getting even more critical and serious day by day and stems from a country that, in the not too distant past, was called the "Vietnam of the Soviets." Now in power and enjoying Democratic majorities in both chambers of Congress, Obama's biggest test case in the foreign policy arena is how to deal with the situation in Afghanistan and in Pakistan.

IMPLICATIONS FOR PAKISTAN

When the US election campaign was going on, in Pakistan three different opinions shaped the country's perception on the possible impact of the election on Pakistan. First, both presidential candidates, Obama and McCain, pursued a convergent approach on sustaining the US military presence in Afghanistan and sustaining pressure on Pakistan to act against what it alleges are terrorist groups sneaking into Afghanistan from the Pakistani Pashtun areas bordering Afghanistan. In such a scenario, the United States would apply more pressure on Pakistan because of what Washington sees as assistance rendered to the Afghan Taliban by their counterparts in the tribal areas of Pakistan. Second, even under an Obama presidency, it may be difficult for him to facilitate any major change in American foreign policy objectives, particularly on those issue areas that the Bush administration had formulated. In this context, policies regarding combating terrorism, especially against the Islamic extremist groups, stand out. The influence of neoconservatives in shaping the policy framework with the blessings of the Bush administration cannot be underestimated, because of their deep penetration in sensitive US intelligence and security bureaucracies. Merely by announcing the closure of Guantanamo Bay in a certain period of time, President Obama will not be able to bring any qualitative change in dealing with issues that cause militancy particularly in the Muslim world. The third opinion held in Pakistan is that US patronage to Israel, which is an important reason for deepening anti-Americanism in different parts of the world, will continue during the Obama administration because the new US President, despite his resolve to strive for a just world order, cannot take a position against the aggressive and militaristic policies of Israel. As a result, it is unrealistic to assume there would be any positive shift in the opinion of people as far as anti-Americanism is concerned, and that holds for the Pakistani people, too.

How Pakistanis thought about the impact of the American elections on their country is summarized by a Pakistani political and defense analyst:

> Pakistanis are faced with a paradox. Barack Obama is a candidate after their own heart but the more pragmatic John McCain is an experienced warrior who is certainly more sensitive to Pakistan. Obama would lean over backwards in avoiding being labeled soft on Muslims because of his middle name "Hussein." While Obama has set the imagination afire, Mc Cain appears too cold for Pakistani calculations. While VP choices really do not matter, Joseph Biden is known to lean towards Pakistan. Sarah Palin would spell disaster for us. As the symbol of the Christian Right she clearly despises Muslims, Pakistan would be in jeopardy should McCain, now 72, not survive his term.[14]

Pakistan's ambassador to the United States, Hussain Haqqani, in his comments given to a private American TV channel was straightforward regarding his views about the impact that the US presidential elections might have on his country. He said that "the outcome of the U.S. presidential election will have no effect on Pakistan. That relations between Pakistan and the U.S. would rather depend on steps taken by the political leadership of both countries. The stance of the U.S. presidential candidates would be different after the elections, as who ever won would make policies in line with the international situation."[15]

A fundamental question raised in Pakistan that concerns the implications of American elections on this country is this: "Should Obama become the next president, will he attack Pakistan?" According to one point of view, that "question has already been answered by Obama himself. Yes, he will. So, how the future relations play out between Islamabad and Washington DC require no brain surgery . If we need money, arms and American goodwill, then jolly well, we will have to do what the new president—Obama and McCain tells us to do."[16]

Another question that is important for Pakistan and raised during the US election campaign was "whether a Republican or Democrat president will be a more advantageous interlocutor for Pakistan?" One response to this question was that,

"the primary answer to this lies within Pakistan itself. How effectively do we negotiate for and are able to promote Pakistan's interests depends on skillful diplomacy, sound politics and governance at home and our use of the leverages available to us at this juncture. This debate on whether the Republicans or the Democrats are 'better' for Pakistan betrays a lack of understanding of how nations seek to promote their foreign policy interests. There are some lessons for Pakistan in the way Indians pursued their nuclear deal and their trade and defense interests with successive U.S. administrations. It is a tribute to India's skillful diplomacy and politics that while the Democrat Clinton initiated in late 1998 the beginning of a strategic opening with India, the Republican Bush was keen to practically implement this strategic relationship."[17]

The question of how the next US administration would deal with the issue of the Indo-Pakistan conflict over Kashmir and the conflict ridden Afghanistan was addressed by Obama himself in his interview given to Rachel Meadow of MSNBC, in which he expressed the hope that, "we should probably try to facilitate a better understanding between Pakistan and India and try to resolve the Kashmir crisis. The most important thing we are going to have to do with respect to Afghanistan, is actually deal with Pakistan…And we have got to say to the Pakistan people, we are not just going to find a dictator in order for us to feel comfortable with who we are dealing with. We are going to respect democracy. But, we do have expectations in terms of being a partner against terrorism."[18]

Finally, how the next US administration may deal with Pakistan on economic, trade, and other related matters also needs to be analyzed, because it is not solely the issue of terrorism that shapes Pakistan-US relations. Critically important is also how Washington approaches and responds to Islamabad's grave economic predicament.

A study, which was conducted by Lisa Curtis of the Heritage Foundation, a conservative US think tank, and other leading American experts on South Asia, produced some suggestions for the next American administration on how to deal with Pakistan on a host of issues. According to the study, "the U.S. should support Pakistan in fields like economy, trade, health, education and infrastructure development and strengthen cooperation in areas which bring economic opportunities to people and this way win hearts and minds of the people...Each strike [by a US drone] carries the cost of undermining US long-term objectives of stabilizing Pakistan and preventing radical forces from strengthening in the country. The next US administration must broaden its cooperation with Pakistan beyond its immediate security interests as a way forward to sustainable peace and development in the region."[19] But, the drone attacks on the tribal areas of Pakistan have continued unabated despite the assumption of power by the new American administration. This has been seen by many in various Pakistani circles as clear confirmation of their worst fears that no qualitative change will take place in American policy toward Afghanistan and the tribal areas of Pakistan despite the change in the White House.

It will, however, be too early to pass judgment on how much continuity in fact exists between the previous and the current US administrations with regard to their policies in Afghanistan and Pakistan. Any role of the United States in dealing with the situation that emanated from the launching of the "long march" by lawyers and political party activists, who demanded the restoration in office of the deposed Chief Justice, also demonstrated the concern prevailing in the Obama administration about the danger to Pakistan's domestic stability. It was probably the involvement of higher-ups in the US administration that helped diffuse the crisis and prevent political chaos. Commenting on the decision of the Pakistan government to reinstate the Chief Justice of the Supreme Court, US State Department spokesman Robert Wood said that, "Secretary of State Hillary Clinton, special U.S. envoy Richard Holbrooke and the U.S. ambassador in Islamabad Anne Patterson were very involved in trying to calm tensions in Pakistan. So the U.S. was involved in that regard."[20] For Washington, the escalation of political crisis would have jeopardized Pakistan's critical role on the "War on terror." Therefore, stability in Pakistan is central to the Obama administration, and the March political confrontation between the government and the opposition was seen by the United States as a major threat to its interests in the region.

NOTES

1. As a result of the campaign launched by the lawyer's community of Pakistan and backed by various political parties, namely PML (N), the government succumbed to popular pressure and announced the restoration of the deposed Chief Justice of Supreme Court, Iftikhar Muhammad Chaudhry, and judges of superior courts on March 16, 2009. For further information, see "People Power Restores Judge in Pakistan," *The Guardian Weekly*, March 20–26, 2009, 4.

2. Javed Ansari, "Challenges for Obama," *South Asia* (Karachi) December 2008, 18.

3. "Tough Talk on Pakistan from Obama," Reuters, August 1, 2007, http://reuters.com/article/domesticNews/idUSNO132206420070801 (accessed February 4, 2009).

4. See "The Obama Era," *The News International* (Karachi), October 18, 2008.

5. Hasan Zaidi, "Do US Polls Really Matter to Us?" *Dawn* (Karachi), October 29, 2009.

6. Yasser Latif Hamdani, "Obama Is Better," *The News International* (Karachi), October 31, 2008.

7. Jehangir Khattak, "Obamanic and Pakistan," *Dawn* (Karachi), October 30, 2008.

8. For further information, see "Pakistan A Major Poll Issue in US," *Dawn* (Karachi), November 1, 2008.

9. Tariq Fatemi, "A Reason for Hope," *Dawn* (Karachi), November 6, 2008.

10. Ayesha Siddiqa, "How We See the US Polls," *Dawn* (Karachi), November 7, 2008.

11. See Hasan Zaidi, "Do US Polls Really Matter to Us?" *Dawn* (Karachi), October 29, 2008.

12. Tariq Fatemi, "A Reason for Hope."

13. Anwar Iqbal, "Obama to Increase Non-military Aid," *Dawn* (Karachi), November 2, 2008.

14. Ikram Sehgel, "US Presidential Home Stretch," *The News International* (Karachi), October 30, 2008.

15. See news item, "U.S. Presidential Election Will Not Affect Pakistan," *Daily Times* (Karachi), October 28, 2008.

16. Anjum Niaz, "America Dream: End or Beginning?" *The News International* (Karachi), October 28, 2008.

17. Nasim Zehra, "US Elections: Four Key Questions," *The News International* (Karachi), October 29, 2008.

18. *Daily Times* (Karachi), November 3, 2008.

19. *Daily Times* (Karachi), November 4, 2008.

20. See "Pakistan Came Back from the Brink: US," *Dawn* (Karachi), March 17, 2009.

12

Support and Apprehension: Chinese Views on the US Presidential Election

Sukhee Han and Kai Jin

The general question is how did the Chinese people perceive the US presidential election of 2008? The United States, as the only real superpower in the contemporary world, plays such an important role in the world that the influence of American domestic politics has extended far beyond its national borders. Because of its status as the only remaining superpower, the presidential election in the United States has been regarded as an important issue not only by US citizens but also by people all over the world. A series of new policies or amendments regarding foreign affairs, trade, energy, and also the environment, and so on, holds a significant impact over the world, and it is especially relevant to China—a key stakeholder for the United States. Since 9/11, Sino-US relations have been relatively stable, but controversies still remain as do their broader underlying causes, such as conflicts over issues like trade, the exchange rate, human rights, and the Taiwan issue. In this context, the Chinese government has been keen on enhanced and more institutionalized bilateral relations with the United States to solidify and possibly give new meaning to the Chinese role of stakeholder in the world at the beginning of the twenty-first century. Since mere economic interdependence based on continuous rounds of dialogue and talks does not always prevent underlying conflicts over other critical issues from breaking open, it has been the intention of both Washington and Beijing to better define China's role. In order for them to forestall major conflicts over problems arising in the context of, for example, regional security, military dominance, energy strategy, and even ideology, both sides have been working hard to clarify and solidify the definition of "stakeholder" through diplomatic means. Key examples in this context are the Sino-US Strategic Talks and the Sino-US Strategic Economic Talks.

SUKHEE HAN AND KAI JIN

In fact, there could be many new opportunities to enhance relations between these two stakeholders, such as President Barack Obama's New Energy Plan. China could utilize this plan to restructure its own huge domestic market and ambitious overseas energy strategy, especially in fields like nuclear energy and eco-friendly or green cars. New strategies and policies could be established in consultation with the new White House and in accordance with Obama's new policies.[1]

It is certainly true that China has paid much attention to the 2008 American election. However, this observation also possibly raises further questions. Does this concern possibly indicate the likelihood of stable and relatively friendly relations with the United States in the immediate future? Or does it rather show the Chinese government's uncertainties about the continuing of this "seven-years' honeymoon"? Put another way, are current Sino-US relations based on a structure of interdependence, or mere inter-compromise? One may argue that common economic benefits, as well as regional or even global security concerns, have made it possible for these two major powers to go beyond compromise and actually aim at genuine interdependence.

Could this be possible? How do Chinese people and scholars view this election in general? In the following discussion, we will focus on the US election from the Chinese perspective in the context of a general discussion of Sino-US relations to provide an appropriate analytical framework on this matter.

KEY VIEWPOINTS OF CHINESE INTELLECTUALS

Various controversies about the issues brought up by the US election are discussed by Chinese experts. Jin Canrong says that there are at least three major issues that take precedence over the US election: first is the current global financial crisis, second is the controversy between the United States and Russia over the issue of Georgia, and third is the rising prominence of China, symbolized by the Beijing Olympic Games. While Yang Yusheng argued that even though the current financial crisis struck the United States rather severely, through this election there will be a new approach to solve the problems. Following an "American Tradition" from the American Civil War, to the two world wars, and on to the present times when US policies need major change, the US presidential election has frequently been utilized as a political mechanism or instrument to solve major US domestic and overseas problems. Thus, the US election is still crucially important to be watched and observed all over the world.

The above debate shows us a first glimpse of the current discussion in China over a widely discussed term—*Xu Jiao* in Chinese, or "illusive pride" in English. Chinese people were concerned about the US election even as early as some ten, twenty, or thirty years ago, simply because the United States was such a mighty superpower that there was no possibility of neglecting developments there. But it seems that the United States has been embroiled over a period in significant problems over many issues, such as, for example, the Iraq War. Moreover, domestically it has been severely affected by the current financial crisis, which raises the question about whether Chinese people still need to be so concerned about the presidential election of this superpower that is bogged down in troubles.

As Yang Hongxi explained, the United States still plays a very important role in East Asia and the regions surrounding China, and the US foreign policy directly or indirectly connects with the security of China's economy, energy needs, food supply, and capital requirements.[2] Yang further pointed out that while the Democrats' fundamental contestations and propositions are important, the national interest of the United States would still come first,[3] which means that disputes over issues such as ideology might have come up in the election campaign but would be relegated to the background soon after the election. This is why China should hold a rational view over this presidential election and the newly elected president, regardless of the outcome in terms of a Democratic or Republican White House.

Zhao Kejin claimed that this US presidential election has been leading to a consensus that transcends the divergence between the two parties.[4] Zhao's arguments may be summarized as follows: first, US economic policy will keep following a social-liberal course; second, America's social policy will keep pursuing moderate conservatism; and third, with respect to US foreign policy and Sino-US relations, a consensus of matured relations and mutual trust has emerged. However, Zhao has also pointed out that the most noticeable challenge for President Barack Obama comes from his Democratic colleagues in Congress who pay much attention to Human Rights, Democracy, and environmental protection. This Democratic agenda has the potential to upset the relationship with China, and President Obama may have to balance these concerns with American economic needs and the US economic relations with China.

China's View of the Democratic and Republican Candidates

When it comes to the candidates, it is not very easy to conclude which candidate China prefers. For Chinese people it is a widely shared consensus that the United States is rather pragmatic when compared to European countries. In this context, Yang Hongxi emphasized that national interest always comes first, including for the United States, and this is true even in the heat of the presidential election campaigns.

Regardless of who actually wins the elections, this argument holds true, a candidate's policy viewpoints may then invariably be reshaped by the logic and immediacy of national interests. Nevertheless, question of what a presidency of either Obama or John McCain would mean for China remained valid and received much interest in China.

In common with general perceptions around the world, Obama has been regarded as an extremely diligent person in China, albeit one who had been almost unknown to the public. First Financial Daily (*Di Yi Caijing Ribao*) described Obama as *Cao Gen*,[5] which in Chinese means "grass roots," and in English refers to the nonelite groups, or someone who not necessarily but quite often holds opposing opinions to the governing administration. However, Obama's experience working in the local community in Chicago allows him to be regarded as a person well acquainted with and genial toward the common concerns of the average American. Obama could easily be seen as a man of the grass roots by Chinese observers.

In 2008, "Commerce Week," a weekly magazine published in China, described Obama during the summer of 2008 as follows:

> During the year of 2008, American polity has been shaken with agitation by an Illinois Senator, Barack Obama, who has ancestral roots in Africa. He seems to have the magic power to call upon the public and subdue them. Some say he is the new Kennedy in the new era. Others name him as the leader and prolocutor of the new American Dream in the new generation. Some are so convinced by his enthusiastic speech that they regard him as the man who stands alongside Abraham Lincoln and Martin Luther King. And some even quote from America's national anthem and describe him as the "man of God."[6]

Interestingly, the Chinese public has shown sympathy or emotional favor to Obama. He was seen as a symbolic figure who rose from the grassroots level through his own hard work, and who also has ancestral roots in Africa. And as for the Republican candidate McCain, his most impressive point is that he is a Vietnam War hero who has also spent over twenty years in Congress. To some Chinese, however, McCain's propositions and claims have been regarded, at least partially, as amounting to, for all practical purposes, an extension of George W. Bush's policies. A key example is his firm belief in winning the "War on Terror." World Affair Press described McCain as:

> A Senator coming back from Vietnam as a War Hero, who is very experienced in foreign affairs and national security issues, with rather strong foreign policy management ability and a mature world view who, on entering the White House, will surely bring some changes in the field of US foreign affairs.[7]

In the eyes of many Chinese, the young Senator Obama seems to be more energetic and attractive than Senator McCain who is over seventy years old. However, winning in the US presidential election is not like winning a reality TV show. Why have people finally chosen a man with a strong grassroots background instead of a war hero?

People Seeking Change and "Renovation"

Americans had become critical of many of President George W. Bush's policies. A strong desire for change and rethinking of many policy approaches developed in the minds of a large segment of the American people. Obama's slogan and major keyword of his campaign for presidency, "change," connected precisely with this widespread desire for new political thinking. His campaign slogan and program were in tune with and appealed to the public's wishes. As Zhang Guoqing explained, Bush's policies, especially over foreign issues like the Iraq War, has been a "mirror" for both candidates—Obama's chance to give a brand new image to the public and McCain's "negative asset," a reminder to people that the latter's policies would be an extension of the major tenets of the Bush administration in foreign policy.[8]

The Matthew Effect of the Current Financial Crisis

Zhang pointed out that it is natural for people to think twice regarding McCain's age and his "negative asset," the carryover of policies from the Bush Administration. With the financial crisis hitting low-income communities with full force, the choice for the 44th President of the United States became closely tied to the question of either further supporting the financial elites who made severe mistakes or saving those ordinary people in trouble. Mainly, people believe that the key to cure this financial crisis is not to save the big corporations but to make sure that small businesses, individual investors, and socially vulnerable groups will be able to recover. Here too, Obama's professional experience in local communities in his early years and his affability to the public has gained him "*Cao Gen*" (Grass Roots) appeal and distanced him from the war hero McCain.

"When US Presidential Election Encounters Financial Crisis," as an article from *China Times* explained, the general public's concern over economic issues gives Obama significant advantages over McCain.[9] Especially during the present difficult times, Obama presented to the people an active, optimistic, and energetic image of himself. By successfully associating himself with "optimism" and "change" in the minds of many, he was also able to gain significantly in the vote count.

INTERNET AND CYBER STRATEGY

The Chinese public and mass media paid much attention to candidate Obama, including his background, his family, and his early experience as a community employee. Wang Mei studied Obama's Internet and cyber strategy during his run for the presidency, and Wang pointed out that Obama's campaign team has been very creative and effective in their efforts to use the Internet and a highly developed cyber strategy.[10] First, they successfully delivered political messages and news releases through the Internet in a very creative and innovative way. This approach proved particularly appealing to younger generations, which paid close attention. It also helped him develop a favorable image not only in papers and on television but also in the cyber world. Wang Mei even concluded that Obama's new strategy in this campaign changed the traditional ways and means of political propaganda completely. Second, Obama's campaign team aggressively utilized social-networking online sites like Myspace and Facebook, which allowed the audience to feel closer and quite literally "connected." It helped create the sense of a bond, much like talking to a friend. And most noticeably, Obama's campaign team quickly, successfully, and effectively responded to numerous side-stories, rumors, and even various instances of slander from the other side by using modern communication tools.

In comparison with Obama, McCain did not show up so much and so favorably in the major Chinese media. For example, a news release by Xinhua News Agency on October 15, 2008, expressed that attitude when it stated: "McCain is still hesitating and stumbling when it is time to vote!"[11] It seems that the experienced and celebrated military expert and war hero McCain had to come back to the issue of the economy and also stop attacking his Democratic competitor Obama. However, right before the vote he realized his mistake, in particular, that his harsh attacks on Obama had not helped him at all. McCain tried hard to change course and overcome his image of being extreme. But as it turned out, it was too late and he had lost much credit in the eyes of the general public already.

In China there was serious concern about whether a possible electoral victory of McCain in the presidential election might in fact mean a second life, a rebirth, of America's neoconservatism. Or would a McCain White House possibly continue the unpopular foreign policy of the Bush administration?[12] It became clear that China was viewing the possibility of a McCain presidency with considerable caution. However, others disagreed with this viewpoint. The Southern Weekly (*Nanfang Zhoumo*) claimed that in light of the likelihood that the Democratic Party would have control of both houses of Congress, the Republican McCain in the White House would be a more favorable choice to maintain the political balance of power. Such a balance might be a particularly prudent requirement if the Democrat Obama, after winning the White House, puts forward bold new legislation that might be well intended but is originated from an inexperienced presidency.[13]

CRITICAL POLITICAL ISSUES SEEN BY CHINA IN THIS ELECTION

Given the overall international situation in 2008, foreign policy issues were generally seen as important in this election. But China did not show up as a major agenda item in the campaigns of this US presidential election, not even in the two candidates' live debates. Still, Obama's campaign disagreed with the opinion that US-China relations should be approached under the terms "engage" and "hedge." Instead, Obama's team favored the attitude of "compete" and "cooperate" to guide US relations with China. As Obama's Chinese Affairs Adviser Jeffrey Bader explained to the Oriental Morning Post (*Dongfang Zaobao*) in August of 2008, competition and cooperation with China were exactly what the United States wants.[14] No matter how each side sees the other, these two powers could never merely step aside and ignore the other, and what happens in one country naturally affects people in the other.

In the summer of 2008, the Chinese people were preoccupied with domestic issues, first and foremost the Olympic Games, but also sadly several natural disasters. Nevertheless, many reasons existed for them to believe that the US presidential election was still one of the most significant international issues for Chinese people to watch, talk, and think about. As already discussed above, the major concerns regarding the possibility of McCain winning in this election were largely focused on US foreign policy and a possible reinvigoration of neoconservatism. However, neither of the candidates made China a major issue in this presidential campaign to begin with. Put differently, they both refrained from criticizing China severely in order to gain credits from a certain portion of the American public. What then are the major political issues from the Chinese perspective, what did China care about in this presidential election? To answer this question adequately, we need to analyze various issues that fall under the context of "political" issues. Within such an expanded framework of political issues and concerns, several issues were continuously brought up in China.

RECONFIRMING AND RESHAPING SINO-US RELATIONS AS GENUINE MUTUAL STAKEHOLDERS

Though to some extend a cliché, reconfiguring US-China relations as a relation between mutual stakeholders is still the most important and most significant issue that China has been pursuing. The concept and term of "mutual stakeholders" was brought up by the then deputy secretary of state, Robert Zoellick. He suggested that China be regarded as a state holding a major stake in the global community, and that, as such, China should be consciously integrated into international affairs. Although Sino-US relations have been through a relatively stable period after 9/11, this does not mean that there are no conflicts and potential crisis today. In fact, China is extremely eager to strengthen and enhance the bilateral relations of stakeholders, and one may actually regard this presidential election as a turning point in this context. That is why China warmly welcomed the visit of Obama's China Adviser, Jeffrey Bader, and also accepted Obama's message regarding China as a "competitor" as well as a "cooperator."

China believes that Obama's propositions regarding China do not imply any significant change in Sino-US relations. Liu Weidong pointed out early in the campaign that trade conflicts could be possible if or when Obama wins. He also claimed, however, that the basic framework of Sino-US relations has been firmly set, and not only are both countries' economies and finances integrated but there has also been a growing consensus and sense of cooperation over security issues. Thus regardless of who would actually occupy the White House from 2009 onward, he would ultimately have to realize that China is much more willing to cooperate internationally.[15]

The most sensitive issue between China and the United States remains the Taiwan Issue. When Taiwan's Democratic Progressive Party stepped down, relations across the straits changed significantly, and there is a widely shared belief that, at least for the near future, there will not be any serious conflicts between mainland China and Taiwan. Both candidates in this US presidential election expressed their conviction that more dialogue will be helpful for both sides across the straits. Even as a strong and firm supporter of the Taiwan Relations Act, McCain expressed several times that he strongly favors and welcomes dialogue between both sides. However, Shen Dingli pointed out that no matter who wins the race for the White House, the United States would most likely insist on pursuing its own national interest in this matter. The principal American strategy to deal with the Taiwan Issue is to maintain the *status quo* across the straits. And though both candidates stood by the "One China Policy," the difference was that Obama appeared more inclined to emphasize the principle of "One China," while McCain looked much more inclined to uphold the American security promise to Taiwan.[16] From the mainland Chinese perspective then, the choice between the US presidential candidates was clearly in favor of Obama, if only the Taiwan issue was considered.

TRADE POLICIES WITH CHINA

When Obama established himself as the clear frontrunner in the campaign, the Chinese believed that once Obama became the next US

President, the Sino-US political relationship would further benefit, although the danger of trade conflicts would remain. In fact, trade conflicts between China and the United States have existed since right after the normalization of trade relations between these two countries. More specifically, there were disputes primarily over textiles, agriculture, and intellectual products. China's huge domestic market has been attracting US capital, know-how, and also products with high added value. However, with regard to Chinese products exported to the US market, things have been complicated. Large quantities of Chinese products have been pouring into the US market, mainly cheap products with low added value. But especially in the field of textile and agricultural products, American workers and farmers have been complaining that cheap Chinese products have been costing them their jobs. During the campaign, Obama expressed support for a very clear hard-line trade policy toward China. Moreover, he urged China to specifically change its policy on exchange rate.

Needless to say, these viewpoints of the presidential frontrunner were major concerns for the Chinese business community and for government officials. The China Trade News reported in this context:

> An inclination to trade protection makes China uneasy. Mei Yuxin, a senior researcher from the Chinese Academy of International Trade and Economic Cooperation, Ministry of Commerce explained that different from McCain, Obama does not lean upon free-trade too much. And his speeches about compelling China to raise the renminbi's exchange rate, and monitoring and limiting Chinese textile products' export have aroused the Chinese government's serious concern.[17]

Liu Weidong further explained the reasons for possible trade conflicts between China and the United States. First, Americans insist that many core issues have not been solved. Second, since there has not been any significant change regarding China's and America's power, and since Sino-US relations have been relatively stable, the overall framework for bilateral relations also remains in place. Also, the major issues that concern both sides are unlikely to change in any major way. Third, Sino-US relations are different from Sino-Japanese relations, in that there have been no conflicts, differences, disputes, and controversies between China and the United States over territorial issues or natural resources. What stands between China and the United States then are mostly differences in ideas and discrepancies of interest.[18]

Although concerned, most Chinese scholars believed that candidate Obama's positions regarding trade with China would not necessarily lead to serious trade disputes or a trade war. Ni Feng was not surprised by Obama's hard-line speeches over trade issues with China, and he pointed out that, generally, the Democratic candidate more or less represents and gives more attention to the interests of labor. The Democratic candidate in each presidential race tends to show more concern for trade issues than does the Republican candidate.[19] Thus, from the Chinese perspective, these critiques are natural and understandable, and good and friendly trade relations between these two countries are still highly possible. Mutual interest has brought China and the United States together, at least in this policy domain. What is more, it was not lost on China that Obama would surely need the support and cooperation from China in order to implement his new economic policies to deal with the economic and financial crisis.

KOREAN PENINSULA SECURITY ISSUES

It might be appropriate to say that the Six-Party Talks have been a regional experimental political stage for China to push forward its ambitious, national grand strategy, and to convince the world of the emergence of a responsible and reliable China. During the US presidential election campaign, both candidates voiced their support for the framework of the Six-Party Talks. However, McCain emphasized that preconditions should be set and met before the new round of talks move on. Recently, the Six-Party Talks have been stumbling back and forth, and China, being the host and regarded as the only country that North Korea would rely on, has been losing face. Given this, Obama's policy over the Korean Peninsula must be a major concern for the Chinese government.

In the context of American policy toward North Korea, the new US Secretary of State Hillary Clinton's recent visit to East Asia offered major insights for China. First, a nuclear-armed North Korea is not acceptable. Second, the Six-Party Talks framework is still the preferred tool to tackle the issue. Third, the United States will enhance cooperation with Japan and South Korea.

However, Beijing wondered whether there was any possibility that the United States would initiate direct high-level bilateral dialogue with North Korea? Moreover, what does the United States expect from China now that the Six-Party Talks have virtually stagnated? Even though Secretary of State Clinton reaffirmed the framework of the Six-Party Talks and that the United States favored cooperation with China, Beijing remained anxious about the long-term policy of the new White House with respect to Korean Peninsula security issues.

During the election campaign in the United States, the situation regarding the Korean Peninsula was rather unstable. In particular, tensions intensified between North Korea and South Korea immediately after the election and after the inauguration of the president. Obviously, North Korea has been flying a kite to the new US President that they expect a breakthrough in bilateral relations with United States. Meanwhile other parties such as China are rather anxious to know Obama's new policy for Northeast Asia. In order to get a clarification and to set the agenda, the Chinese government repeatedly emphasized the importance of the Six-Party Talks—the framework that binds China and the United States more tightly and perhaps more cooperatively than other regional security issues.

Perception of the US Presidential Election and Domestic Politics in China

For several decades China has been "going out" even to the most remote corners of the world, sending large delegations and meeting with government officials, business CEOs, and local people. Furthermore, for decades China has been actively involved in various international issues, from the Middle East to North Korea, from East Timor to Congo (Kinshasa). Moreover, with respect to the world economy, China has been regarded as a powerful economic engine for years. China has insisted on a long-established pattern to deal with its domestic politics, and has built its foreign policy on the basis of the Five Principles of Peaceful Coexistence—mutual respect for sovereignty and territorial integrity, mutual nonaggression, noninterference in each other's internal affairs, equality and mutual benefit, and peaceful coexistence. China has been particularly insistent on its firm proposition of noninterference in each other's internal affairs.

Though Chinese society is, by and large, firmly behind the government's rejection of what it considers outside interference in its domestic politics, there are still connections between US domestic politics, such as, for example, the US presidential election, and China's domestic affairs. One of the major issues that connects this US presidential election and domestic politics in China are the economic policies that the candidates represented. After the election outcome was clear, the possible course the newly elected US President would take to deal with the current global economic and financial crisis moved center stage. Therefore, China paid close attention to Obama's new economic plans as they were unveiled, and particularly watched out for hints of possible US trade protectionism. This concern gained a sense of urgency when candidate Obama criticized China over its policy on foreign exchange and said that he would stop importing certain Chinese toys once elected.[20] As a major trading partner and foreign market for Chinese exports, any intent by the United States to replace part of its imports from China with its own products would directly affect the Chinese government's recent economic campaign and further reforms. The recent shutting down of many small businesses in the southern provinces such as Guangdong due to a lack of overseas orders has urged the Chinese government to be even more concerned regarding the impact of possible changes in US foreign economic policy initiated by the new US administration. This concern sparked a major discussion in China over Obama and McCain's different attitudes toward free trade policy. McCain seemed to be supportive of free trade with other countries, including China, while Obama was regarded as representing labor's interests and was seen as more concerned with the trade issue than was the Republican Party.[21] In fact, in China Obama's position on trade was frequently associated with protectionism.

However, other policy issues further complicated and changed China's initial preference of McCain for his stance on trade. Again, the key issue was that of Taiwan. Although both candidates favored a process of dialogue across the Taiwan Straits, McCain showed a more "hard-line" tendency, evidenced by his firm support for the Taiwan Relations Act. Even though the Chinese government has long been claiming that the Taiwan Issue is a part of China's domestic affairs, the United States still plays a critical role in it, and the reaffirmation of former policies, or any change to the former policies, over the Taiwan Issue by the new US President would touch China's most sensitive nerve. In this policy domain, McCain lost considerable sympathy in the eyes of China.

Other issues also entered the equation. Political issues such as freedom of religion, human rights, and environmental protection, for example, are also claimed by China to fall, at least in part, under domestic Chinese affairs and would thus be off-limits to interference by any foreign government. Nevertheless, given the nature of these issues and their relevance for the United States, they were also viewed in China in the context of the US election. Here, the general consensus in China was that the Democrats are traditionally more critical about these issues than the Republicans.

MAJOR IMPLICATIONS OF THE ELECTION OUTCOME FOR CHINA

Overall, China welcomed the outcome of the 2008 US presidential election. Wang Jisi pointed out that only a short period of time will be needed for the Obama administration to get acquainted with China.

> The period of time needed for Obama's administration to get acquainted with China will be relatively short. In fact, China has been anticipating Obama's final victory in this presidential election, and has been negotiating with his colleagues and advisers, sending the message that China hopes Obama will get more familiar with China and issues related with China as soon as possible before he wins the election. Obama has many advisers in the field of diplomatic affairs, and they are very experienced in dealing, coping and working with China.

Thus, a shorter period of time will be needed for Obama's administration to get acquainted with China.[22]

The assumption in China is that Sino-US relations will be kept on the present track and that the main framework will not be changed. The Democrats might insist on putting some issues like trade and human rights on the agenda. More importantly, as Beijing sees it, for the past decades, from Carter to Clinton, the Democrats have gained lots of experience in contacting and coping with the Chinese governments. The expectation in China is that former US policies regarding China will continue under the Obama administration.

It is too early to evaluate the full scale of the new White House policies and how they may impact US-Sino relations. However, certain issues must be added to the previous discussion. First, though Obama's New Energy Plan could be a chance for the Chinese government to enhance cooperation with the United States in the field of energy policy and technology, disputes remain a real possibility when it comes to issues such as environmental policy and climate change. Second, disputes over intellectual property rights remain unsolved, and China's ambitious overseas strategy for gaining access to natural resources, in particular oil, also carries in it the threat of conflict with the United States.

Nevertheless, the general consensus in China is that Sino-US relations will be enhanced under the new White House. The newly elected President Obama implied that dialogue and negotiation are the best means to solve global problems, and in this context he included China as a "cooperator," a message that was not lost on Beijing.

CONCLUSION

If the newly elected US President actually makes good on the propositions he made during the presidential campaign, his respect for cultural differences, his promise to bring change, and his belief in world peace, the international community should congratulate him and cheer for the first black president in American history. After eight years of the Bush administration, any adjustments and changes in a number of issue areas, from the Iraq War, to reconstruction in Afghanistan, to the Middle East Peace Process, and on to many other transnational problems like climate change, for example, will be welcomed by China. The world still needs US leadership to cope with many global issues, and, most urgently, the current world economic and financial crisis.

Talking about China, Obama once proclaimed: "neither our enemy nor our friend, they're competitors." The point here is that the United States under Obama may take a rising China seriously and Sino-US relations may transcend barriers of misunderstandings. As the Chinese proverb says, "crisis means both challenge and chance." Today, when the world is faced with a huge economic and financial crisis, China expects President Obama to end America's former unilateralism and pursue multilateralism in all areas. Beijing also looks to be seen and treated not merely as a competitor but more as a responsible and reliable partner. After the 2008 US presidential election and Obama's victory, people might hope that Sino-US relations would not necessarily follow the former narrow "V-Shape" track, and that this event might be a turning point in Sino-US relations, relations that may be enhanced and thus truly regarded as relations between two genuine stakeholders. That is certainly what China will be looking for from the Obama White House.

Notes

1. Li Ke, Gao Hongyan, Zhongguo Ke Jiejian Aobama Nengyuan Jihua (China Could Utilize Obama's New Energy Plan), *Zhongguo Maoyi Bao* (*China Trade News*), November 11, 2008.

2. Yang Hongxi, Meiguo Daxuanzhinian Kan Zhongmei Guanxi Fazhan—2005 Nian Yilai Zhongmei Guanxi De Huigu Yu Zhanwang (Sino-US Relations from 2005), *Shijie Jingji Yu Zhengzhi* (*World Economy and Politics*), Vol. 5, 2008.

3. Yang Hongxi, Meiguo Daxuanzhinian Kan Zhongmei Guanxi Fazhan—2005 Nian Yilai Zhongmei Guanxi De Huigu Yu Zhanwang (Sino-US Relations from 2005), *Shijie Jingji Yu Zhengzhi* (*World Economy and Politics*), Vol. 5, 2008.

4. Zhao Kejin, Meiguo Daxuan Yunniang Kuadang Gongshi (US Presidential Election Prepares for Consensus of Parties), *Shijie Zhishi* (*World Affair Press*), Vol. 23, 2008.

5. Feng Yuqing, Caogen Yingxiong vs. Yuezhan Yingxiong: Shui Gengneng Dadong Meiguoren De Xin? ("Grass Root Hero" vs. "War Hero": Who is American People's Favorite?) *Diyi Caijing Ribao* (*First Financial Daily*), June 5, 2008.

6. Kuangre Aobama (Enthusiastic Obama), *Zhaoshang Zhoukan* (*Commerce Week*), Vol. 6, 2008.

7. Zhang zhixin, Maikaien Shi Ge Zenyang De Ren? (What Kind of Person is McCain?) *Shijie Zhishi* (*World Affair Press*), Vol. 12, 2008.

8. Zhang Guoqing, Weishenme Shi Aobama? (Why Obama?) *Zhongguo Shehuikexueyuan Bao* (*Chinese Academy of Social Sciences Journal*), November 6, 2008.

9. Li Nan, Li Xiaojia, Niu Wenxin, Dang Meiguo Daxuan Zaoyu Jinrong Weiji (When US Presidential Election Encounters Financial Crisis), *Huaxia Shibao* (*China Times*), November 8, 2008.

10. Wang Mei, Aobama Zai Meiguo Daxuanzhong De Wangluo Chuanbo Celue (Obama's Internet and Cyber Strategy in His Run for Presidency), *Zhonghua Xinwen Bao* (*China Press Journal*), November 19, 2008.

11. Wu Zheng, Doukuai Toupiao Le, Maikaien Haizai Zuoyou Yaobai (McCain Is Still Hesitating and Stumbling When It Is Time to Vote), *Xinhua Meiri Dianxun* (*Xinhua Daily Telegraph*), October 15, 2008.

12. Zhang zhixin, What Kind of Person is McCain? *World Affair Press*, Vol. 12, 2008.

13. Wu Li, Aobama, Maikaien, Nage Shangtai Hui Genghao? (Obama and McCain, Who Is Better?) *Nanfang Zhoumo* (*Southern Weekly*), October 2, 2008.

14. Ma Yida, Aobama Duihua Jianchi Jingzhenghezuo Kuangjia (Obama Persist in Competitive and Cooperative Framework with China), *Dongfang Zaobao* (*Oriental Morning Post*), August 28, 2008.

15. Liu Weidong, Aobama Dangxuan, Mei Duihua Zhengce Buhui Datiaozheng (US's China Policy Will Not Face A Big Change After Obama's Victory), *Xin Jing Bao* (*The Beijing News*), November 6, 2008.

16. Ma Yida, Aobama, Maikaien Yazhou Zhengce Guwen Jibian Taihai Zhengce (Advisers for Obama and McCain Debate over Taiwan Issue), *Dongfang Zaobao* (*Oriental Morning Post*), October 22, 2008.

17. Li Ke, Gao Hongyan, Aobama Dangxuan, Zhongmei Jingmao Guanxi Zouxiang Hefang? (Obama Elected, and What Will Happen to Sino-US Trade Relations?) *Zhongguo Maoyi Bao* (*China Trade News*), November 11, 2008.

18. Liu Weidong, Aobama Dangxuan, Mei Duihua Zhengce Buhui Datiaozheng (US's China Policy Will Not Face A Big Change After Obama's Victory), *Xin Jing Bao* (*The Beijing News*), November 6, 2008.

19. Li Ke, Gao Hongyan, Aobama Dangxuan, Zhongmei Jingmao Guanxi Zouxiang Hefang? (Obama Elected, and What Will Happen to Sino-US Trade Relations?) *Zhongguo Maoyi Bao* (*China Trade News*), November 11, 2008.

20. Yuan Rongjun, Aobama Dangxuan Dui Zhongmai Jingmao Yingxiang Jihe (Impacts over Sino-US Economic Relations by Obama's Victory), *Jinrong Shibao* (*Financial News*), November 6, 2008.

21. Li Ke, Gao Hongyan, Aobama Dangxuan, Zhongmei Jingmao Guanxi Zouxiang Hefang? (Obama Elected, and What Will Happen to Sino-US Trade Relations?) *Zhongguo Maoyi Bao* (*China Trade News*), November 11, 2008.

22. Ma Yida, Aobama Yu Zhongguo Moheqi Hui Gengduan (Shorter Time Needed for Obama to Get Acquainted with China), *Dongfang Zaobao* (*Oriental Morning Post*), November 7, 2008.

13

JAPAN AND THE US PRESIDENTIAL ELECTION OF 2008

Robert Dujarric

The aftermath of Japan's capitulation in 1945 radically altered Japan's place in the world as a Great Power. Following the US occupation (1945–1952), Japan recovered its independence. It did so, however, as a weak nation relying on American protection. America not only defended Japan against the communists during the Cold War, but also provided a security system that allowed Japan to establish normal economic relations with its Asian neighbors, which it had invaded or colonized in the preceding decades. Japanese dependence was not totally unilateral. The United States could not have waged the Cold War in Asia without access to its numerous bases in Japan. But overall, the relationship was profoundly unequal. The United States could exist without Japan, whereas Japan, at least in its post-1945 liberal democratic incarnation, could not remain free without the United States.

In the two decades since the demise of the Soviet empire, a new picture has evolved, but without any fundamental transformation. The Soviet Union vanished, replaced by a declining Russia with a decrepit military, but Japan continues to face several threats. A war in the Korean Peninsula is unlikely, but the Japanese are understandably worried by the menace from North Korea, which now fields ballistic missiles and may possess a crude nuclear arsenal. Korean unification itself is seen in Tokyo as potentially dangerous if a unified peninsula turns out to be anti-Japanese or too closely tied to China. Sino-Taiwanese relations improved since the electoral victory of the Kuo Min-Tang (KMT) in Taipei in March 2008, but the possibility of a military confrontation remains. Any war between Taipei and Beijing, or even just an increase in tensions, would have severe repercussions on Asian security and Japanese interests. Moreover, besides the Taiwan issue, Japanese analysts are concerned by China's growing strength and Beijing's designs in the region.

Japan has a sizeable military of its own, known as the Self-Defense Forces (SDF), but its strategy requires that, should a major conflict arise, the United States come to its rescue. Additionally, Japan's policy relies on American diplomacy and deterrence to keep Northeast Asia peaceful. Were the United States to abandon its role as Japan's protector and Asia's stabilizer, Japan's entire security architecture would disintegrate. The most logical alternative to prevent such a scenario would be to spend much more on defense, a step that in itself would fuel tensions internationally, and domestically it is most likely to split the Japanese public.

On the economic front, Japan's economic welfare is, despite decades of economic development since 1945, still reliant on the health of the US economy. Thus, Japan's stake in America includes not only defense and diplomacy but also economics and finance.

Finally, there is a psychological element that must not be overlooked. Many conservatives who are labeled as "pro-American" in Japan are ambivalent about America. They are thankful for its role as a bulwark against communism and now against China, but they resent the democratization of the United States imposed on their fatherland and the other liberal reforms introduced by SCAP (The Supreme Commander of Allied Powers, i.e., the US occupation). Many of them, those who were convinced that Japan's actions during the Asian and Pacific Wars of 1931–1945 were justified, also view the US bombings of Japanese cities and the US-led Tokyo Trials of Japan's war leadership as despicable acts. Nevertheless, regardless of whether they love or hate America in their hearts, almost all members of the conservative establishment believe that the alliance with the United States is critical to Japan's very survival. They consider that Japan has no friends except for the United States (and perhaps Taiwanese nationalists). The term "friend" anthropomorphizes international relations, but it best describes the sort of psychological dependence of postwar Japan on the United States. Therefore, there is a feeling of dependence on the United States among the Japanese, which is not felt as acutely by the other major allies of the United States. For example, whereas most Europeans care little about whom the US president sends as ambassador to their countries, Japanese observers are reassured when the US envoy is a man of great stature, and they are disturbed if he is not.

Consequently, signs that America is abandoning Japan are scrutinized in the hope that it will prove to be false, and good omens are a cause to rejoice. For example, they perceived Secretary of State Hillary Clinton's decision to make Japan the first stop on her maiden trip as a cabinet member, in February 2009, as a sign that America values Japan, rather than realize that US policymakers thought that it cost nothing to have Tokyo be the first city Clinton visited and that this had no real policy implications. Unlike all other major US allies, Japanese officials attach a lot of importance to the selection of the US ambassador to Japan, taking great pride if he/she is a political heavyweight. The reaction of Japan's elites is similar to that of spouses living in constant fear their partners may be contemplating other alternatives. They pore over the numbers of Americans studying Japanese, comparing the data with statistics on those learning Chinese; they analyze the relative frequency of Congressional delegations stopping in Tokyo and Beijing, and other small details, with much trepidation.

The Japanese Audience of the American Election

Obviously, it is impossible to speak of "Japan" as having an opinion on the US election. Countries are not individuals; they are agglomerations of citizens and organizations. However, when it comes to the elite, defined as the ruling party (the Liberal Democratic Party, LDP) and its coalition partners, the main opposition party (the Democratic Party of Japan, DPJ), the permanent senior civil servants, the business community, and a large segment of the intellectual and media establishment, we can refer to a relatively unified view of the 2008 US presidential election.

Unlike South Korea, Japan is not sharply divided between conservative and progressive camps. The struggles against the US alliance of the 1960s have been replaced by a consensus on the need for a strong relationship with the United States. The Democratic Party opposed Japan's SDF carrying out operations in support of the US military in the Indian Ocean and Iraq. This opposition is neither anti-American nor against a strong alliance with America. There are pacifists and leftist academics and journalists who do not share these views, but their influence is negligible. During the Iraq War, enormous crowds gathered to protest the US-led invasion in Britain, Italy, and other countries whose governments supported the US action, but in Japan the demonstrators were few and public interest was low.

Therefore, when we talk about "Japan's reaction" to the election, by focusing on the mainstream establishment we in fact capture the great majority of the population whose views matter on this issue and indeed are relevant to policy.

Japan's Stake in the US Elections

When carrying out an analysis of international reactions to the US election, there is a danger of projecting the dominant attitudes of intellectual elites in Western Europe, Canada, and other western nations, and subordinating the attitudes of the rest of the world. Therefore, there may be a danger in assuming that in Japan, too, most of the thinking classes had a similar image of the US President, and that they held

George W. Bush not only in low esteem politically, but generally considered him to be incompetent and with a narrow outlook, and his policies at times even dangerous.

However, it is crucial to fully appreciate how different the situation was in Japan. President Bush's severe unpopularity in Western Europe had several reasons, none of which are particularly relevant to the Japanese scenario. Most importantly, western elites and societies in general were immensely critical with regard to the Iraq War and other issues related to the administration's actions in the Middle East, namely, the Israeli-Arab conflict, and also torture, and the Guantanamo prison.

In Japan, however, the Iraq War did not resonate much with the public. Most Japanese were against it, but with little intensity. Very few considered or realized the extent of the consequences for the United States, and indirectly for Japan, of the invasion of the Mesopotamia. For most Japanese, the common man as well as those of the educated elite, Iraq is, to paraphrase Neville Chamberlin's comments about Czechoslovakia during the Sudetenland crisis of 1938, "a faraway country of which we know little."[1] Unlike Western Europe, Japan did not have any of its citizens interned at Guantanamo, nor was Japan involved in flying US detainees through its airspace and airports, as far as is publically known. The Israeli-Arab struggle is also much less salient in Japan. Japan is a country that is far more removed, geographically and psychologically, from the Levant than Europe. Therefore its elite (as well as the average Japanese) lacks spiritual ties to the birthplace of Abrahamic faiths. For all practical purposes, Japan's citizenry counts practically no Jews, Muslims, Arabs, Turks, and Kurds, among its citizenry, and has very few Christians as well. Therefore, US policy in the Middle East had far less impact on Japanese opinion than it did in Europe.

Second, there was a cultural aspect to the hostility President Bush generated in Western Europe. To western Europeans, including moderate conservatives, Christian Democrats, and liberals (in the European meaning of the term, i.e., advocates of political and economic liberalism), there was something loathsome, or at least ridiculous, about Bush. He had practically never travelled abroad, knew little world history, and displayed a fundamentalist faith that looks simplistic to many in Europe and downright imbecile to others.

Japan, however, is not a western society. Consequently, except for a small minority, these aspects of Bush's personality and philosophy that were striking to Europeans were much less apparent to the Japanese. For Europeans, there is a wide difference between John Kerry, who knew Europe, spoke several continental European languages, and married a cosmopolitan African-born, Geneva-educated Portuguese, and the provincial Texan with an all-American wife. In Japan, however, Americans who know Japan and Japanese (of whom there are very few) stand apart, but the difference between Kerry and Bush is far less obvious.

Moreover, in some countries the 2008 US election directly led to a discussion on the contrast between domestic politics and those of the United States. For Western Europe, as well as Canada and Australia, Barack Obama's candidacy and subsequent victory was obviously relevant to the status of ethnic minorities in these nations. Japan, however, has very few ethnic minorities. There are Asian-Japanese (Korean-, Chinese-, and Taiwanese-Japanese), as well Okinawans, a few Ainus (indigenous population of Hokkaido), burakumin (ethnically Japanese but descendents of the "eta" class of "untouchables" of the pre-Meiji era), and citizens of mixed races, who are different from the mainstream population. The total size of these minority populations is hard to measure given the ill-defined burakumin category, but the best estimates are in the range of several million residents in a country of 125 million total citizens.[2] Moreover, the Okinawans live on an island that renders them geographically peripheral to Japanese society. The Asian-Japanese and buraku have little in common with the majority Japanese, but they do not stand out in a Japanese crowd since there are no discernable pigmentary or physionomical differences between them and the rest of the Japanese. Finally, minorities loom large in a country if they are exceptionally successful in some fields and geographically concentrated, if they are poor and concentrated in poor neighborhoods, or seeking to secede through violence. But in Japan none of these factors apply. The minorities remain thus largely invisible to the average Japanese who, unlike white Americans or native European citizens, does not really think of Japan as having minorities as the word is understood in the United States and nowadays in Western Europe. Therefore, the question heard frequently in Europe, "where is our Obama?" does not resonate in Japan.

The rise of a young politician with a short résumé, who defeated Hillary Rodham Clinton and had vast support in the Democratic Party and could build on the political network of her husband, and the decorated war hero John S. McCain, should have led the Japanese to look in the mirror at their sclerotic politics. The Japanese Prime Minister in January 2009, Aso Taro, is the grandson and son-in-law of premiers, and he brought into his cabinet ten other politicians from political families, including another grandson of a prime minister and son of a foreign minister, and two children of premiers. He succeeded Fukuda Yasuo, son of a prime minister, brother-in-law of a former cabinet member and uncle of a Diet member, who had taken over from Abe Shinzo, son of a foreign minister, grandson of a prime minister, and grandnephew of another prime minister. Abe's predecessor, Koizumi Junichiro, indicated in 2008 that he would retire from Parliament, offering his seat to his son. Assuming he succeeds in what most expect will be an easy election for him, the young and totally inexperienced Koizumi junior will become a fourth generation Diet member, following in the footsteps of his father, grandfather, and great-grandfather in the Lower House.

In light of this, one might expect that the winds of change that brought Obama to the White House would make the Japanese envious. However, this certainly did not occur, nor did it impact Japanese politics in the least. The ruling Liberal Democrats may well lose the next general election. The reasons will be the continuing decay of the Liberal Democratic Power, a succession of hapless premiers (Abe Shinzo, Fukuda Yasuo, and Aso Taro), and the economic crisis. But the demise of the LDP, if it occurs, will thus be purely caused by domestic factors rather than by an "Obama effect."

In countries that have very similar politics, the outcome of elections in one nation can have an impact on the other. But Japan is truly sui generis. It is the only parliamentary democracy in East Asia. The Japanese have no close cultural or geographic ties with any other nation, comparable to those that bind European nations, or link the former Spanish and British dominions to Madrid and London. Moreover, very few Japanese understand a foreign language and few outside of their country speak the Japanese language.

Looking at the major political actors, the ruling LDP and the US GOP are both "conservative" parties, but it is hard to argue that they have much in common. Japanese conservatism has a communitarian, statist, and mercantilist bend that is at odds with American individualism and economic liberalism. Moreover, the Christian fundamentalist influence on the Republican Party has no equivalent in Japanese society, where religiosity is low, syncretism common, and Christianity confined to one percent of the electorate.

The Democratic Party of Japan (DPJ) shares the same name with America's Democrats, but that is about the extent of the intersection between both organizations. Like the LDP, it is the product of an old-world society with values fundamentally different from America's. The societal and cultural issues that have defined American Democrats in recent decades, namely, ethnic diversity, affirmative action, gender equality, legalized abortion, and homosexual rights, have little or no traction in Japanese society. Race and ethnicity are obviously not very relevant to Japan's fairly homogenous society. Female empowerment should be a mobilizing issue in Japanese politics, but in truth it is not. Abortion is legal in Japan. The absence of Christian opposition to reproductive choice makes it a nonissue. Equal rights for homosexuals are rarely discussed in Japan, but neither does homophobia have the same mobilizing potential as it does have with some segments of religious voters in America.

As of January 2009, Ozawa Ichiro is the leader of the DPJ. He has little if any in common with Obama. Ozawa, nineteen years older than the new US President, was elected to the Japanese Diet in 1969, when

Obama was in primary school. He first joined the cabinet in 1985, before Obama even entered Harvard Law School. His father was a member of parliament, whereas Obama's was a Kenyan studying in Hawaii. Ozawa himself learned politics from Tanaka Kakuei, one of the most powerful "godfathers" of Japanese politics. Thus, it is hard to see any similarity between the Japanese and the American leaders of their respective Democratic Parties.

In many parts of the world, the 2008 US presidential election morphed from "an American election" to "The American election of the Century," and in some ways to a "world election" due to the intense feelings it generated. In Europe, Africa, the Middle East, and other regions, there was a sense of excitement generally not felt when the United States votes. But, in Japan, President Bush did not generate the intense hostile feelings that he generated in Europe and the Middle East. There were reasons for that. Few members of the Japanese political and intellectual establishment realized the negative impact of the Bush presidency on US interests. The Japan-US cultural gap played a role, too. Finally, as I will explain in more detail later, the Republicans, and Bush in particular, were seen as particularly "pro-Japan." While Bush had a better image in Japan than in most other countries around the globe, Obama did not crystallize hopes about America and their own country in Japan the same way he did in Europe. Japanese followed the US campaign, but, unlike what took place in most other countries, it did not spur the same excitement and fascination.

JAPANESE FAVORABILITY OF PRESIDENTIAL CANDIDATES

There is no doubt that Senator McCain was Tokyo's preferred option. This did not reflect any particular dislike for Obama, about whom little was known, or even a wave of support for McCain as a person. It was the consequence of the establishment's dislike of the Democrats and preference for the Republicans. Had Hillary Clinton been the standard-bearer of the Democratic Party, it is probable that the tilt away from the Democrats would have been even stronger. Whereas Obama had been totally unknown, Clinton was, by definition, seen in the light of the policies of her husband. These policies were seen by the ruling party as having been too much "pro-China" and not sufficiently attentive to Japan.

Japanese news organizations deploy impressive levels of manpower to cover the news and have sizeable operations in the United States. Therefore, the events during the campaign were duly reported. On balance, it is probably fair to say that neither candidate really developed a strong brand image in Japan. In Japan, except for a small cadre of Japanese who lived and studied in America, Obama and McCain remained names rather than fascinating characters, as was the case in other countries.

Had Hillary Clinton been the Democratic candidate, there might have been more "personality coverage." Obama's African-American background was largely irrelevant to the Japanese experience of race and ethnicity. But in a country that lags behind the rest of the developed world in empowering women, the sight of a female campaigning for the highest office of the United States might have generated more attention.

Moreover, when, in 1998, President Bill Clinton undertook a nine-day trip to China without stopping in Japan, this "Japan passing" traumatized the Japanese establishment. In fact, it frightened them. If the "Most Powerful Man in the World" did not think that their country was worth a stop, it could mean that one day the United States would abandon them to their fate.

Overall, Clinton's decision not to stop in Japan revealed more about Japan's neuroses than about US policy. Under Clinton's presidency, the so-called Nye Initiative (named after the then assistant secretary of defense, Joseph S. Nye) set in motion the reinforcement of the operational mechanisms of the Japan-US alliance. This improved interoperability enhanced the effectiveness of US forces in Japan and strengthened the military relationship between the two nations. In 1996, the US Navy sailed two aircraft carriers close to Taiwan to express American concern over China's threats to the island's security, demonstrating the US commitment not only to Taiwan but also to Japan. The actual Clinton record in Asia did not indicate a lack of concern over Japan's security needs.

In fact, concern about Japan-passing was, and remains, linked to China. As China's economy continues to grow more and more, the Japanese fear that Japan may cease to be the lodestar of US policy in Asia. This is a frequent, one could even say constant, topic of discussion among Japanese officials, academics, and journalists.

The fear of "Japan passing" can hardly be overestimated. For Japan, Clinton's choice of route was a worrying sign of possible abandonment. Moreover, as China grew economically, Japan noticed that American policymakers were devoting more and more attention to the relationship with Beijing. Victor Cha describes the tensions between the fear of abandonment and alignment in Japan (and in South Korea).[3] In Japan's case, it is abandonment that now frightens the Japanese.

If Japan perceived that the Democrats carried negative baggage going into the 2008 election, the Republicans had a positive one. First, the Japanese establishment perceived the Republicans to be stronger supporters of free trade and less likely to press Japan hard on market-opening moves.

Second, the Japanese government considered the Republicans to be stronger on national security, in general, and more particularly strong on the Japan-US Alliance. The composition of the main opposition party in Japan, the DPJ, is complex and spans a broad political spectrum, making it impossible to identify the party's outlook on security policy. Some in the DPJ prefer a stronger military alliance with America, whereas others are more inclined toward pacifism. Again, Japanese political alignments did not mesh with American political party affiliations.

On the surface, this predilection for the Republicans may be surprising, because it is hard to see a causal relationship between the party affiliation of the US President and policies that favor or hurt Japan. For example, the two biggest financial crises of the postwar era, neither of which were good for Japan, occurred under Republican presidencies: the severing of the fixed dollar parity under Richard Nixon and the financial meltdown that marked the end of George W. Bush's tenure in the White House. Moreover, free trade and open market-advocate Ronald Reagan himself did not hesitate to support "voluntary restraints" on Japanese car imports, a euphemism for barriers against Japanese automobiles and thus a protectionist policy when he occupied the White House. In contrast, the Democratic Clinton administration did push the North American Free Trade Agreement (NAFTA) and similar measures successfully through the legislative process. These policies benefited international trade significantly—including Japanese companies that gained easier entry for their Mexican-manufactured goods into the US and Canadian markets.

As far as security policy is concerned, President Clinton's eight years were favorable for the Japan-US Security Treaty. Clinton's desire to work on ties with China benefited Japan. Tokyo's interests can only be hurt by Sino-American confrontation. At worst such a development would mean war, probably over a Chinese attack on Taiwan. Regardless of the outcome of such a conflict, it is hard to see how Japan would benefit. Even if tensions do not lead to armed conflict, saber rattling between Americans and Chinese would be most frightening to Japan. It would make dealing with North Korea more difficult, since doing so requires Sino-American cooperation, possibly frighten investors, and put pressure on Japan to spend more on its armed forces. Even if Sino-American problems are limited to economics and trade, this is also damaging to Japanese interests. Many Japanese companies export to the United States products that rely on Chinese inputs. Thus a Sino-American trade war would automatically create severe collateral economic damage in Japan.

It is worth noting that the George W. Bush administration continued to emphasize the importance of building a good relationship with Beijing. During President Bush's first year in office, in 2001, a Chinese jet fighter collided with a US Navy aircraft, forcing it to land in China. The US reaction to the accident and the internment of the US Navy fliers was rather cautious and diplomatic. Washington sought to avoid confrontation at all costs. Later in the administration, Treasury Secretary Paulson developed an extremely ambitious program to engage China in high-level economic policy discussions with several US cabinet members.

Clinton's North Korea policy was not a great success, but the Bush administration also similarly failed to produce a positive outcome. Moreover, Bush's legacy, the deal negotiated with Pyongyang in 2008, led to the United States removing North Korea from the list of "state sponsors of terrorism." In practice, this has little importance. But it inflicted a severe blow to Japanese prestige. For years, the Japanese government emphasized the need to free Japanese citizens abducted from Japan by North Korean agents.[4] It is unclear what can be done for these victims, nevertheless, the "abductees" gained some salience in Japanese conservative circles in the 2000s. Until the 2008 US-DPRK (Democratic People's Republic of Korea) agreement, the United States had stood side-by-side with its Japanese allies. President Bush even met in the White House with the mother of Megumi Yokota, the most famous victim of North Korean kidnappers. Thus Tokyo lost a lot of "face" when the United States removed Pyongyang from the terrorism list without a satisfactory resolution of the abductees issue. It is therefore difficult to agree with the proposition that the administration of the Democratic Bill Clinton was worse for Japan's interests than that of the Republican successor Bush.

Japan is the world's second largest economy as well as America's largest ally (by the size of its GDP) and a key economic partner. Therefore, one would expect Japanese officials to enjoy strong ties at all levels of the US government, from the president down to more junior officials in the executive branch. One would also assume that Japanese diplomats and politicians would have a solid relationship with Congress and members of the business and intellectual establishment. Since neither Republicans nor Democrats have been intrinsically hostile to Japan in the past decades, connections should be equally developed with both US political parties.

The reality, however, is different. Japanese government officials like to deal with Americans whom they think understand them and have a positive attitude of the Japan-US relationship. This means that their contact is limited largely to Americans who are either very familiar with Japan or at least seem to have a strong knowledge and empathy for it. In the first term of the second Bush administration, this role was fulfilled primarily by two individuals: Deputy Secretary of State Richard Armitage and Senior Director for Asian Affairs on the National Security Council staff Michael Green. Armitage is not a full-fledged Japan expert, but has a strong knowledge of Japanese affairs and a long experience dealing with East Asia. He also coauthored the 2000 "Nye-Armitage Report," sometimes called only the "Armitage Report," on strengthening Japan-US relations.[5] Green, a real specialist in Japanese security affairs and fluent in Japanese, was actively involved as a consultant during the Clinton Administration in the modernization of "The

Guidelines for Japan-US Defense Cooperation." Japanese officials felt reassured by Armitage's and Green's familiarity with their nation and support for its policies. However, they failed to realize that it is not a country specialist or a deputy secretary that sets issues that affect Japan's vital interests. The decisions of the previous Bush White House that most affected Japan's interest were the conduct of the war on al-Qaeda and its consequences, the invasion of Iraq, North Korea policy, China policy, trade policy, and, given the effect of America's economy on Japan, US fiscal and monetary policies. Thus, to have an understanding of these American policies, and if possible to try to influence them, dealing with different and more senior individuals was needed.

Japan has a stable and mature alliance with America. Therefore, the real issues are not those that pertain to the management of the bilateral relationship. What Tokyo needs to focus on are US policies that affect Japan indirectly, such as American policies toward the world economy and global security. This demands deep and extended contacts in Washington.

Both Armitage and Green were known to support John McCain in 2008. On the Obama side, however, there was no one seen in Tokyo as a "friend of Japan." There were large numbers of high-quality Asian experts, several of whom, such as Frank Januzzi, Michael Schiffer, Sheila Smith, had spent time in Japan and were first-class Asia hands, but no one was seen as having the affinity that Armitage and Green, in Japanese eyes, had for Japan in general and, perhaps more importantly, for the more hawkish elements of its ruling establishment. To some conservative Japanese, elements within the Democratic Party looked suspiciously like "panda huggers," the pejorative term given to those who embrace China, often at the expense of Japanese interests.

It may seem strange that Japan feels such need for *friends* in the political realm. In fact, for a state of major importance for the United States, such as Japan, relying on ties with relatively low-ranking individuals, even if they are considered to be reliable friends, makes little or no sense at all. In essence, with its approach on relying on individuals that are perceived as friendly but are lower in the US executive's hierarchy, Japan is not getting the access that corresponds to its weight and overall importance. Instead, Tokyo would be better served if it dealt directly with the president, his top advisers, the key cabinet officials, and the Congressional leadership.

THE KEY POLITICAL ISSUES OF
THE CAMPAIGN THROUGH JAPANESE EYES

Though the Japanese media followed the US campaign, Japanese coverage was not dominated by any particular angle. Asia in general did not figure prominently in the US election. Asia was mentioned mostly in the context of trade. However, even with respect to international trade, the domestic US debate and discussion during the campaign period was centered on NAFTA much more than on Asia. In this sense, the US election had little direct and immediate relevance for Japan. Consequently, Japanese coverage tended to be mostly a summary of what was discussed in America, without any particular emphasis.

In many nations, the "ethnic" angle of the campaign, being the first US presidential election with a viable African-American candidate, was a focus of the local press coverage. In Japan, this had less resonance. The overall consensus was that neither the election nor the outcome generated major interest in Japan. Japanese, in general, were aware that Obama's father was African. Nevertheless, this only fascinated a small number of Japanese who followed American affairs closely and who are thus aware of the significance of this in the US political context.

IMPLICATIONS FOR JAPAN

If Japanese analysts had been asked in early 2008 or at the time of the presidential conventions in August and September 2008 about the implications of the presidential election, they would most likely have focused on security affairs. Most Japanese commentaries on US affairs focused on these issues, as did most discussions with Japanese officials and academics. They had noticed that the candidates rarely, if ever, mentioned Japan. For example, Hillary Clinton published an article in *Foreign Affairs* on her foreign policy priorities without ever mentioning Japan.[6] Evidence like this convinced Japanese observers that there was indeed again a great risk of "Japan passing." Even worse, the United States might even decide to make China its principal partner in Asia, or indeed in the world. In an n article entitled "A partnership of Equals," Fred Bergsten, one of America's most respected political economists, called for a G-2 type relationship between Washington and Beijing (G-2 referring to a hypothetical Group of two countries, the United States and China). Both would lead the world in many issues, the way currently the G-8 does. For Japan, being the only Asian state in the G-8 is seen as an important sign of its unique position and role in Asia. For Japanese policymakers, this was again evidence of a possible shift in US policy away from Tokyo and toward Beijing.[7] Justified or not, these scenarios cause major concern among Japanese policymakers.

However, the Japanese concern about "Japan passing" reflects a profound misunderstanding of the nature of the Japan-US relationship and of international relations. The so-called Japan passing does not reflect a lack of appreciation of the role that Japan plays in sustaining American hegemony. American policymakers of both parties are aware that Japan is vital to US interests. On the military side, the United States needs bases in Asia, backed up by first-rate infrastructure, in a country with a strong commitment to the US alliance. Only Japan fits the bill for several reasons. First, it boasts a modern military that can provide valuable assistance to the United States. Its first-rate airports, ports, trains, roads, and hospitals allow it to provide rear-area support and a logistical infrastructure unmatched in Asia.[8] Second, it is politically stable and in the past decades the parties and groups opposed to US alliance and American policies have become increasingly weak and marginal. Additionally, since Japan is by far the largest US ally in Asia, it is important for the US military to develop a close relationship with its Japanese counterparts and to gain an understanding of Japan. These goals therefore require a large US presence in Japan.

By comparison, South Korea's politics are inhospitable to a much larger US presence. Moreover, the country is very vulnerable to Chinese and North Korean pressure. Taiwan cannot even be considered as a locale for large permanent US bases because stationing tens of thousands of US troops in Taiwan would most likely trigger a military confrontation with China. Southeast Asian states are either politically too unstable (Philippines, Thailand) or too small (Singapore). In any event, all are too far from the economic and strategic center of gravity of Northeast Asia. Finally, Australia is simply located too far away from the geostrategic center of Northeast Asia.[9]

On the economic side, regardless of the persistent stagnation of the economy, Japan will still remain for a long time the most important economy in the world after America. Not only is Japan's economy of enormous size, but, even more importantly, many of its high-tech products are essential for the United States and the rest of the world. America's and many other countries' own economies depend on Japanese products and technology. In other words, the Japanese economy is indispensable not only for the United States but also for the world economy.

Given Japan's importance to the United States in security and economic matters, there is broad consensus among decision-makers in the United States about maintaining the Japan-US Alliance and continuing the American commitment to defend Japan against foreign enemies. To the extent that some American thinkers favor "Japan passing" or the establishment of a G-2 with China, it does not reflect a desire to endanger Japan. What this lack of interest in Japan indicates is a belief that, despite its economic clout, Japan's capacity to make significant contributions to international security is limited by a host of constitutional, political, diplomatic, and psychological factors that prevent Japan from playing much of a role in military affairs.

Moreover, the American wish to form a much stronger relationship with China does not entail ignoring Japan. On the contrary, American efforts to better and deepen ties with Beijing are premised on the assumption that Tokyo is an ally with a stable relationship with Washington. If the United States had doubts about Japan's ally status, American policy would clearly be different. In particular, the United States would not be investing, as it has for more than a decade, considerable amounts of resources in enhancing its military ties with Japan. To be sure, the relationship may require fine-tuning from time to time, but certainly no major transformation is required. Positively enhancing the relationship with China, a partner in many respects but also a potential enemy, fits well with the goal of protecting Japan. Therefore, the policy of bringing China into the world system as a stakeholder, as described by then Deputy Secretary of State Robert Zoellick during a speech at the National Committee on US-China Relations on September 21, 2005, is in fact part of America's strategy to keep Japan secure.[10]

Additionally, even if one assumes that China's position will evolve along lines that are compatible with US interests and thus lead to the creation of a G-2 Sino-American condominium in Asia, this in itself would still not be detrimental to Japan's interests. Under such a possible arrangement, basic Japanese interests, namely, protection by the United States, stability in the region, and a liberal international trade regime, would be secured because they exactly match America's own general and regional interests.

In the final analysis, this Japanese fear of being "passed over" reflects reluctance on the part of Japanese policymakers to accept a basic fact about their country. Since the end of World War II, the Japanese people have wanted their country to maintain a low profile in international affairs. This entails first and foremost avoiding the use of military force, and thus remaining passive. There is no international treaty, or obstacle deriving from the international system, that prevents Japan from obtaining and maintaining a larger defense budget, from taking on a much larger military posture, or from participating prominently in peacekeeping operations or even US-led wars in Iraq or Afghanistan. Similarly, there is nothing external that makes it impossible for Tokyo to have a much more assertive diplomacy. However, the wishes of the majority in Japan demand a low profile.

Furthermore, it is not obvious that a really higher political or military profile would really serve Japan's interests or those of the United States. Consequently, as much as Tokyo loses sleep over "Japan passing," at the same time they would react disfavorably if the American President asked Japan to take on a significantly larger role in world affairs, one that is commensurate with its role as a major ally.

Given the economic importance of the United States to Japan, Japanese officials and business executives also normally follow American discussions of trade-related issues. Now that the financial crisis followed by the economic downturn has taken center stage in the United States and throughout the globe since the second half of 2008, it became certain that economic and financial issues would have to be the primary focus of the next US administration. But most of the Japanese focused on what the Bush administration and Congress where doing in the last months of the Bush presidency (both after and before the November ballot) than on the policies of the two competing candidates, which were never clearly defined.

It is in this context that the Japan-US relationship may be affected. During the Bush administration, Tokyo mildly succumbed to American pressure to act more visibly in military affairs by "showing the flag" and putting "boots on the ground." The price to satisfy these American demands was extremely low: a few refueling ships and escort vessels to help coalition forces in the Indian Ocean, a battalion deployed to Samawah in Iraq, and a few C-130 transport planes to help with logistics in Iraq. The naval deployment entailed very few risks in the absence of enemy navies. In Iraq, the Japanese forces deployed in a fairly calm area and were provided with protection from Dutch and later Australian army units tasked with shielding the Japanese soldiers from insurgents. As for the Japanese transport aircraft, they were based in peaceful Kuwait and flew to fairly safe air bases in Iraq. As the Iraqi insurrection lacked a credible threat to aircrafts, the Japanese fliers only incurred minimal dangers. Nor was the financial burden of these small operations of any consequence for Japan's economy.

However, the world recession could generate tensions with the United States if Washington decides to put very strong pressure on Japan to boost consumer demand (especially for imported goods), sustain an appreciation of the yen (to assist US exports and cut down on Japan's structural trade surplus and America's structural deficits), and to further open its markets to foreign—and in particular American—products.

Though Japan obviously watches the United States with much interest, by international standards Japanese paid relatively little attention to an event that seems to have mobilized passions on a global scale. The Japanese establishment will regret the departure of the Republicans but will strive to work with the Obama administration. Most Japanese analysts do not view the result of the US elections as having an enormous impact on the country or even the region.

NOTES

1. Mark Steyn, *America Alone: The End of the World as We Know It* (Washington DC: Regnery Publishing Inc., 2006), xxvii. http://books.google.com/books?id=thP_UKhPbP0C&pg=PR27&lpg=PR27&dq=a+faraway+country+of+which+we+know+little&source=bl&ots=kYABK4wew4&sig=dvkomT_WZ9A1DaAsnRUdgO4O3CY&hl=en&ei=MDqhSYy8O9XLkAXLp5jGCw&sa=X&oi=book_result&resnum=11&ct=result#PPR11,M1 (accessed February 22, 2009).

2. There is no realizable data on the total "minority" population in Japan, especially due to the impossibility of knowing how many Japanese are (and more importantly are considered to be) descendents of the eta class. See Encyclopedia Britannica Online, *Burakumin* http://www. britannica.com/EBchecked/topic/84894/burakumin (accessed February 22, 2009).

3. Victor Cha, *Alignment Despite Antagonism: The United States-Korea-Japan Security Triangle* (Stanford: Stanford University Press, 1999).

4. These individuals were reportedly used by North Korea to teach Japanese language and culture to North Korean operatives.

5. "The United States and Japan: Advancing Toward a Mature Partnership," National Defense University, Institute for National Strategic Studies (2000), http://www.ndu.edu/inss/strforum/SR_01/SR_Japan.htm. (accessed February 22, 2009.)

6. Hillary Rodham Clinton, "Security and Opportunity for the Twenty-first Century," *Foreign Affairs* 86, 6 (2007).

7. C. Fred Bergsten, "A Partnership of Equals: How Washington Should Respond to China's Economic Challenge," *Foreign Affairs* 87, 4 (2008).

8. See: William E. Odom and Robert Dujarric, *America's Inadvertent Empire* (New Haven CT: Yale University Press, 2004).

9. The Military Balance, published annually by the International Institute of Strategic Studies (IISS), provides military and economic data on these issues. See Kent E. Calder, *Embattled Garrisons: Comparative Base Politics and American Globalism* (Princeton, NJ: Princeton University Press, 2007).

10. "Prepared remarks of Deputy Secretary of State Robert Zoellick to the National Committee on U.S.-China Relations. Subject: Whither China: from membership to responsibility." *Federal News Service*, September 21, 2005, http://libproxy.temple.edu:2210/us/lnaca-demic/results/docview/docview.do?docLinkInd=true&risb=21_T58 46403280&format=GNBFI&sort=RELEVANCE&startDocNo=1& resultsUrlKey=29_T5846403283&cisb=22_T5846403282&treeMa x=true&treeWidth=0&csi=8104&docNo=20 (accessed February 22, 2009).

Conclusion

A "GLOBAL EVENT" WITH GLOBAL STAKEHOLDERS: OBAMA'S ELECTION AND THE "IDEA" OF AMERICA

Matthias Maass

The previous chapters centered on a set of larger questions. First, did the 2008 US presidential election matter with respect to the various countries considered in this volume, and if so, how and why? The fact that the United States is globally too relevant for its major domestic political events to be ignored emerged quickly and repeatedly in the individual studies discussed in various chapters. The US continues to maintain a hegemonic position in the early twenty-first century, and hence there is a need for practically all countries across the globe to pay close attention to key events in Washington.

However, the global reach and the level of interdependence of the United States, mainly but not exclusively economic, have created a feedback mechanism. Today the United States must also be cognizant of how it is perceived abroad, because the image it has overseas constitutes part of the foreign policy environment in which any US administration has to work. Thus, the previous analyses of how countries worldwide viewed the US election do not only tell the story of why the US election gained such international prominence, but also begins to lay out part of the foreign policy context with which the Obama White House will have to deal with.

Second, and particularly if considered together, a picture emerged of how "globalized" the US presidential election, at least in 2008, had become. The world paid attention and felt it had a stake in the outcome. Such concern, however, was not simply the product of concrete bilateral relations different countries had with the United States, but also an expression of preference for a particular type of America. In fact, in many countries, one could sense that the people there wanted a particular "idea" of America to be reconfirmed in these US presidential elections.

In other words, many countries worldwide held the view that a particular notion of what the United States was or was supposed to be, even if this notion remains rather diffuse, was also on the ballot in 2008. The joy that was generally shown internationally over the outcome of the election was thus not only for the success of Obama the person and politician, but also for the type of America he seemed to represent.

Related to the ideational argument is, third, the confirmation of the overall claim that the US presidential election may in fact amount to a "global event," as postulated in the Introduction. The international attention and sense of "being part" of the election was, by and large, so substantial and on such a high level as to warrant special consideration. This was in fact, in many ways, a "global election" with global "participation." Moreover, given that only very few countries worldwide would have preferred to see McCain enter the White House, it was also an election with a general, even if not complete, international consensus.

Fourth, and finally, each chapter investigated the impact that the choice of Obama as the 44th President of the United States may have from the overseas perspectives. While there are significant individual differences, overall, one could detect a sense of relief and approval that the United States would now fundamentally reevaluate its foreign policies. This election offered the opportunity for the United States to rethink the substance and style of its foreign relations, and the world was glad that this opportunity was not missed.

NATIONAL PERSPECTIVES BECAUSE OF NATIONAL PRIORITIES AND DEFICIENCIES

As in domestic elections, the world as a whole did not reach a full consensus regarding the 2008 US Presidential election. Viewpoints differed across the globe in many respects. In all countries the perception was a mix of concrete policy concerns, mostly regarding bilateral issues, and an interest in, and sometimes fascination with, the person Obama, and whether this individual might be able to change some of today's international and domestic political dynamics. Between these two foci, countries struck very different balances. However, as the previous chapters have demonstrated, both aspects formed part of the perceptions of practically all countries.

For a number of countries investigated here, US foreign policy plays a very critical role; for these countries a pragmatic view of the US Presidential candidates' respective positions on certain bilateral issues dominated the way the US election was viewed. For Pakistan, Iran, Palestine, and, to a good degree, Israel, US policies in the Middle East and Southwest Asia are critical. Logically, their perception was shaped largely by the possible implication of the US election on America's foreign policy toward their regions. China's viewpoint was shaped largely by its desire not to be opposed by the United States in claiming a larger international role, its place as a responsible international "stakeholder." As in China, Russia also preferred Obama over McCain, but in an almost cynical way. The broader perception assumed that neither Obama nor McCain would be able to change US-Russian relations. These were seen as largely determined by power considerations, a logic neither candidate would be able to escape. In short, for a good number of countries, US foreign policy was pretty much all that mattered in this election.

The coverage of the US election in Mexico and Israel indicated each country's interest in some of the broader issues touched off by the candidacy of Obama. To be sure, both countries had their particular concerns regarding their bilateral relationship with the United States. Still, in each country one could also detect a certain degree of fascination with some of the tangible aspects of the election, in particular the notions of "hope" and "change," possibly on a historical scale. In Brazil and in Japan, Obama's run for the White House did not generate as much interest as in other parts of the world. In Brazil, Obama's overall policy priorities as well as what his personal story represented was largely in line with the country's own political and social priorities and ambitions. Only a possible conflict over trade loomed in the background. In Japan, Obama's personal success as a minority candidate did not really compute, given Japanese society's overall homogeneity. In other words, in some countries the notion that Obama's success might indicate a larger development, a possibly historic change, or a reinvigoration of certain American values, did not really take off, but for a variety of reasons. Sometimes this dimension of the election did not overcome the immediacy of foreign policy issues, in other cases it did not translate well enough or seemed unspectacular.

A third group of countries, represented here by Venezuela and Iran, appeared to have shaped their perception of the US election consciously on a preexisting notion of the United States. Obama, too, had to fit that image, and the election was denied any real relevance for the perception of America or for US bilateral relations with either of these countries. Nevertheless, to a limited degree, the appeal of Obama and his policy positions was too hard to ignore, even in Teheran and Caracas, and both seemed willing to at least allow Obama a first diplomatic move.

Finally, in many countries, such as France and the UK, the tangible meaning of Obama's candidacy and his ultimate success in winning the White House trumped concrete policy concerns. To be sure, Obama's French and British audience expected concrete policy changes, essentially a rollback of the major tenets of his predecessor's foreign policy actions. However, here, as in many countries across the globe, the expectation of a reversal of US foreign policy was paralleled by an intense admiration of the political success of a minority candidate and a passionate desire for America to "change."

GLOBALLY SHARED PERSPECTIVES ON A "GLOBAL EVENT"

The purpose of this volume has been twofold, to analyze various individual countries' perceptions of the US election, and, by doing so, to investigate common themes and perceptions that were shared worldwide. While each country's perspective is, of course, unique, a set of common themes constitute a general, "global" viewpoint.

It is remarkable how quickly the international discussion centered on the issue of race and Obama being an Africa-American. The fact that Obama had to beat Hillary Clinton in order to come that far, and thus turn the election into a contest between two male candidates, was quickly overshadowed by the dynamic of "race" as part of the presidential campaigns. This is not the place to judge such a development. However, it is important to point out that, even overseas, few lamented the loss of the aspect of "gender equality" in politics when it was replaced with "racial equality" during the primary campaign. To be sure, for many countries the question of integrating racial minorities successfully appears more pressing than empowering women. But even if that were the case more generally, the ease with which the focus on Clinton as a legitimate female contender for the Democratic nomination faded worldwide stands out. Moreover, even in racially rather homogenous societies, that is to say countries in which the race issue did not resonate nearly as much, the defeat of the female candidate Hillary Clinton did not appear to have caused much stir. Globally, it turned out that the gender issue was much less appealing than the racial dimension in the 2008 presidential election.

Even the racial issue was then overtaken by concerns with the overall direction of the country and, most critically, economic policy issues, in light of the growing financial and economic crises worldwide, and US security policy.

Not surprisingly, at a time when crises in security and economic affairs were converging, the world paid close attention to the policy record and political viewpoints of each party's candidate. These policies, it was clear, would matter in a significant way particularly in a time of crisis, as was the case at the end of the first decade of the twenty-first century. It was already clear during the campaign stage in mid-2008 that practically all states would experience effects of the economic crisis. By the same token, ever since 9/11, the world had to deal with the US response to this particular event, the so-called War on Terror and the wars in Afghanistan and Iraq. Especially in times such as these, the choice of the American electorate would greatly matter outside the borders of that country.

These general but still very pressing concerns were in some cases compounded by more concrete issues that hit closer to home. South Korea, for example, was very concerned with the future of the just recently signed Free Trade Agreement with the United States. Its neighbor Japan was worried about any weakening of its security partnership with the Americans, particularly in light of the rise of China.

A further dimension may be added that underlined the relevance of this election, though not exclusively in the eyes of major European countries, and that is the degree to which this election was perceived to be a final "vote of no-confidence" for President George W. Bush. For some, the election was more "anti-Bush" than "pro-Obama." In this context, the 2008 presidential election was seen in parts of the world as an important confirmation on the part of the American people that it had erred at least in reelecting Bush in 2004. Put differently, the 2008 election was seen as crucial because it signified formally a political change of heart of the majority of the American electorate.

It is likely that a successful candidacy of Clinton would also have been celebrated overseas, though not as much as the candidacy of Obama. Clinton would have signified the end of the Bush presidency in a similar way, probably garnering some initial international support from that fact alone. On the flip-side, McCain suffered in the eyes of many from being associated with the Bush administration's policies and thus viewed, for all practical purposes, as representing a continuation of the Bush White House. Needless to say, both images were oversimplifications, but, nonetheless, this was the "hard" political reality overseas.

Still, Obama's message, his promise of "change," caught on in many countries overseas in a way and with a magnitude neither McCain's political viewpoints did nor Clinton's opinions could have. Obama clearly hit a nerve with many overseas audiences in a way none of his competitors was able to do. As a relatively fresh face in Washington, his promise of a new start was much more convincing, not the least to the overseas audience. Moreover, his simple message of "change" translated easily. It could be filled abroad with content, depending on the circumstances. "Change" could mean a fundamental shift in Middle Eastern Policy for the regional audience, but it could just as well mean a new emphasis on multilateral policy for Europeans. Obama's message could and did mean different things to different peoples. What is critical in this context, though, is how Obama's vision of a "changed" US foreign policy connected with a universal desire for significant new approaches in international relations. The world seemed to be drifting toward a more conflictual environment, and major adjustments were needed. Obama seemed to be the needed "agent of change."

More specifically, most countries worldwide expected substantial corrections in the substance and style of US foreign policy and America's interaction with the world. The previous chapters investigated in detail exactly what changes are desired by the various countries, and how they expect the United States to conduct itself internationally.

In 2008, the world was, by and large, welcoming renewed US leadership in international affairs provided such leadership would come in a different form and if the United States reconsidered some of its policy goals and objectives. After widespread rejection of the major tenets of the Bush administration's foreign policy, one could detect a willingness in many parts of the world to accept US leadership in major policy areas if that would also mean a less hawkish and unilateral policy and a fundamental overhaul of the concept of the "War on Terror." A critical component of what the world desired from an Obama White House was also a retooling of how the US conducts its foreign policy, away from the self-assured, even brash, application of hard power, and toward a heavy reliance on soft power tools. In this sense, in 2008, many countries were hoping for a change in Washington that would bring with it "soft leadership" on the part of the United States.

As significant as the evolution of a worldview on the US election already was—the development of a world opinion on a domestic political event in the United States, no less—the 2008 presidential election can be interpreted as a "global event" for two more reasons: the election in the United States was, first, directly relevant for domestic politics in many countries around the world, and, second, it rekindled parts of the American Dream abroad.

As has been pointed out in a number of case studies above, the way the US presidential election, with all its aspects, played out had an impact on aspects of the domestic politics in numerous countries across the globe. Obviously, the United States is not the only country with a history of minority discrimination. However, the meteoric rise of an African-American politician and him occupying the White House right away put the finger on a sore spot of countries as far apart as India and France or England. Many countries with large minorities began a process of self-reflection. Why had their country not produced a star politician like Obama? And still worse, why did it seem rather unlikely to happen in the foreseeable future? In particular, some countries in Europe that had indulged themselves in ridiculing the United States during the past eight years over what they perceived were democratic deficiencies now began to doubt themselves and their own political systems. Obama's rise and ultimate victory pointed out how poorly minorities remain integrated in the political process in many countries worldwide, including in Europe. The enthusiasm shown toward the African-American presidential candidate can therefore partly be viewed as a response to the skepticism regarding their own domestic political setup. Obama was cheered on because he had achieved something that seemed so utterly unrealistic in many countries around the world.[1]

This sentiment extends further than just admiration for the personal achievement of Obama and it enjoins some of the other countries to a process of self-questioning. The US political system was proving its capability to revitalize itself and to bring forward new thinking and new personalities. Many other countries had to admit that they have come up short in this regard. The US political system was demonstrating its permeability when it allowed a young, unproven minority candidate to contest for the highest office in the country. Other democracies looked at their track record in this regard and felt it lacking. The US political system seemed to have transformed itself with ease, while in so many other countries, even in a moment of converging crises, the political systems remained rigid and fairly closed. Thus, a good deal of the eagerness with which the US election was followed can be explained by the domestic desire overseas to be able to replicate "the Obama story."

Furthermore, Obama's victory and the call for major changes it represented demonstrated in an impressive way the vitality of the US democratic system in general. At least at a moment of crisis, such as in 2008, it seemed that the US political system still maintained the capacity to generate urgently needed change. This implied message was not lost overseas. Democracy, at least in the United States, remained capable of responding to new situations in a hurry.

In large parts of the world, the outcome of the US presidential election was also interpreted in part as a reaffirmation of the "American Dream" in certain ways. To be sure, the "American Dream," both the myth and the reality, has been played up for a long time. For centuries the American Dream stood for the possibility that anybody in the United States can rise "from rags to riches" and to pursue his (later also her) goals regardless of any "glass ceilings." American society was organized in such a way that each citizen was guaranteed a shot at success and wealth, but not success or wealth themselves. Soon the United States came to represent individual possibilities in the eyes of many, within and outside the nation.

Even in its early stages the image of the United States as a place where each individual was granted the opportunity to succeed became very relevant overseas too. The pursuance of their very own "American Dream" was what lured thousands of European immigrants to the United States in the nineteenth and twentieth centuries. Later on, in the twentieth century, Latino immigrants to the United States also chased their "American Dream," as did immigrants from many other nations. And the "American Dream" still remains alive and well—and politically relevant—in the early twenty-first century. What is critical in the context here is that this "American Dream" has already been known and valued abroad for a long time.

Today, the relevance of the "American Dream" goes far beyond its physical manifestation, that is, a promise tied to a geographic location. It has become a source of inspiration and aspiration for many across the globe. This in turn allows people worldwide to "experience" the "American Dream" even without migrating to the United States. In its mythical form, the "American Dream" can be shared and lived from abroad.

For many across the globe, Obama is proof of the vitality of the "American Dream" today. His rise to prominence despite his minority background, his success over Hillary Clinton for the nomination despite her strong party connections, and his victory over the much more experienced politician McCain were seen as living proof that the opportunity to build one's own success still existed—at least in the United States. From the outside, Obama "was" the "American Dream."

The last point needs further elaboration. Obama was seen as evidence of what was possible in the United States. In a more abstract way, the "American Dream" has become a global phenomenon. In many ways, this American idea now stands for an aspiration that can be shared even by people outside the United States with no intention or opportunity to migrate to that country. Even if the same opportunities available in the United States are not offered in their home countries, the fact that the idea of unhindered progress exists somewhere may serve as an inspiration. Obama's success has helped reinvigorate this inspiration. Around the time of the election in 2008, it seemed that the world, by and large, longed for such affirmation of the "American Dream," which was understood as a global phenomenon.

Building on this observation, it may be possible to take this line of reasoning one step further. In the year 1630, John Winthrop presented the concept of a "City Upon a Hill" to his fellow colonists, the ambition to set up an exemplary Christian community in America. Because of its purity and success, it would then serve as a model for others. Even though this concept was applied only by a small religious splinter group, it nevertheless found its way into the American psyche and has remained a politically viable concept.[2] However, for centuries, the "City Upon a Hill" remained an American ambition.

Today it appears as if the world is sharing in this ambition. Of course, the world does not, nor does it want to, look up to the United States in the way Winthrop envisioned it for his religious colony. Nevertheless, given that the concept of a "City Upon a Hill" has become broader and more diffuse even in the minds of Americans, it appears as if the notion of parts of the United States serving as a source of inspiration for other countries is not universally rejected. Major parts of the world, one may conclude, want the United States to fulfill a role as a source of inspiration. It is in this sense that one may claim that the "City Upon a Hill" has by now become a globalized phenomenon. Obama's success seems to have validated such thinking.

All in all, it has been argued here that the 2008 US presidential election amounted to a "global event" and produced a global audience that shared in it. The world, by and large, felt it had a stake in the US election and participated in it, in a manner of speaking. However, this participation was strong enough to remake the election, in large part, into a "global election," with stakeholders worldwide.

Moreover, this election produced not only a variety of individual views on it across the globe, but also a set of common worldviews. To be sure, there was significant variation, different foci, and distinctive expectations from country to country. Nevertheless, this "global event" also brought to light a set of opinions and attitudes that were shared widely across the world.

The overwhelming international support for Obama and the de facto international acclamation of his electoral win also indicated the substantial international desire for a renewed and recalibrated type of "soft American leadership" in international affairs. Last but certainly not the least, it appears that the world viewed the US election and its outcome as a revitalization of the United States as a source of inspiration and aspiration.

Notes

1. Steven Erlanger, "Historic U.S. Election Has Europe Looking at Its Own Racial Issues," International, *International Herald Tribune*, November 13, 2008, 5.
2. "Governor John Winthrop Envisions a City Upon a Hill, 1630." In Dennis Merrill and Thomas G. Paterson (eds), *Major Problems in American Foreign Relations* (Boston: Houghton Mifflin), 1:30–31; See also, for an example of the continuous political relevance in the US, Ronald Reagan. "Farewell Address to the Nation," *Ronald Reagan Library*, http://www.reaganlibrary.com/reagan/speeches/farewell.asp (accessed February 14, 2009).

CONTRIBUTORS

Moonis Ahmar is Professor and Chair, Department of International Relations, University of Karachi and Director, Program on Peace Studies and Conflict Resolution. He was previously the Visiting Scholar or Visiting Professor at the Program in Arms Control and Disarmament, University of Illinois at Urbana-Champaign, Stimson Center, Washington DC; Center for Strategic and International Studies, Washington DC; Middle East Institute, Washington DC; Kroc Institute for International Peace Studies, University of Notre Dame, Indiana; Department of International Relations, University of Dhaka, Bangladesh; and Asia Research Center, London School of Economics and Politics Science. He specializes in conflict resolution and confidence-building measures with a focus on South Asia, Central Asia, and the Middle East. He is the author of two books, four monographs, and numerous research papers.

Ruchi Anand is Associate Professor at the American Graduate School of International Relations and Diplomacy in Paris, France. Additionally she teaches at the Centre d'Etude Franco-Américain de Management (CEFAM) in Lyon, France and is a Faculty Member for the summer programs of the Junior Statesmen of America at Princeton University. She received her Doctorate from Purdue University. She also holds graduate degrees from the Jawaharlal Nehru University, Delhi. She published *International Environmental Justice: A North-South Dimension*, in 2004. Currently, Dr. Anand is finishing up her second book entitled *Self-Defense in International Law*. Dr. Anand's research interests include international relations, international law, international organizations, foreign policy, environmental policy, politics of developing countries, and women's studies.

Lesley Martina Burns is a doctoral candidate in the department of Political Science at the University of British Columbia. She also consults on political risk. She has spend several years in Venezuela where she was a visiting research fellow at the Instituto de Estudios Superiores de Administración. Her research focuses on the rule of law and democratic stability, with a focus on Latin America.

Grace Cheng is Assistant Professor of Political Science at Hawai`i Pacific University. Her specialization is in comparative political theory and political development. She has traveled to Iran and is currently developing cooperative projects with Iranian scholars.

Kenneth Christie is Professor and Director of the Program on Human Security and Peacebuilding at Royal Roads University, British Columbia, Canada. Previously, he taught and conducted research at universities in the United States, Singapore, South Africa, Norway, and Dubai, concentrating on issues of human rights, security, and democratization. Christie is the author, coauthor, editor, and coeditor of eight books, the most recent being America's *War on Terrorism: The Revival of the Nation-State versus Universal Human Rights* and *US National Identity* and *Foreign Policy in the 21st Century*.

Thomas Cieslik is Lecturer at the Institute for Political Science and Social Research at the University of Würzburg in Germany. Earlier he worked in Mexico City as professor in international relations at the University Tecnologico de Monterrey, Campus State of Mexico. He also directed the Mexico-project of the liberal political German Friedrich Naumann Foundation. Cieslik earned his PhD in Political Science from the Catholic University of Eichstätt (Germany). His research interests include geopolitics, migration, and comparative foreign policy.

Robert Dujarric is Director, Institute of Contemporary Japanese Studies at Temple University, Japan Campus in Tokyo. He is a former Council on Foreign Relations/Hitachi Fellow. He is a graduate of Harvard College and holds an MBA from Yale University. His publications include *America's Inadvertent Empire* (with William E. Odom), *Korea After Unification, Europe 2005* (with Gary Geipel), *Commonwealth or Empire? Russia, Central Asia and the Transcaucasus* (with W. E. Odom).

Jeremy Dwyer is Adjunct Research Associate at the School of Political and Social Inquiry, Monash University, where he has taught courses in Soviet and post-Soviet Russian politics. At present his work focuses on the intersections between politics and Russian culture.

Sukhee Han is Assistant Professor at the Graduate School of International Studies, Yonsei University in Seoul, Korea. Before joining Yonsei University, he held positions at the Institute of Korean Unification Studies, the China CEO Advanced Management Program, both at Yonsei University, at the School of Government, Peking University, and at the Institute for Asia-Pacific Studies, Chinese Academy of Social Sciences. He was trained at Yonsei University and received his MA and PhD degrees from the Fletcher School, Tufts University. Han's main research interests are Sino-American relations, Sino-Korean relations, Sino-North Korean relations, and China's interactions with international institutions.

Kai Jin is a PhD Candidate at the Graduate School of International Studies, Yonsei University, South Korea. He is currently working on his dissertation that evaluates the transformation of China as a rising power. He was trained at the School of Political Science and Public Management, Wuhan University, China and served as professional officer at the Headquarters of the General Staff, Chinese People's Liberation Army.

Kai Michael Kenkel is Assistant Professor at the Institute of International Relations of the Catholic University of Rio de Janeiro. He was previously a Postdoctoral Fellow at the Centre of International Relations of the University of British Columbia and has been Visiting Researcher at institutions in Canada, Brazil, and South Africa. He holds an AB from The Johns Hopkins University and MA and PhD degrees from the Graduate Institute of International Studies in Geneva. He is a specialist in peace operations and intervention and has also published in the areas of civil-military relations, small arms, and defence policy decision-making.

Peter Lentini is the cofounder and Director of the Global Terrorism Research Centre (GTReC), at Monash University, Victoria, Australia. He received his BA from the University of Rhode Island and his PhD from the University of Glasgow. He has written extensively on contemporary Russian politics, political violence, and comparative extremisms.

Matthias Maass lectures on International Affairs. Before joining the faculty of Yonsei University's Graduate School of International Studies in Seoul/Korea, he taught International Relations in Singapore, Hawaii, Seoul, Paris, and Hanoi. He was educated in Germany, Australia, and the United States. In addition to the United States, his research focuses on East Asia, and Small States and Governance.

Mohammad Masad is Assistant Professor in the Department of Humanities and Social Sciences at Zayed University in Dubai (UAE). His research interests include Medieval Divination, Islamic History and Culture, and the Middle East, particularly Palestine and the United Arab Emirates.

João Pontes Nogueira is Professor of International Relations at the International Relations Institute at the Pontifical Catholic University of Rio de Janeiro, Brazil. He received his PhD from the University of Denver. His areas of specialization include international relations theory, the geopolitics of knowledge in the discipline of IR, humanitarian interventions and international human rights. He has published *Peru vs. Ecuador: peacemaking amid rivalry* (coauthored with Monica Herz), *Teoria das Relacoes Internacionais: correntes e debates* (with Nizar Messari), and is coediting with Rob Walker and Nizar Messari, *Displacing the International* (forthcoming).

Ronnie Olesker is Assistant Professor at St. Lawrence University, and she is specializing in comparative politics and international relations.

She holds a Law Degree (LL.B) with specialization in International Law from Israel and worked for the district attorney's office in Tel Aviv before entering academia. Her research focuses on majority-minority relations and the decision-making processes of minority groups in adopting political violence against the state. Other areas of interests include the nexus between political violence and violations of human rights, particularly in the Israeli-Palestinian context.

Adam Quinn is Lecturer in International Studies at the Department of Political Science and International Studies, University of Birmingham, England. He is co-convenor of the US foreign policy working group of the British International Studies Association (BISA) and founding editor of the group's online newsletter-magazine, *Argentia*. His book, *US Foreign Policy in Context: National Ideology From the Founders to the Bush Doctrine*, is forthcoming in 2009.

INDEX